10. Special equipment
What special equipment is required, and what are its space requirements? Is security a factor?
22, 36, 43, 46, 50, 74, 100–2, 106, 167, 199, 206–7

11. Materials
What materials need to be uniquely considered or rejected?
71–110, 191–92

12. Acoustic control
What special acoustical considerations affect the design?
140

13. Lighting design
What special lighting (day and artificial) considerations affect the design?
56, 74, 76–87, 102, 168–75, 185, 190

14. Interiors issues
What special considerations (scale, color, texture, finishes, furnishings, special features) affect the planning of interiors?
31–37, 43, 49, 50, 71–110, 167, 171

15. Wayfinding
What special factors determine signing systems?
46, 87–96, 175–82, 185, 189

16. Preservation/modernization
What special considerations (historical authenticity, infrastructure retrofit) arise when renovating a facility of this type?
16–17, 21–22, 26–29, 213

17. International challenges
On international projects, what special considerations influence marketing, design, presentations, document production, and field presence?
8, 22, 25, 41, 154, 157, 170–71, 200–1, 216–17

18. Operation and maintenance
How will design decisions influence the operation and maintenance of the completed facility?
43, 50

19. Key cost factors
What are the principal determinants of the total construction cost?
39, 43, 127–29, 130, 163, 173

20. Finances, fees, feasibility
What are the typical techniques for financing this facility?
111–12, 116–27, 129

BUILDING TYPE BASICS FOR

retail and mixed-use facilities

BUILDING TYPE BASICS FOR

retail and mixed-use facilities

Stephen A. Kliment, Series Founder and Editor

THE JERDE PARTNERSHIP
with VILMA BARR

WILEY

JOHN WILEY & SONS, INC.

Copyright © 2004 by John Wiley & Sons, Inc. All rights reserved

Published by John Wiley & Sons, Inc., Hoboken, New Jersey
Published simultaneously in Canada

For general information on our other products and services or for technical support, please contact our Customer Care Department within the United States at (800) 762-2974, outside the United States at (317) 572-3993 or fax (317) 572-4002.

Wiley also publishes its books in a variety of electronic formats. Some content that appears in print may not be available in electronic books. For more information about Wiley products, visit our web site at www.wiley.com.

Library of Congress Cataloging-in-Publication Data:

Building type basics for retail and mixed-use facilities / by the Jerde Partnership.
    p. cm.—(Building type basics)
Includes bibliographical references and index.
  ISBN 0-471-20322-X (cloth : alk. paper)
 1. Retail trade. 2. Stores, Retail—Planning. 3. Shopping
centers—Planning. 4. Shopping malls—Design and construction. I.
Jerde Partnership International. II. Building type basics series.
  HF5429.B672 2003
  658.8'7'00682--dc21
                                        2003008387

Printed in the United States of America.

10 9 8 7 6 5 4

CONTENTS

PREFACE

STEPHEN A. KLIMENT *Series Founder and Editor*

Any review of trends in retail architecture must consider a wide array of project types, ranging from stand-alone stores and strip centers to regional shopping centers and large-scale urban mixed-use projects. Within these project types, too, there is a broad range of uses, including cinemas, restaurants, entertainment venues, and corporate showcases. A project's success is dependent, to a great degree, on the artful blending of retail with these other uses.

Myriad factors, such as location, access, adjacent uses, the political environment, the consultant team, the construction industry, leasing, economic timing, the insurance and banking industry, and the vision of the development team, enter the planning and design equation. All must work together to produce successful and profitable retail projects. When imbued with inspired design, retail projects transcend purely commercial and social values by breathing life into our communities.

The designer's role is to help clients build their future by thinking about opportunities they create together. The decisions they make together today affect tomorrow in both the United States and across the world. The concepts that prove successful in stores and shopping centers in one part of the world often find themselves reformatted for adaptive reuse elsewhere.

High-caliber design for retail creates a viable environment to support all forms of merchandising. Moreover, a the truly successful retail project fits seamlessly into the preconditioned patterns of ordinary life.

This volume in the Wiley "Building Type Basics" series provides answers, guidelines, and cautionary advice, as well as the lessons to be learned from actual completed buildings. Its goal is to steer architects and their specialty consultants, developers, members of corporate boards, and financial institutions toward making sound decisions early in the planning cycle of a retail facility. Students at architecture schools will also find the volume useful, as a kind of Cliffs Notes to get a head start on an assigned studio problem. The text is concise and supplemented by diagrams, drawings, lists, and illustrations.

Like other volumes in the series, *Retail and Mixed-Use Facilities* is tightly organized for ease of use. The framework for this book is a set of twenty questions most commonly asked about a building type in the early phases of its design. For a complete listing of these twenty questions, see the inside of the front and back covers of this book. You can also use this list as a supplementary index.

Retail and Mixed-Use Facilities begins with the origins of retailing, a description of the entrepreneurs and trend setters who shaped the industry, and the scope of the retail marketplace today.

The early chapters cover the basic steps in the planning and design development phases that are applicable to all types of retail environments. Examples of store layouts, display fixtures, and background elements that stimulate sales are described and illustrated. *Retail and Mixed-Use Facilities* includes the most current trends in lighting and signage that add excitement to store interiors and exteriors.

Chapters 6 and 7 cover the planning and design of retail centers and mixed-use complexes. These have an added dimension of intricacy that takes them beyond the realm of retail store planning and design. Recommended planning and design procedures are supplemented by case studies from around the world.

Chapter 8 covers topics common to shops, stores, shopping centers, and mixed-use complexes. These include engineering issues, technical lighting information, codes, acoustics, sustainability, operation and maintenance, and security.

Chapter 9 offers a sharp look at the future of retail.

ACKNOWLEDGMENTS

The co-creative process was the vehicle for generating this book. And for that, we are very grateful to the many contributors. The expertise necessary to create legendary retail and mixed-use projects is wide-ranging and vast. We have tried to include the thoughts of many architects and consultants who are distinguished by their own long lists of successful projects. Their ideas herein will help anyone seeking a working knowledge of the design of retail and mixed-use projects.

CONTRIBUTORS
In Chapter 4, the sections titled "Program Development" and "Basic Store Layouts" were prepared with the assistance of Charles E. Broudy, FAIA, Charles E. Broudy & Associates, PC, Architects, Philadelphia, Pennsylvania. The section titled "Exterior and Store Entrance Design" was prepared with the assistance of Kenneth A. Nisch, AIA, JGA, Inc., Southfield, Michigan.

In Chapter 5, various sections were prepared with the assistance of the following contributors: "Colors, Materials, and Finishes," Kenneth A. Nisch, AIA, JGA, Inc., Southfield, Michigan; "Lighting," Joe Kaplan, Senior Principal, Kaplan Partners Architectural Lighting, Los Angeles, California; "Signs and Graphics," Robin Perkins, Selbert Perkins Design Collaborative, Santa Monica, California, and Cambridge, Massachusetts, and Charles E. Broudy, FAIA, Charles E. Broudy & Associates, PC, Architects, Philadelphia, Pennsylvania; "Displaying Merchandise," Joseph Weisbar, New Vision Studios, New York.

In Chapter 6, the section titled "Defining the Market" was prepared with the assistance of Thomas Consultants, Vancouver, British Columbia, Canada.

In Chapter 7, the section titled "Lighting Design" was prepared with the assistance of Joe Kaplan, Senior Principal, Kaplan Partners Architectural Lighting, Los Angeles, California. The section titled "Environmental Graphic Design" was prepared with the assistance of Deborah Sussman, Principal, and Sam Fidler, Senior Project Manager, Sussman/Prejza Co., Inc., Culver City, California.

Chapter 9, "The Future of Retail," was prepared in collaboration with Stephanie Smith, founder of Architecture-NOW, Los Angeles, California.

Last, but certainly not least, we owe a tremendous thank you to Vilma Barr, without whose retail expertise and steadfast dedication this book would not have been possible.

CHAPTER 1

INTRODUCTION

This book is not only about designing environments for buying and selling goods, it is also about creating enjoyable places in which to spend time. Retail projects, or projects with retail at their core, at their best can provide a strong sense of community and social interaction for today's increasingly global culture.

Successful shopping environments—from small boutiques to large mixed-use projects—are places where people want to be. People visit retail environments to go shopping, but often to do more: to dine, to recreate, to socialize, and to be entertained. Retail projects have become more than just shopping centers; they have transformed our cities and changed the way we interact with each other. The evolution of retailing has also transformed how we plan and design civic infrastructure as well as commercial and cultural projects.

◀ Retail projects have transformed our cities and influenced how urban centers are planned and designed, including civic infrastructure, cultural facilities, and other commercial structures. Beursplein, Rotterdam, The Netherlands. Designed by The Jerde Partnership in collaboration with T+T Design and de Architeckten Cie. (Photo: Max Kroot Studio.)

▶ The Gateway, Salt Lake City, Utah. The Boyer Company, developer. Designed by the Jerde Partnership. (Photo: Michael McRae.)

▶ Rue du Faubourg Saint Honoré, Paris. (Photo: ©Robert Holmes, Corbis.)

RETAIL IS UNDERRATED

Retail design is underrated as a form of applied art. It has received little critical analysis; however, this is changing. Perhaps it is because this is the one branch of architectural design that can be considered to have a direct impact on an area's financial health. Stores, malls, street vendors, and signs surround us. In the United States alone, there are more than 45,000 shopping centers with a total of more than 5.6 billion sq ft of leasable space. Annual retail sales at the close of the twentieth century accounted for more than $3 trillion annually, nearly one-third of the U.S. gross domestic product (GDP).

Of total retail sales, catalog and Internet sales accounted for approximately $111 billion, or about 5 percent. The rest of retail transactions took place in stores, ranging from 200 sq ft boutiques to multi-million sq ft shopping centers.

RETAIL IS THE NEW PUBLIC REALM

Retail responds to, but also transcends, commercial goals. People love to shop, but there is another reason why retail space has become ubiquitous: Shopping is the foundation of communal life. Whether in the form of a shopping center, a freestanding store, or a street-level shop, retail space makes up the bottom 30 feet of every city. It is the "glue" that holds the city together. Moreover, retail encompasses many types of commercial, civic, and cultural exchange. Within the retail environment we not only exchange goods and services but also share experiences. This is the heart of what is best about vital communities at any scale. Great environments are the foundation of today's global public realm.

Historically, the trade of goods and services has been a fundamental function of good cities.

With the evolution of the suburbs in America, a desire for memorable communal experience has become more pronounced. The mass-produced aspect of suburban sprawl has left many new communities without a public sense of belonging. They lack communal identity and social memory, the ingredients of a "sense of place."

Today, throughout "placeless" suburbs and blighted cities, we are experiencing a

▲ Shopping is at the core of today's urban renaissance. San Francisco Center, San Francisco. The curved escalator, the first to operate at a major commercial establishment, carries visitors to the various levels of this vertical shopping center, which includes a Nordstrom branch. (Photo: Hedrich Blessing.)

renaissance of the urban communal scene, and retail is at its core. Retail and mixed-use designs are answering a desperate need for communal spaces, creating projects that reinvent the authentic urban experience and communal settings that renew a public life of rich variety.

HOW THE MALL TRANSFORMED OUR CITIES

The Jerde Partnership's reinvention of community started 25 years ago with the design of shopping malls.

Why? The death of Main Street, the blight of the inner city, the increasing move to the suburbs, the sterility of so much contemporary development had resulted in a major disconnection between the human community and the built environment. The shopping center was the last place left where American communal life existed; malls remained the de facto meeting points for citizens living and working in the endless suburban sprawl.

We believed the shopping center could again create a communal urban experience and renew a public life of richness and complexity that was denied in the suburban version. This experiment began with Horton Plaza, San Diego, California, a design that broke many rules of the suburban shopping center industry and became a catalyst—drawing a crowd of people, who, once there, experienced a stimulating environment to connect to and share with those around them. Horton Plaza's opening brought to its blighted downtown environment more than $2.5 billion in reinvestment and, 18 years after opening, achieves the highest sales per sq ft rates in the area.

When retail design is done well and properly, it enhances a sense of community in urban spaces and results in lasting social and economic value. Two innovative approaches to design that we, along with many of our peers, have been developing over the last 25 years use retailing as a basis for creating urban life; we call them *placemaking* and *experience design.*

PLACEMAKING: CREATING A BACKDROP FOR URBAN LIFE

To understand placemaking requires, first, an understanding of the idea of *place.* Place includes the physical, human, and emotional qualities of a space. Places are spatial-

ly defined entities with recognizable identities and distinct characters. A *sense of place* is the quality of the visitor's or resident's experience when he or she is in a place.

Great places become so by anonymous editing over time. For example, Paris, Venice, or a Balinese village all took hundreds, even thousands, of years to develop into their present formats. Long periods of trial and error, of tuning and refining, have gone into their creation. They evolved out of deep and continuous cultures and were acted upon by individuals and groups throughout the years. Great places are more than bricks and mortar; they are vessels for collective memory, the accumulation of a kind of public mind.

In this way community consciousness and physical space are joined.

Today, market forces require similar evolutionary processes acting on space to be completed in a much shorter time. Participants in the global economy no longer have the patience for slow growth. Our landscapes and environments are now designed as instant worlds.

Fortunately, we think the communal experience is a designable event. The challenge is to inspire—to trigger—unity out of the dismembered and specialized parts of the once-cohesive city, within the abbreviated time frames of our fast-paced world.

Creating places requires a focus on designing unique spatial experiences using a

◀◀ ▲ Horton Plaza revitalized downtown San Diego, California. It succeeds in drawing crowds of visitors who experience and enjoy its stimulating environment for shopping, dining, and entertainment. More than $2.5 billion was invested in the area in the 15 years after it opened in 1985. Designed by The Jerde Partnership. (Photo: The Jerde Partnership.)

▶ "Placemaking"—creating a backdrop for human life—is not limited by any one aesthetic or visual approach. Creating places utilizes a tool kit of urban, architectural, landscape, and public space elements. Del Mar Plaza, Del Mar, California. Designed by The Jerde Partnership. (Photo: The Jerde Partnership.)

▶ Universal CityWalk, Los Angeles. Designed by The Jerde Partnership. (Photo: Jim Simmons/ Annette Del Zoppo Photography.)

tool kit of urban, architectural, landscape, and public space elements. Placemakers are not limited by any one aesthetic or visual approach. Places can have an urban, suburban, or rural flavor, they can be sophisticated and expensive or simple and functional; but the ways in which the elements are combined give places distinct identities.

We think places are more identifiable in their signature characteristics than an anonymous cityscape or a typically alienating suburban environment. For example, Del Mar Plaza (shown at left) used its hillside site in the beach town of Del Mar as a primary design component. Successful places do more than provide shopping for residents and tourists; they also solidify a sense of place and identity for the cities where they are located.

EXPERIENCE DESIGN: DRAWING A CROWD

For the most part, the retail industry has been focused on function and economics. From the 1960s to the early 1990s, standard market-formula shopping centers spread like wildfire across the United States. Originally designed solely as machines for shopping, these malls lacked the kind of complex experience found in existing urban conditions.

Since the 1990s, however, an increasing number of retail centers have focused on entertainment as an anchor comparable to more typical "soft goods" anchors. For instance, the typical food court has evolved to include a wider selection of restaurants, some with a nationally branded identity. New entertainment anchors

◀ Movies, dining, and entertainment have joined shopping to produce projects that have become more experience oriented. To the feelings of comfort and familiarity, basic attributes of any successful retail establishment, successful shopping centers and stores have added layers of activity and excitement to encourage visitors to explore and discover. Denver Pavilions, Denver, Colorado. Developed by Denhill Denver LLC, a partnership of Arthur Hill & Co., LLC, and Entertainment Development Group. (Photo: Timothy Hursley/ELS.)

also include sophisticated high-tech games, bowling, and other attractions geared to teenagers and families with younger adults. In addition, recent technical evolutions in the cinema have allowed theaters in malls to utilize the latest in stadium seating and sound systems.

As the retail product offering became more experience oriented (movies, dining, and entertainment), so did the project's design. Our newer designs, following the principles of the older prototypes, also add moments of surprise and excitement. In our latest projects, we have tried to create a magical quality of intensity and activity; thereby stimulating the senses. At the same time, we try to preserve a certain comfort level, encouraging in the customers/guests a willingness to explore. The intention is

to allow the practical and the magical to coexist and enhance each other.

IMPACT OF PLACEMAKING AND EXPERIENCE DESIGN

Today's shopping center developers and retailers are recognizing the fundamental role they play in animating urban life. They are extending their reach by providing facilities and services that are part of their community's activity base. In New York City, the Hugo Boss store on Fifth Avenue has a dramatic four-level, glass-enclosed atrium used for art shows and receptions. The new Prada store in the city's Soho district has a grandstand-like seating area that can be used to display shoes and allow customers to try them on, as well as for visitors to view live performances from

▼ *The first floor and lower level at the Prada store in New York City's Soho section is joined by "The Wave." One side is formed of grandstand-like tiers displaying casual shoes and doubling as try-on seating. After store closing, the tiers can be occupied by an audience watching a performance on a stage, out of sight during the day, that can be lowered from the opposite side of The Wave. Designed by OMA Office for Metropolitan Architecture. (Photo: courtesy of Prada.)*

a stage that emerges from a curved wall in front of them.

Both new and renovated retail projects reflect current consumer lifestyle preferences; they are designed with the consumer experience in mind. They are more casual in atmosphere and entertaining in visual amenities. Shopping centers that create a local streetscape, rather than typical enclosed malls, are attracting customers who stay longer and buy more.

In addition, retail and entertainment elements are increasingly being inserted into other building types as a way to draw crowds. Placemaking and experience design are reflected in the new approach that cities, planners, developers, and architects are taking in response to the power of retail. Developers are paying more attention to exterior design than they did 20 years ago. The hard-edge, monolithic look has been replaced by designs that are welcoming, that fit into the neighborhood context, and that utilize landscaping and water features to provide a sense of well-being.

In-store dining, from coffee shops to white linen restaurants, is a major attraction at retail stores. Cafés at bookstores like Barnes & Noble are usually crowded with patrons. The Nicole Farhi upscale women's apparel store near Fifth Avenue in New York City has a handsome restaurant that occupies most of the store's lower level. Marshall Fields's flagship State Street store in Chicago invested in an extensive renovation of its seventh-floor food services areas to bring more shoppers to the store's upper levels. Museums' bookstores and cafeterias are becoming an ever greater part of even these institutions. Sports stadiums are integrating retail and restaurants that are open for business on game day and even when the venue is dark, to take advantage of infrastructure.

▲ Shopping center structures have evolved into designs that fit into the context of the surrounding communities. Landscaping and water features add to the image of an environment that welcomes visitors of all ages. Town Center Drive, Valencia, California. Developed by Newhall Land & Farming Company. Designed by RTKL, Skidmore Owings and Merrill, Johnson Fain, Altoon + Porter. (Photo: Newhall Land & Farming Company.)

▼ The Gateway, Salt Lake City, Utah. Developed by The Boyer Company. Designed by The Jerde Partnership. (Photo: Michael McRae.)

RETAIL WILL CONTINUE TO EVOLVE

How can we keep up with changes in consumer desire? We can make better retail, but can we also learn from retail?

Retail influences cultural, economic, and social trends, and tracks them as well. Retail can be categorized as belonging to the world of pop culture. Pop culture constantly changes. Its mutability represents a challenge for designers. We must constantly probe more deeply into the source of human experiences and into the dynamics of community.

Because retail is flexible and changing with culture shifts, store owners eager to create repeat business are always looking to refresh the product offering, often remodeling in the process. This environment of change is fertile ground for new technology, new brand and marketing techniques, and new design approaches.

▶ *Giants Dugout Store at Pacific Bell Park, San Francisco. Developed by San Francisco Giants/Kajima Urban Development. Designed by Callison Architecture, Inc. (Photo: Chris Eden.)*

THINKING BEYOND RETAIL—CO-CREATIVITY AND THE INTEGRATION OF USES

Retail has much to offer. When properly designed, it can be the common thread knitting together our urban fabric—the bottom 30 feet of every city. We believe that for retail to fully realize its potential, we must not look at it solely as an isolated specialty but properly integrate it with other uses. Integration is one of the most important trends we see for the future of the industry.

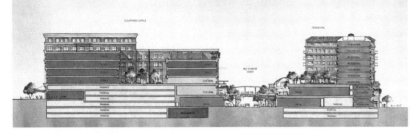

◀ ▼ *Retailing follows shifts in culture and consumer lifestyles. To grow their businesses, merchants and shopping center owners remodel and renovate their facilities, incorporating new design approaches, technology, and services. The Gateway, Salt Lake City, Utah. Developed by The Boyer Company. (Photos: The Jerde Partnership, Michael McRae.)*

▶ *Libby Lu Club, Schaumberg, Illinois. Designed by Chute Gerdeman. (Photo: Michael Roberts, Chicago.)*

For example, in many countries, on many mixed-use projects, we collaborate with other architects who specialize in office, hotel, or cultural venues. Our role is to bring these uses together, usually at the base of the building where retail is the glue. And even though the retail specialty is just as rule bound as any other, there are principles that can be skillfully applied to create a transcendent value for all uses.

Successfully organizing the dozens of design consultants, engineers, client groups, and community workers who influence a project is critical. The process we have developed for this type of collaboration we call "co-creativity." We liken it to playing in a jazz band, with a basic

◀ MGM Grand, Las Vegas, Nevada. Designed by JGA, Inc. (Photo: Laszlo Regos Photography.)

melody and beat, and plenty of room for improvisation by soloists.

We would like the reader to keep that collaborative approach in mind as we explore the principles of the industry in the following chapters. We hope to set a tone that is more observational than prescriptive. We offer "rules" for creating top-notch retail spaces, but we have found that for every rule, there is an exception and a successful example that defies the standard. Our hope, therefore, is that the reader will gain knowledge from exposure to a range of successful retail approaches, and then, with that knowledge, will bend the rules.

CHAPTER 2

THE EVOLUTION OF RETAILING

Events that affect retail evolve, revolve, and change. This process is inherent in the industry and has been since the first entrepreneurial nomads set up tents, displayed their wares, and competed for business. The design for retail has to be resilient yet strong enough to hold up even as other forces come, go, or shift.

HISTORICAL PRECEDENTS

Trade, the bartering of goods and services, has always been a part of the human experience. With the advent of agriculture, however, the nomadic existence of humans was replaced by a more stable lifestyle that fostered the specialization of activities and functions within a permanent community. In the agrarian society,

the basic food needs of an entire community could be provided by a small percentage of the total population, allowing others to pursue different occupations, including the production of goods.

The marketplace, often the commercial and social focal point of early towns and cities, enabled people to access the goods and services of multiple vendors in a convenient manner. The marketplace provided a venue to compare similar goods based on quantity, quality, and cost; it initiated competition for customers—the foundation of modern retailing.

The introduction of currency sparked a revolution in retailing. Currency provided a common basis for the exchange of goods and services. No longer did people with

◀ Outdoor marketplaces such as this one in the plaza of Wiesbaden, Germany, and traditional market halls in towns and villages brought together vendors and buyers. Some operated daily; others blossomed on market days, when farmers and artisans brought their produce and goods to a central location to trade and exchange. (Photo: Bettmann/CORBIS.)

▲ Looking the same today as in this vintage photo circa 1875, Milan's Galleria Vittorio Emanuelle II is at an important crossroads of the city at the Duomo. The elaborate facades unify its restaurants, bars, and shops. Adaptations, most smaller, of the Galleria's signature vaulted glass and iron roof structure can be found in many European cities. (Photo: Bettmann/CORBIS.)

goods need to find others to trade with directly for items they desired. Currency allowed for the "value" of a particular good to be readily transferable for exchange at a later time or in another location.

EIGHTEENTH- AND NINETEENTH-CENTURY DEVELOPMENTS

When retail moved from outdoor, open-air markets to interior spaces, the temporary nature of retailing changed. Arcades, such as the Milan Galleria, created covered streets that allowed for comfortable shopping even in rain or snow and estab-

lished a new context for visual spectacle and continuous movement. Providing the first opportunities for shopping as a leisure time experience, arcades paved the way for the modern shopping mall.

Unlike earlier arcades, the Galeries de Bois offered a diversity of goods for sale; it also attracted a very diverse crowd of strollers/shoppers. After the French Revolution, these galleries became a meeting place for Parisians of all classes. Balzac and others describe the mix of foreigners, burgers, nobles, demi-monde criminals, gentlemen flaneurs, whores and so on, who flocked here for shopping, people watching and much discussion and debate. Here the proto arcade offers a space within the city that can serve as a site for the activities of . . . the newly emerging "public sphere" of interactive debate. At the bookstores here or at the Café American in Galeries de Bois, Parisians entered what was termed a lively verbal "bourse" registering minute changes in reputations or in public values or in public opinion — in this marketplace of ideas — with at this point apparently quite a free trade in ideas. These political, aesthetic or social debates benefited from a liberty not found elsewhere at this time.

— Peter Gibian, lecture, McGill
    University, November 21, 1997

The invention of the price tag fostered another revolution in retailing. No longer did retail depend on face-to-face contact between customer and proprietor. The price tag allowed customers to browse goods and make selections based on a preestablished cost.

Convenience also influenced retailing in the late nineteenth century. Retail stores began to carry more than one item or line of goods, creating the original one-stop shopping experience. The rise of the "department" store represented a milestone achievement in retailing format. Composed of multiple departments, it offered a comprehensive selection of goods and services under one roof.

As competition among retailers increased, the notion of "customer service" evolved. John Wanamaker of Philadelphia and Marshall Field of Chicago moved retailing from a haphazard, "buyer beware" interchange to a deliberate focus on customer service. "Give the lady what she wants!" Field is reputed to have told an inquiring clerk. A few blocks from Field's store, Louis Sullivan designed the

Schlesinger and Mayer store, now Carson Pirie Scott, on State Street, from 1899 to 1904, with its signature first-floor facade.

EARLY TWENTIETH-CENTURY DEVELOPMENTS

When Henry Ford developed the mass-produced automobile at the turn of the century, the opportunity for the modern shopping center industry was born. The automobile afforded easy and convenient transportation, unhindered by schedules or fixed routes. Very quickly it became apparent that traditional patterns of city development could not accommodate the

▼ *Major urban thoroughfares became shopping destinations for the buying public through the first decades of the twentieth century. Examples include Fifth and Madison Avenues in New York City; Washington and Newbury Streets, Boston; Walnut and Chestnut Streets, Philadelphia; Chicago's State Street; Oxford and Bond Streets, London; and the Rue du Faubourg St. Honoré, Paris. This is Calle St. Congalio, Buenos Aires, Argentina. (Photo: Hulton-Deutsch Collection/CORBIS.)*

▲ *Country Club Plaza in Kansas City, Missouri, first opened in 1922, was the first multitenant U.S. shopping center. This view was taken about 1940. (Photo: Special Collections, Kansas City Public Library, Kansas City, Missouri.)*

THE RISE OF THE SHOPPING CENTER

In 1944 the federal government passed the Servicemen's Readjustment Act, commonly known as the GI Bill, which included guaranteed loans for veterans to buy homes, farms, and businesses. With the end of World War II, hundreds of thousands of veterans returned home to restart their lives. Their search for land on which to build homes and businesses, combined with the mobility of the automobile, triggered a mass exodus from the city to the suburbs.

With the availability of television in 1948, product advertising became popular. The age of the consumer dawned, and as new households were being formed in the cities and suburbs (heralding the baby boom), the shopping center and supermarket industries began to take shape.

The 1950s—The Birth of the Shopping Center Industry

From 1950 to 1954, suburbs grew seven times faster than cities, forever altering the physical and social landscape of America. The new, instant communities demanded instant commercial retail centers, and the retail industry responded. Instead of the freestanding structures they had built in the 1930s, department stores began to develop larger projects that included smaller individual tenants. In 1950, the Northgate Shopping Center opened in Seattle, featuring a full-line department store, The Bon Marché, with an open pedestrian mall. Northgate quickly became a model for other shopping centers.

In 1954, the J. L. Hudson department store opened Northland Mall in suburban Detroit, Michigan. The project, which encompassed 700,000 sq ft of retail space in addition to the 600,000 sq ft Hudson's

parking requirements for the rapidly growing number of automobiles.

In Kansas City, J. C. Nichols, a residential developer, anticipated the age of the automobile and began to buy swampland on which to develop a commercial project designed for people who would arrive by car. In 1922, Nichols opened Country Club Plaza, the prototype for the suburban shopping center. Country Club Plaza unified multiple tenants in a single structure, managed by a sole entity, and offered convenient, free parking.

In 1932, Hugh Prather opened Highland Park Shopping Village in a Dallas suburb. The project was unique in that it was centered by an internal parking field; its tenants encircled the parking, their storefronts facing away from the perimeter public streets.

By 1947, the Urban Land Institute had formulated standards for the planning and design of suburban commercial centers.

store, replicated the traditional downtown mix of uses, including a Kroger grocery store and a Kresge furniture store.

In 1956, Dayton Hudson opened the Southdale Mall in Edina, a suburb of Minneapolis, Minnesota. Designed by Victor Gruen & Associates, Southdale Mall broke all the rules of current shopping center design. Unlike the typical model, combining one department store with a single-level, open-air strip, South-dale had two major department stores and two levels of tenant shops. It was also fully enclosed and offered air-condition-ing and heating. To ensure equal access to both levels of tenant shops, Southdale's parking areas were split, with half serving the first level and the other half the sec-ond level. Both department stores placed their fashion apparel on the second level, thereby encouraging fashion tenants to locate on the upper level. The enclosed

◀▲ In the mid-1950s, department store branches in shopping centers began to locate their fashion apparel departments on the second level, drawing traffic through the store to the upper floor. Victor Gruen was the architect for both shopping centers shown here. J. L. Hudson, Northland Mall, suburban Detroit, Michigan. Southdale Mall, Edina, Minnesota. (Photos: Ben Schall, courtesy of Gruen and Associates; Chester Freden, courtesy of Gruen and Associates)

mall provided year-round comfortable shopping, in contrast to the 126 ideal shopping days identified in a 1952 Minneapolis study.

Soon after opening, Southdale became a magnet for other development, including office buildings, a supermarket, strip and other retail centers, a hospital, a medical office building, and apartments. Southdale foretold the power of the shopping center to siphon the economic energy of the city to the suburbs. In 1956 the federal government increased its contribution to the interstate highway system to 90 percent of the total cost. The resulting boom in highway construction provided the accessibility necessary to support the development of the suburban regional shopping center across the country.

In 1957, J.C. Penney, a cash-only department store since its founding in 1902, began to offer credit purchases as a way to attract younger married customers. Consumer credit on a mass basis instantly magnified the purchasing power of consumers and provided additional growth to the rapidly expanding shop-

ping center industry. Also in 1957, the International Council of Shopping Centers (ICSC) was established to provide a forum for shopping center developers to share their experiences and begin to formulate standards that would define the industry. By the end of the 1950s, there were 2,640 shopping centers with an average size of 500,000 sq ft and anchored by one or two department stores.

THE 1960s AND 1970s: GROWTH AND DOMINANCE

The movement to the suburbs provided shopping center developers with almost unlimited opportunities for growth. By 1960 the evolution of the supermarket and the development of the department store were in full swing. America's economy had entered an unprecedented growth cycle, and almost any kind of retail concept met with immediate success. According to an ICSC study, within six years there were 8,420 shopping centers, and within ten years the total had risen to 11,580.

Federal legislation in the 1960s outlawed price fixing, which had previously permitted manufacturers to control the sale of their products at higher prices through traditional department stores. This change allowed the creation of E. J. Korvettes discount department store, which was followed by others, including Wal-Mart, Kohl's, and Target.

The age of consumerism and advertising, coupled with the continued growth of suburban life, dominated retail development in the 1960s and 1970s. The advertising campaigns and national name recognition of department stores reinforced their power in the development of larger-scale retail projects.

Experiments in the development of new towns were conducted in Columbia,

▼ In 1962 customers flocked to the opening of the newest Wal-Mart store in Rogers, Arkansas. Under the leadership of the late founder Sam Walton, Wal-Mart grew to be the largest company in the United States, ranked number one in the Fortune 500, with sales in 2001 reaching $2.2 billion. (Photo: courtesy Wal-Mart Stores, Inc.)

Maryland, and Reston, Virginia, where the shopping center was designed as the community focal point.

The regional shopping typology began to make its way back to the city as a tool to revitalize derelict and abandoned urban cores. In 1962, the Victor Gruen-designed Midtown Plaza opened in Rochester, New York, and was immediately praised as a successful model for downtown revitalization. It is credited with triggering the construction of a number of new office towers in downtown Rochester, an extensive skyway system connecting the towers with Midtown Plaza, and a seven-level office and retail complex that was ultimately integrated into the project.

Midtown Plaza was followed by a number of urban revitalization efforts with shopping centers at their core. And as shopping centers began to spring up in other cities, they took on new forms to fit within the urban context. Water Tower Place, for instance, which opened in Chicago in 1975, was the first vertical center to be built in the United States. The 74-story mixed-use complex, combining eight levels of shopping with a luxury hotel, dining, offices, and residential and parking, helped transform Michigan Avenue into a world-class shopping area.

In 1976, Faneuil Hall opened in Boston, revitalizing the important historical structure (built in 1742, it has hosted many famous speakers and is where George Washington toasted the nation's first birthday), which had fallen into disrepair by the mid-1900s, as the city's central meeting place. Today it serves as a tourist destination and includes 70 shops, 14 restaurants, and 40 food stalls.

Horton Plaza opened in downtown San Diego in 1985. Horton Plaza was de-

signed by The Jerde Partnership, not as a project or a building, but as a unique multiuse, six-block district of the city. To create a compelling urban place, Jerde employed a multilevel, double-curved diagonal "street" linking the four department store anchors. The street, which became the axis connecting downtown with the waterfront, was designed to provide a sense of surprise and discovery. According to the Centre City Development Corporation, Horton Plaza has helped trigger more than $2.5 billion of reinvestment and development in the downtown core. (See pages 4-5.)

▲ *Water Tower Place on Chicago's North Michigan Avenue has eight levels of stores reachable by clear enclosed elevators. Lord & Taylor and Marshall Field's are the anchors. Designed by Loebl, Schlossman & Hackl. (Photo: Hedrich-Blessing.)*

▲ *Faneuil Hall Marketplace in Boston, one of the Rouse Company's highly successful festival marketplaces. Architects: BTA Architects, Inc. (Photo: Steve Rosenthal.)*

The new technology of the time also affected the retail environment. For instance, the invention of the bar scanner and new forms of merchandise distribution allowed for tighter inventory controls, almost completely eliminating the need for storerooms in the typical specialty store.

1980s TO TODAY

Mass media, globalization, and the Internet have brought great change to our lives—and to retail. The influence of American culture is more palpable worldwide, and American architects are beginning to do more commercial work in foreign countries. Americans are moving from mass consumption to the experience economy, leading to a boom in travel, tourism, and themed environments. Consumers are also becoming more educated; comparison shopping, consumer reports, power centers, big boxes, and outlet centers, and now the Internet, are creating increasing competition for price and value.

In the 1980s and 1990s the department store industry consolidated. Shopping centers throughout the United States have the same four or five department stores. Industry consolidation has also affected mini-anchors, such as The Gap, The Limited, and Crate & Barrel, to name a few. Developers are turning to credit-worthy national chain tenants that use most of the leaseable space, thereby reducing the number of small ma-and-pa shops.

There has also been a counter swing to rejuvenation of the downtown main street and traditional shopping arcas. Local governments are investing in area improvements, such as parking. Examples include Melrose Avenue in Los Angeles and Montana Avenue in Santa Monica; Old Town Pasadena; Old City, South Street, the University area, and the Manayunk section in Philadelphia; the Lower East Side and the East Village in New York City; Fifth Street in Seattle; the North River area and Navy Pier in Chicago; the South End and Boylston Street in Boston; and Union Street in San Francisco.

During the 1990s urban entertainment centers spread worldwide. A popular destination for residents of Budapest, Hungary, for example, is Duna Plaza, a shopping and entertainment center featuring an indoor ice rink and nine movie screens, and the first of many malls planned for that city. Such centers are springing up on obsolete industrial sites and in the suburbs of old cities in Europe and Asia.

The elements that lead to a successful project are changing constantly and at a hyperaccelerated pace. Previously, if a shopping center developer had two or three good department stores lined up for a new mall, the success of the project was virtually guaranteed. Today, fewer department stores are opening in shopping centers. Their strategies are focused on appealing to a new generation of customers and making their existing real estate more productive.

LIFESTYLE SHIFTS

Today's savvy retailers have their fingers on the pulse of the consumer. By analyzing the bundles of information gleaned from electronic data capture, they know more about what their customers do and the products they purchase to support their lifestyles.

The buying public is increasingly sophisticated today: people know they have choices. In years gone by, consumers went to the department store as their main destination for clothing and home goods because there were few specialty retail operations. They bought what the store carried. Now, because there are far more retailing formats, including the Internet, in just about every merchandise category, consumers are a lot more knowledgeable. They will drive 40 miles to shop at an outlet center if they think they will get better value.

One of the remarkable and interesting evolutions of retailing of the last 10–15 years is the recognition that better service and improved customer interaction benefits the entire community. Sporting goods superstores operated by Bass Pro and Cabela's demonstrate how a service-oriented approach to buying and selling can upgrade the entire commercial life of a community.

These retailers are creating demand for their products where there was previously no demand. Nike is probably the best example. There was no such thing as a "sport shoe" 30 years ago. Nike's marketers created a product and a way of merchandising that product that has to do with lifestyle and intangibles, com-

municated in physical space through Niketown and by print and electronic advertising.

Thematic shopping is another kind of design storytelling that began in high-traffic tourist destinations such as Las Vegas and Orlando. It is an outgrowth of the relationship between entertainment, media, and retailing. By combining environments that dazzle the senses with fairy-tale-like settings and extended hours, retailers in The Forum Shops at Caesar's Palace average $1,200 per sq ft in gross sales, as compared with a typical boutique average of $300–400 per sq ft.

Mass merchant Target's campaign of high-quality ads and sophisticated store display and merchandise selection has won over a middle-market consumer. Target has created a dialogue between the way it merchandises its brand and its store design. It is now more related to its customers' sense of style and shopping patterns than it was 15–20 years ago.

▲ *Mizner Park in Boca Raton, Florida, is an example of a successful "Main Street" project. Such projects draw on traditional downtown environments for scale and diversity of activities, interpreted in a contemporary setting. (Photo: courtesy of Cooper Carry, Inc., Stephen Traves Photography.)*

TRENDS

Most large retail companies are publicly owned and have to show growth. They must keep their assortments fresh and, at the same time, determine how to expand. They can continue to grow by buying other stores or firms, by conglomerating, or by introducing brand new products.

Units of chains have replaced the small independent stores in many markets across the United States. There are few operator-owned bookstores, candy stores, hardware stores, pharmacies, groceries, or banks. House to Home is a home decorating version of Home Depot. It has a patio department, plant nursery, and lawn care section. Its competitive position, between Bed Bath and Beyond and Crate & Barrel, is a good example of creating a focused niche market. Walgreen's drugstore chain has begun to deemphasize broad retail and concentrate on the pharmacy. It is seeking to provide other services, such as smaller drive-throughs so customers need not leave their cars.

Significant cosynergies are occurring. Home Depot now has joint ventures with McDonald's. Taco Bell and Kentucky Fried Chicken are co-locating in the same stores. Burger King is testing a dual location with an enterprise with a Mexican menu. They will save on real estate and the number of employees each would normally have. A facility in Culver City, California, offers in-store service with a window to the outside. Service stations with convenience stores and take-out food are becoming more common.

Retail venues are utilized to support other main uses. Museums, transportation facilities, and sports stadiums now have stores, open seven days a week. At a rehab at the America West Sports Stadium in Phoenix, developers are carving out the space beneath the seats. Retail is being attached to create an arcade that is tucked into the stadium so that it will have year-round vitality. Such spaces are typically dark 90 percent of the day. San Diego Stadium has an open park outside the outfield, surrounded by commercial enterprises. This is quite a sophisticated and high-quality concept in a very high density urban situation.

CHANGES THAT WILL CONTINUE TO AFFECT CONSUMERS AND RETAILERS

Demographic and Lifestyle Changes
An aging population
More working women
A focus on leisure
A demand for value
Dilution of the traditional family unit
Less discretionary time
More eating away from home
A demand for personal services

Operating Issues
Limited labor availability
Technological changes
Competition
Capital-intensive requirements
Growth of nonstore shopping modes
  (Internet, catalogs, TV, telemarketing)

Concept Changes
Stores that dominate a merchandise category at retail,
  also known as "category killers"
Wholesale clubs
Niche retailers
Enlarged grocery stores
Changes to the traditional department store

New Retailing Formats
Urban revitalization and redevelopment
Airport redevelopment
Entertainment retail formats
TV shopping, infomercials
Catalogs

Source: *The Jerde Partnership*

The Internet has made the buying public extremely savvy and well prepared. Increasingly, researched shopping, based on price, availability, and desirable features, is done on-line.

Transportation and the relationship between the public and private realms will continue to be one of the most interesting and challenging design problems. As more third-world countries obtain private automobiles, the issues of circulation, public transport, scale, pollution, sprawl, garaging, and the like will need new and better solutions.

Energy efficiency and environmental sustainability will become increasingly important components of retail design, even in light of the extremely cost-conscious, short-term interests of the typical commercial developer. Particularly in Europe, green building techniques are a require-

ment of all large-scale projects, especially semipublic enterprises. In Asia, demonstration of environmental sustainability is becoming more a requirement than an option in projects in which the government (or a government agency) is a partner.

When the California energy crisis began in 2000, retail shop owners were asked to turn off the lights after closing—an example highlighting the need for greater efficiency and sustainability. New thinking on technical issues of heat recovery, watershed control, passive design, solar collection, cogeneration, and central cooling systems will be more commonly applied to retail projects.

Stores that offer greater personal service, unique merchandise, high-quality display, product testing, and other such benefits will be rewarded with greater local patronage, leading to a greater local identity.

▼ *No Problem on Melrose Avenue, Los Angeles, invites customers inside with an open storefront that spans the width of the store.*

SOME EARLY GIANTS OF U.S. RETAILING

Samuel Carson was co-founder, with John T. Pirie, of the LaSalle, Illinois, store Carson, Pirie, Scott & Company (1854), which in the 1860s moved to Chicago. Carson pioneered the idea that costs could be cut if wholesalers were bypassed and goods were bought directly from the manufacturers. The famous facade of the State Street store was designed by architect Louis Sullivan.

Marshall Field began his career as a Chicago wholesaler, but he is best known for the store he founded in 1881, Marshall Field & Company. Field, who believed in refinement and the personal touch, adopted the motto "Give the lady what she wants." He was responsible for such store policies as "money back if not satisfied," free delivery, emphasis on imports, and many other retailing innovations.

William Filene opened a successful store in Salem, Massachusetts, in 1856, and some years later, two small stores in Lynn, Massachusetts. In 1881, Filene opened his Boston store (later known as William Filene's Sons Company). By 1890 the store was the largest in Boston retailing women's ready-to-wear. The business was carried on by Filene's two sons, Edward and Lincoln.

Adam Gimbel opened his first store in Vincennes, Indiana, in 1842, where he gained a reputation for honesty and his insistence on a fixed price policy for the goods he sold. The organization was carried on by his sons after his death as Gimbel Brothers, Inc. In 1910 a store was opened in New York City, in direct competition with Macy's, under the direction of Adam's grandson Bernard Gimbel. The last Gimbel's store closed in 1987.

Edwin Goodman went to work as a tailor (1899) for the New York retailer Bergdorf-Voight and, after assuming control of the firm, built what is now Bergdorf Goodman. A man of taste and judgment, Goodman moved his elegant establishment to its present location at Fifth Avenue and 58th Street in 1928. It is now part of the Neiman Marcus Group.

Joseph Lothian Hudson opened his Detroit store in 1881 after having operated an Ionia, Michigan, store for some years. By 1890, the J. L. Hudson Company was a true department store and on its way to becoming a Detroit institution. Hudson was known for his aggressiveness and competitiveness, his integrity, and a sense of responsibility to the community. The Dayton Hudson Corporation was formed through a merger of the Dayton Corporation and the J. L. Hudson Company in 1969. The Corporation acquired Mervyn's (1978), Marshall Field's (1990), Rivertown Trading Company, and the Associated Merchandising Corporation (1997). In 2000 the company changed its name to Target Corporation. Currently there are 1,000 Target stores in 46 states, 64 Marshall Field's stores in 8 states, and 267 Mervyn's stores in 14 states.

Eben Dyer Jordan founded (1851) the Jordan Marsh Company, Boston, with partner Benjamin L Marsh. The early success of the store was largely due to Jordan's extensive buying trips across the country in search of quality merchandise. He was one of the first American merchants to use the phrase, "The customer is always right." An innovator, he introduced the first telephone to be used in a department store.

Fred Lazarus, Jr., was the grandson of Simon Lazarus, founder of F. & R. Lazarus, Columbus, Ohio. Fred served as store president for many years and, in 1939, was responsible for organizing the movement that culminated in President Franklin D. Roosevelt's designating the fourth Thursday in November as Thanksgiving Day. Lazarus was at heart a showman and used many promotional gimmicks to attract customers to the store. In 1945, Lazarus took command of Federated Department Stores, which he had helped found, and was responsible for expanding the member stores to include Foley's (1945), Burdine's (1957), and Bullocks (1964).

Frieda "Mamma" Loehmann took the emerging concept of discounting and brought it upscale. In 1921 she opened a store in Brooklyn that she stocked by going around to Seventh Avenue apparel manufacturers, buying overstocked items, cutting out their labels, and selling them. Eventually the company became a chain of stores, with headquarters in the Bronx. Loehmann's innovations gave rise to a whole generation of discount retailers.

Samuel Lord founded in 1826, with his wife's cousin George W. Taylor, a store that was to become Lord & Taylor. Lord never entered into price competition with other stores, always regarding his customers as the carriage trade.

Rowland H. (R. H.) Macy, born in 1822, opened a small dry goods emporium in New York City in 1857, where first-day sales totaled $11.06. During the first year, Macy spent $2,800 on advertising and finished the year with $85,000 in sales. Later, Macy's moved uptown on 34th Street at Herald Square, opening the largest retail store in the United States. Macy's set new holiday standards with elaborate illuminated window displays and an in-store Santa Claus. It is also famous for its Thanksgiving Day Parade and Spring Flower Show. Currently, there are 137 Macy's stores in operation on the West Coast and 117 stores on the East Coast.

Herbert Marcus founded, with his sister Carrie and her husband A. O. Neiman, Neiman-Marcus in Dallas, Texas (1907). From the beginning, Marcus insisted on style and quality in his store.

Stanley Marcus in 1926 joined the family business, the Neiman-Marcus retail store. By the 1940s he had put his imprint on the store, and he took it over when his father (Herbert) died in the early 1950s. Marcus developed nationally recognized advertising and sales-promotion events, such as the annual Fortnight celebrations that feature the entertainment, culture, and luxury offerings of countries such as France, Italy, and elsewhere. He developed the *Christmas Book,* the catalog that features the renowned "His and Her Gifts," ranging from matching camels to mummy cases. The Neiman Marcus Group achieved a record $3 billion in revenues in fiscal 2001. The company operates 32 Neiman Marcus stores across the United States and two Bergdorf Goodman stores in Manhattan. Marcus died in January 2002 at the age of 96.

David May, after having successfully run a store in the boomtown of Leadville, Colorado, opened a larger store in Denver (1888). Four years later he took over the Famous Company in St. Louis (now Famous-Barr). A promoter by nature, May continued to add stores to his group until, in 1910, it became the May Department Stores Company.

James Cash Penney's first store, the Golden Rule, opened in 1902, operated strictly on a cash basis because Penney considered the extension of credit immoral. The store was noted for its one-price policy and its emphasis on good customer relations. By 1913 there were 36 Golden

Rule stores, which were incorporated that year as the J. C. Penney Company. There are 1,050 stores in all 50 U.S. states, Puerto Rico, and Mexico. The company also operates 49 Renner department stores in Brazil.

Morris Rich, founder of Rich's in Atlanta shortly after the Civil War, is perhaps best remembered for his policy of accepting returned merchandise without question and for the general air of Southern hospitality associated with the store. Currently there are 26 stores in three states.

Alvah Curtis Roebuck, a watchmaker, became involved with R. W. Sears when he answered an ad for a watchmaker for Sears's watch company. Roebuck organized an assembly line for watchmaking in 1887. The company did not become known as Sears, Roebuck and Company until 1893, but by 1895 Roebuck had sold his interest in the firm.

Horace Saks, son of founder Andrew Saks, became president of Saks and Company upon his father's death in 1912. He is largely responsible for the fashionable, gracious image Saks reflects even today. The company operates 359 stores in 39 states, with more than $6.5 billion in annual revenues.

Richard Warren Sears began with R.W. Sears Watch Company in 1886. He first conceived the idea of a small Sears catalog and wrote all the copy for it. The company became known as Sears, Roebuck and Company for the first time in September 1893. At the close of its 2000 fiscal year, Sears operated 863 mall-based retail stores, most with co-located Sears Auto Centers, and an additional 1,200 retail locations including hardware, outlet, and tire and battery stores, as well as independently owned stores, primarily in smaller and rural markets. Sears, Roebuck and

Company is also the majority owner of Sears Canada Inc., one of Canada's largest retailers. Sears Canada operates 125 full-line stores, 176 specialty stores, and 1,550 independently owned catalog agents and dealer stores.

Harry Gordon Selfridge began as a Marshall Field executive, where he instituted Field's bargain basement. Selfridge also introduced the first restaurant to the store. In 1909, Selfridge emigrated to London where he founded his own store, Selfridge & Company.

Dorothy Shaver was president of Lord & Taylor from 1945 until her death in 1959. She is best remembered for making the store a fashion leader and for her promotion of American fashion designers.

Alexander T. Stewart, in 1846, erected at Broadway and Chambers Street a five-story retail giant, in Italian renaissance style, that was known as the Marble Palace. Wildly successful, it was the first self-service department store and spawned a host of copycats in the 1850s, transforming a section of Manhattan along lower Broadway into a retailing mecca, a center of fashion and trends in the United States. In 1862, Stewart built an even larger store, dubbed the Iron Palace, on Broadway at Ninth Street. By the mid-1860s, Stewart's business was grossing $50 million a year, and he became one of the city's wealthiest residents.

Justus Clayton Strawbridge, with his business partner, Isaac Hallowell Clothier, opened a small dry goods store in Philadelphia in 1868, which later became Strawbridge and Clothier department store. The company was bought by the May Department Store Company in 1995.

Charles L. Tiffany started a jewelry importing firm in 1841 with two partners.

Twelve years later, he brought them out and founded the influential Tiffany & Company. He was active until 1902. The store set new standards for style and prestige in retailing and has since become an international chain of stores selling jewelry, watches, gifts, and tableware. As of 2001, Tiffany had 42 U.S. and 77 international stores.

Sam Walton (1918–1992) was the founder of Wal-Mart Stores, Inc. In 1962 he opened his first Wal-Mart in Rogers, Arkansas, offering a wide selection of discount merchandise. Walton based his stores in small towns where there was little competition. With the use of this strategy, the chain expanded to 800 stores by 1985 and to 1,700 by 1992. Today it is the world's largest retailer, with nearly 3,500 facilities in operation in the United States and more than 1,000 units in Mexico, Puerto Rico, Canada, Argentina, Brazil, China, Korea, Germany, and the United Kingdom.

John Wanamaker, considered the greatest merchant of his day, opened his first store in 1861, the Oak Hall Clothing Bazaar in Philadelphia. It was the largest space devoted to retail selling on a single floor of that era. In 1896, Wanamaker bought the Cast Iron Palace in New York and opened his New York store. Among Wanamaker's "firsts" in a department store are the first white sale, the first restaurant, the first telephones, the first ventilation fan system, and the first to use U.S. Parcel Post for delivery. He also led in the hiring of women; the granting of bonuses, insurance, pensions, and health benefits; in providing recreational facilities for employees and establishing employee relations.

Aaron Montgomery Ward founded, in 1872, the first firm to sell a wide variety of products by mail from Chicago. His slogan was "Satisfaction Guaranteed, or Your Money Back." Ward also established testing labs for his merchandise and was the forerunner in offering several grades and price ranges in each class of goods. The company is no longer in operation.

Frank Winfield Woolworth opened his first "Great 5-Cent Store" in February 1879 in Utica, New York, and it was a failure. In May of the same year, however, he moved to Lancaster, Pennsylvania, and opened the world's first five-and-ten. Woolworth used quantity buying to obtain the lowest possible prices and often tied up entire factories for extended periods of time. In 1913 he completed the Woolworth building in New York City, the 50-story "Skyqueen." The company now operates as Foot Locker, Inc.

Brigham Young, the Mormon leader, was the founder of Zions Cooperative Mercantile Institution. Zions, founded in 1868, claims to be "America's first department store," which is its current slogan.

CHAPTER 3
WHERE PEOPLE SHOP

In a competitive retailing environment, superior design can be the critical difference between success and failure for an individual merchant or a multitenant shopping center. To succeed, a merchant or shopping center must offer an enhanced buying experience to distinguish itself from others.

THE EXPERIENCE OF SHOPPING—WHY RETAIL DESIGN IS IMPORTANT

Today, excellence in retail design is more important than ever. Not only does a retail store have to compete with other retail stores for customers, but shopping, as a social activity, also has severe competition. In *Why We Buy: The Science of Shopping*, author Paco Underhill (2000) notes, "The routine shopping trip is no longer the great

escape. It's now something that must be crammed into the spaces between job and commute and home life and sleep. It's something to be rushed through over a lunch hour, on the way home or at night."

A pleasant shopping experience will not only attract customers, but it will also allow goods and services to be sold at a higher price. *The Experience Economy,* by Pine and Gilmore (1999), describes customer perception of value at four levels: as commodities, goods, service, and experience. Consider coffee as an example. Coffee beans purchased as a commodity on the wholesale market will yield a price of $0.03 per cup of coffee. If the customer buys the coffee as a good in a grocery store, then the value is $0.10 per cup. If the cup of coffee is purchased in an aver-

◀ Many factors contribute to providing the customer with a positive shopping experience. These include the image of the shopping area, the exterior and interior designs of individual stores, and the quality and value of the merchandise offered and presented by the merchants in freestanding, urban, or shopping center locales. Newbury Street, Boston, has upscale shops located in buildings that are more than a century old in the city's Back Bay section. Art galleries and residences occupy the upper floors. (Photo: courtesy Newbury Street Merchant's Association.)

▶ Signage and choice of exterior materials help to communicate REI's message to the customer. (Photo: courtesy MulvannyG2 Architecture.)

▶ Rodeo Drive in Beverly Hills, California, is a thoroughfare devoted to high-end shopping. This prime corner location is occupied by a unit of the Bulgari chain of jewelry and accessories stores. (Photo: courtesy Rodeo Drive Committee.)

age coffee shop, it will cost $1.00–$2.00 per cup. But if the consumer wants an experience to go with the cup of coffee and stops at Harry's Bar in Venice, Italy, facing a fifteenth-century piazza, the bill could be as much as $15. More retailers, like Starbucks, are creating experiences to enhance the value of their product. The price for a cup of coffee at Starbucks is not so much for the coffee bean as for the cost of the design of the store and the experience created. Consumers are willing to pay a premium in return for enjoying a better experience.

WHY PEOPLE SHOP

How do designers create environments that enhance the buying experience? What are the fundamental components to making that happen, whether the project is the interior of a store or a regional shopping center? What are the basic principles designers need to understand?

What brings the customer to a store?

- Quality
- Need
- Value
- Price
- Impulse

What attracts the customer, prompting him or her to enter a store?

- The store's "image"
- Architectural design
- Signage
- The store's interior

What motivates customers to buy?

- Perceived value
- Design
- Price

- Ambience
- Merchandise presentation

Underhill (2000) identifies the following critical aspects of successful retail design.

Psychology of Movement and Circulation

It is possible to anticipate and even determine how and where people will walk—people go in predictable paths and speed up, slow down, and stop in response to their surroundings.

Where shoppers go, what they see, and how they respond determine the very na-

▲ *This men's wear boutique attracts shoppers with open-back windows that allow viewers to see into the store and a header over the main entrance carrying the logo of the highly promoted Ralph Lauren line. (Photo: Vilma Barr.)*

▶ Shops in transportation hubs cater to travelers and commuters. Their design has become a specialty for such firms as Silvester Tafuro Design, Inc., which has created facilities like this Euro Café combination newsstand and coffee bar at Dulles International Airport, Washington, D.C., for its client, Hudson News Co. Fixtures are cherrywood veneer; flooring and countertops are granite. (Photo: Peter Paige Photography.)

▶ Shoppers can be encouraged to examine product displays by the combining of such elements as the shape and placement of the fixtures; the dynamics of the merchandise arrangement, lighting, signs, floor covering patterns, background and accent colors; and the overall appeal of the ambience created. Club Libby Lu is targeted to girls aged 7–12. This 1,600 sq ft store in the Woodfield Mall, Schaumburg, Illinois, is divided into four main activity rooms: bath and body, T-shirts, jewelry, and dress-up. Colors in the floor covering and display fixtures help guide visitors through the store. Design: Chute Gerdeman. (Photo: Michael Roberts, Chicago.)

◀ Sentry Foods, Madison, Wisconsin, promoted its brand with the theme "America's Market." Expanding the space to 54,000 sq ft, the designers worked with millwork and fixture manufacturers to create the fronts of cases to be merchandisable. Architects: Strang Associates; interior design: Marco Design Group; lighting: Creative Lighting Design & Engineering. (Photo: Laszlo Regos Photography.)

ture of their shopping experiences. They will either see merchandise and signs clearly or they won't. They will reach objects easily or with difficulty. They will move through areas at a leisurely pace or swiftly—or not at all. All of these physiological and anatomical factors come into play simultaneously, forming a complex matrix of behaviors that must be understood if the retail environment is to adapt itself successfully to the "animal that shops."

Maximum Exposure to Merchandise

A good store is, by definition, one that exposes the greatest portion of its goods to the greatest number of its shoppers for the longest period of time—in other words, the store that puts its merchandise in our path and our field of vision in a way that invites consideration.

Architects have to design stores with sight lines in mind. They must ensure that shoppers will be able to see what is in front of them but also able to look around and see what is elsewhere.

Getting shoppers to the back wall of any store is usually a challenge. Blockbuster Video has trained its customers to go directly to the back wall—because that is where the new releases are kept. Wisely, most retailers do not sell their bread-and-butter merchandise from the back wall. Still, every square foot of selling space is equally expensive to rent, heat, and light.

Merchandise Presentation— What Do Shoppers Love?

- *Touch.* Almost all unplanned buying is a result of touching, hearing, smelling, or tasting something on the premises of a store. That is why the

▼ *A sense of discovery keeps shoppers moving from one display to another. "Never Stop Exploring" is the trademark motto for the North Face chain. Entry to the 7,500 sq ft store is a winding path. The interior design was based on interpreting the technical aspects of exploration and the athletes and the places they go. Design by JGA, Inc. (Photo: Laszlo Regos Photography.)*

Internet, catalogs, and home shopping on TV will complement but never seriously challenge real-live stores.

- *Mirrors.* Mirrors slow shoppers in their tracks. Stores generally fail to provide enough of them, much less put them in the right places.

- *Discovery.* Stores should seduce shoppers through the aisles with suggestions and hints of what is to come. The aroma of bread can be enough to lead supermarket shoppers to the bakery aisle.

- *Talking.* If you can create an atmosphere that fosters discussion of an outfit, say, or a telephone, the merchandise begins to sell itself.

- *Dressing rooms.* Men and women who design clothing stores do everything possible to allow us to touch all that is for sale. Yet when it is time to design the dressing rooms, they show how completely they misunderstand what happens inside that space. When the customer is in the dressing room, he or she is in total buying mode. But instead of taking advantage of that moment, most stores squander it.

◀ Sales in 2001 for Swedish international retailer Hennes & Mauritz AB totaled $1.1 billion. It operates more than 780 H&M stores worldwide, selling fashionable and popular-priced male and female apparel and accessories. Its stores are characterized by wide open, inviting entries to support its high-traffic, high-volume operation. (Photo: Courtesy Joseph Weishar.)

▼ Retailers and manufacturers are emphasizing brand identity, starting with young consumers. This "Kids Korner" is in the entertainment area of Bell World Flagship Store at Eaton Center, Toronto, Canada. Design by HOK Canada. (Photo: courtesy Ronald Ng Photography.)

Service

Bad times are times when the customer is made to wait. In study after study, the single most important factor in determining a shopper's opinion of the service he or she receives is waiting time. Quite simply, a short wait enhances the entire shopping experience and a long wait poisons it.

In truth, retailers compete with every other demand on consumer time and money. The era of the visionary retailer or manufacturer king is over. In the twenty-first century the consumer will be king. Just as fashion now comes from the streets, making its way up to the trendy designers, the world of retail is about following shoppers where they are going.

Today's shoppers are fickle, and their loyalty to a brand name—of a product or of a store—lasts only as long as the afterglow of the most recent shopping experience.

CHAPTER 4
RETAIL STORE PLANNING

PROGRAM DEVELOPMENT

During the planning snd design process, the store designer is part of a merchant's operating team. The project program becomes the roadmap to creating sales-stimulating, profit-building environments.

From its inception to the completion of a store design and construction project, the program is the basis for verbal communication between the merchant and the designer. It is the designer's job to ask the relevant questions that provide the database for the design development phase. The client's merchandising goals will translate into the program's backbone.

The Objectives of Store Design

Prior to initiating a store design, an understanding of the basic objectives is essential.

- Recognition factor: A store, large or small, needs to stand out from its surroundings and its competition, regardless of its size.

- Strategic advantage: A distinctive, memorable personality is a necessary component of a successful, profitable store.

- The designer's proposed solutions to the retail client's needs must be responsive to basic merchandising concept. For any type of retail-related assignment, the designer needs to understand the following:

  The context and location of the project

  The customer base the store will attract

  The circulation and basic flow pattern of interior and exterior traffic

  The architectural objectives

  The merchandise spatial allocations

Other areas to which the retail designer should be sensitive include the following:

- Consumer trends in spending, buying patterns, and fashion trends

- The corporate culture, if the retailer is a large organization

- The image that the owners wish to project

- The appeal of the merchandise, including price points and the fashion outlook

- Budgets

- Codes, including life safety, and the requirements of the Americans with Disabilities Act (ADA)

- Schedules, including those of other consultants and the trades

- Societal aspects: Malls and individual store types, such as bookstores, have become social nodes where people meet and spend time together as well as purchase products.

Design Program

During the planning of a retail store, the program becomes a reference for the designer and the client throughout the design process. It is used to define the needs of the client, the constraints within which the design will be developed, and the budget required to make the design feasible. Depending on the scope of the project, the program can be as simple as a one-page checklist or as complex as a multiple-page document of questions and answers. The program summarizes such issues as functional requirements, building areas, and so forth.

RETAIL STORE PLANNING

▶ Planning for a retail store requires an understanding of the image that the merchant hopes to project and, if it is a large organization, the corporate culture. When Petro-Canada embarked on a countrywide upgrading of more than 2,000 of its service stations and convenience stores, the new design upgraded the company's overall image. (Above right) Plan of the convenience store and (right) photo of the interior. Architect Charles E. Broudy, FAIA, worked closely with Petro-Canada's marketing and operations executives to understand the objectives of the company's "revitalization" program. He sat in on focus group sessions and reviewed extensive customer profile information. The final scheme utilized long-wearing, low-cost products, and has boosted sales volume beyond expectations. (Photo courtesy Charles E. Broudy & Associates.)

Sensitivity to the national or global economy is a historical trait of the retail industry. When the economy is strong, retailers aggressively renovate existing stores, add new units to the chain, or launch new formats. When the steam goes out of the economy, as it did following the decade of the 1990s and into 2001, a slowdown or a recession may cause the retailer to limit expansion. Still, the designer can maintain a flow of work in this field by proposing cost-effective, traffic-building ideas to retailers that will put them ahead of the competition as the economy recovers.

Basic Programming Considerations

The following topics will give the designer who is new to the current retail market a quick overview of the scope of information that contributes to the working pro-

gram for a retail store. Readers can adapt the information presented here as a questionnaire, checklist, or agenda topics for a client meeting.

Store type/location

Type of Store Ownership: Independent, chain, franchise, manufacturer owned, operated by an overseas company

Project Name: Placement and type style of store name; logo design if applicable

Location: Enclosed mall, strip mall, freestanding, urban

Size: Selling areas, support areas

Number of Floors: Above and below grade phase

Exterior environment

- What is the nature of the surrounding neighborhood?

◀ To communicate their concepts for The North Face prototype store in Beverly Hills, California, designers JGA, Inc., presented an Image Board that contained photos of the outdoors and elegant interiors. An eclectic, subtle use of materials provides the contrast to simulate the environments in which the products will be used, outdoors and indoors. A large stonelike sculpture arch element spans the width of the store and frames the product displays inside. (Laszlo Regos Photography.)

▶ Located in the Charlotte, North Carolina, Douglas International Airport, Simply Books presents a warm and gracious environment, a distinct contrast to the bustling pace of the airport itself. The design solution includes a graphic communication system that facilitates the purchase process. Three pendant lighting fixtures help the customer identify the cashwrap. Chute Gerdeman (Michael Houghton Photography.)

▶ Customers combine shopping with in-store dining to enhance the retail experience. Retailers today are also expanding their roster of services, ranging from banking to child care. Bloomingdale's restaurants, such as this one in the Aventura Mall near Miami, Florida, are sleek and contemporary, with extended counter seating for customers with limited time. Robert Young Associates. (Photo: Paul Bielenberg.)

- Define the adjacent commercial area: shopping center or block; strip or freestanding stores?
- How will existing colors, textures, architectural styles, and graphics affect the store's design?
- Is traffic primarily vehicular or pedestrian?

Schedule/budget

- Estimated opening date: for new construction; for renovation, completion date by phase
- Time frames
    Consultants and various trades
    Building code and other agency approvals
    Advance ordering of equipment and supplies
    Construction budget

Operational issues

Type of service
- Full service
- Self-service
- Combination

Special services
- Dining facilities: coffee bar, cafeteria, sit-down restaurant
- Child care facilities
- Auditorium, meeting rooms
- Coat check
- Gift wrap
- Beauty salon, spa
- Financial services: investments, banking

Technological considerations

- Scanning equipment (stationary or portable)
- Internet stations for customer use
- Owner's computerized inventory control system
- Information kiosks and selling kiosks
- Checkout configuration: placement of cashwrap(s); cashier stations

Storage

- Concealed stock in floor displays
- Stock stored in drawers or behind doors on the sales floor
- Stockroom and backup areas
- Remote off-site storage

▼ *Stores that specialize in wireless communication and other technology products are proliferating. The placement of Internet stations, kiosks, and interactive displays at this Cingular store are sculptural, colorful, and inviting. Callison Architecture. (Photo: Chris Eden.)*

Characteristics of the merchandise

What will be sold in the store? The following are some classifications:

- Clothing: men's, women's, children's
- Accessories: belts, scarves, hats, hosiery, jewelry
- Shoes: men's, women's, children's
- Home furnishings: furniture, carpeting, lamps and lighting, wall décor
- Food: supermarket, bread store, coffee shop, sandwich shop, gourmet shop
- Office supplies
- Gifts
- Cosmetics and beauty products
- Underwear, sleepwear, and loungewear
- Holiday merchandise
- Luggage and leather goods
- Electronic equipment
- Cameras and photographic equipment
- Home entertainment products
- Drugs and pharmacy

How often will the store's display fixturing have to be moved to accommodate changes, and how will this affect the interior layout?

What will influence the store's merchandise assortment?

- Style point of view: basic, classic, trendy, promotional
- Weather
- Themes: seasonal, special holiday
- Calendar: back to-school, cruisewear
- Impulse shopping or big-ticket items
- Full markup or discount; outlet store, big box store
- Tie-ins with media, local events

What is the merchandise breakdown?

- Number of stock keeping units (SKUs)
- Percent each major location contributes to total sales
- Sales per square foot for each category
- Stock turns per year
- Other

▶ The 1,200 sq ft Colour Studio for Lancôme at Macy's Union Square in San Francisco offers customers different styles of service, from a quick purchase to a full makeover. Products are arranged in open sell displays for self-service and stored under individual makeover workstations in curved and rounded units. Kenne Shepherd Interior Design Architecture PLLC. (Photo: Peter Paige.)

Customer profile

- Age range, particularly for female age segments below 25. Entire stores are now catering to preteen (8–12) , 'tween (13–16), young junior (17–20), and college/young career (up to 25).

- Geographical distribution: Super-regional malls and several of the destination sporting goods and home furnishings stores can draw from a radius of 300–400 miles.

- Income level

- Size range: In some areas of the country, a rise in the number of Asian American consumers, who are shorter and smaller than consumers of other backgrounds, requires departments of sufficient size to carry a profitable selection of petite-size clothing.

- Ethnic influences on color used in the store, light level, and product presentation: Hispanic Americans have shown a preference for brighter background colors in the stores they patronize, as well as a high ambient light level (minimum of 100 foot-candles).

- Special needs, including maternity, plus sizes, sports participation.

▲◀ Major specialty and department stores such as David Jones in Adelaide, Australia, have numerous classifications within each product category—basic, fashion, promotional, special purchase, in-house brand, and seasonal are some examples. The women's apparel department makes a strong fashion statement with seated and standing mannequins bordering the broad main aisle. In housewares, the demonstration kitchen is the central focus of the department. Robert Young Associates. (Photos: Tim Griffith.)

The profile for an upscale customer fits the target markets for Brookstone.
The branch at the Walt Whitman Mall in Huntington Station, New York, appeals particularly to shoppers looking for innovative, functional, and stylish products in categories related to home and office, health and fitness, lawn and garden, and travel and auto, shown here. Designed by JGA, Inc. (Laszlo Regos Photography.)

Sign considerations

- Image signs, interior and exterior, two- and three-dimensional
- Product information signs for floor and counter use
- Wayfinding
- Environmental, such as photographic blowups
- Electronic, including flat panel video, light-emitting diodes (LED)

Merchandise displays

- Open-sell departments (for cosmetics, hosiery, some accessories)
- Flexibility required for departmental reconfiguration
- Wall displays, accessible by customers and sales personnel
- Wall displays, above 80 in.
- Island displays
- Vignettes (small wall, table, or free-standing displays)
- Secure displays, under glass
- Manufacturer-supplied displays

Construction considerations

- Enforcement of broader code requirements will increase a project's cost. For example, more sprinklers are needed to satisfy life safety codes; ramps and larger fitting rooms are part of the far-reaching ADA building guidelines. Cashwrap desks now have a lower counter area to serve customers in wheelchairs.
- Changes are expected to heighten security code requirements, especially for multistory buildings, following the terrorist attacks in the fall of 2001.
- For retailers who want to roll out a successful prototype, modular design created by computer-aided design and drafting (CADD) will reduce the cost of additional units. The process will involve adapting a prototypical plan to site-specific locations.

Local codes

- Sprinkler system
- Fireproof materials
- Watts/square foot requirements or other energy usage limitations

BASIC STORE LAYOUTS

Basic Floor Planning Guidelines

Six Basic Plans

The basic plans illustrated on page 48 are not the only solutions that can be developed for the owner's consideration. Designers can utilize them as foundations on which variations can be created.

Curved plan

For boutiques, salons, or other types of stores carrying high-end merchandise, the curved plan creates an inviting, special environment for the customer. Construction costs for such a plan are higher than those for retail interiors designed on an angular or straight plan. The curved theme can be emphasized with walls, ceiling, and corners. To complete the look, specify circular floor fixtures.

Varied plan

For products that require backup stock to be immediately adjacent (shoes and men's shirts, for example), the varied plan is highly functional. Box or carton storage is created off the main sales floor with perimeter wall stocking. Typical of the varied plan is a "bellows" effect, a tapering of the space that focuses on a special-purpose area in the rear. Service departments in stereo, jewelry, or hardware stores can be located in this narrow end.

Straight plan

The straight plan is economical and can be adapted to any type of store, from gift shops to apparel stores, from drugstores to shoe stores. It uses walls and projections to create niches and smaller spaces. The straight plan lends itself well to pulling customers to the back of the store. To define transition from one section of the store to another, displays can be placed to help lead shoppers. For a change of pace, floor levels can be elevated.

Pathway plan

Applicable to virtually any type of store, the pathway plan is particularly suited to stores of more than 5,000 sq ft and on one level. A good architectural organizer, it pulls shoppers smoothly from the front to the rear without interruption by floor fixtures. The pathway plan, which can take a variety of shapes, is especially applicable for apparel stores where shoppers do not want to feel that they have to fight their way to the back through a maze of merchandise. The floor and ceiling can be used to create directional elements off the path.

Diagonal plan

For self-service stores, a diagonal plan is optimal. It permits angular traffic and design interest around the store's perimeter and encourages movement to all areas. Both soft goods and hard goods stores can take advantage of the diagonal plan. The cashier is in a central location, with sight lines to all areas.

Geometric plan

The geometric plan is the most exotic of the six basic plans. The designer creates forms and shapes derived from showcases, racks, or gondolas and can use wall angles to restate the shapes dominating the sales floor. This plan comfortably allows for fitting rooms without wasting square footage, making it especially suitable for apparel stores. It can nicely accommodate adjacent storage, making it an alternative to the varied plan for shoe stores and gift shops. Ceilings and floors can be lowered or raised to create zones and departments.

▶ *Six basic plans. Straight plan, pathway plan, diagonal plan, curved plan, varied plan, geometric plan. (Charles E. Broudy & Associates)*

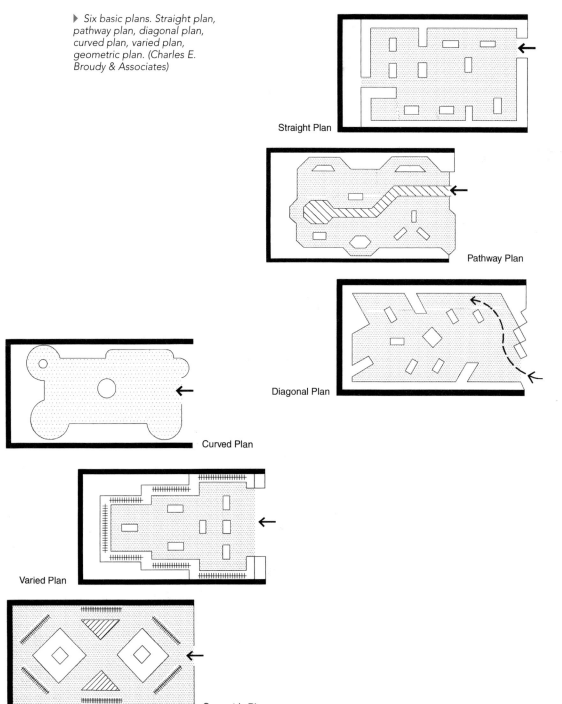

Straight Plan

Pathway Plan

Diagonal Plan

Curved Plan

Varied Plan

Geometric Plan

Layout Planning

After the initial project program is defined, the actual design process begins. In the development of a retail store floor plan, there are three basic floor layout planning principles to follow:

1. Use 100 percent of the space allotted in the lease.
2. Do not sacrifice function for asthetics. Successful plans combine *both* to the fullest.
3. Do not create a maze.

Interior Traffic Flow Characteristics

The proper direction of the traffic flow of shoppers within a store stimulates sales. Numerous studies, involving analysis of hundreds of hours of videotapes taken by cameras positioned high above the sales floor, reveal the instinctive patterns of shoppers' movements. Shoppers create pathways as they move from section to section. The most common patterns observed are:

- Entrance to exit
- Front to back
- Side to side
- Diagonal

In creating a main traffic aisle plan, the entrance position, the walls, and the columns are three basic considerations. Most stores use an aisle directly in front of the main entry. Large stores with distinct and different merchandise categories use large, wide aisles to separate major categories.

Merchandise Siting and Aisle Planning

Customers respond to the placement of products within a store. Staple items are often placed at the rear to draw the traffic from the front to the back of the store. Merchants count on customers getting to view additional merchandise displays along the way. And because a high percentage of consumer purchases is unplanned, this strategy is a proven impulse-purchasing stimulator.

As customers see and move, they do not move in a straight line, but rather meander and "bounce" from sequential points, which are within the control sphere of designers and merchants. In determining how merchandise will be viewed by customers, the plan should allow for the displays to create a "pinball" effect so that it will drive traffic not only from the front to the back of the store, but also from side to side.

Three feet is the minimum ADA aisle width requirement. The designer should check for any exemptions or variations that are allowed.

Merchandise Display

Merchandise displays can be freestanding, ceiling mounted, or wall mounted. They can be composed of mannequins, props, massed arrangements of merchandise or stacked boxed items, or electronic items, used singly or in combination. Fashion displays can be mounted on pedestals for additional impact, encouraging viewing from all angles.

Walls hold more merchandise than any other fixture in a department. The height and extent of a wall make it the most formidable fixture for the full variety of purposes in a store. *The concept of departmental penetration is to get customers to move to the wall.* The advantages are as follows:

- Once at the wall, customers have passed many items shown on floor stands. Customers are then out of the main traffic pattern and will shop more slowly.

- When finished selecting merchandise, customers will turn to the main aisle and exit the department. On the way, they see the other 50 percent of the stock housed on the backs of floor fixtures.

Utilizing Columns

Columns are the highest points on a sales floor. Because the eye will focus on high points, the merchandise on a column will be the first merchandise seen, increasing the chances of its being bought. The rate of sale of merchandise presented on a column is two to eight times the typical rates in other parts of the store.

In a large store, columns are approximately 30–35 ft on center, the general distance from the wall to one of the main traffic aisles. Columns are rare in mall specialty shops because the operating sales area is between the support columns of the center's structure. Most support columns, square or round, measure 6–8 in. in diameter in one-story structures. The width of a column with cladding designed to hold merchandise should be approximately 36 in. so that it can hold two garments, faced out, or a

reasonable width of vertically stacked shelf merchandise.

The orientation of the axis of the columns should be 45 degrees to the main traffic flow. Columns that are set at 90 degrees to the traffic flow show only one side well from the aisle.

Security

Visual surveillance of the sales floor from a central point is part of a store's overall theft-deterence program. Mirrors or cameras compensate for tall displays or partitions. Electronic article surveillance (EAS) systems require electronic pedestals, usually at store exits.

Other Considerations

- Cashwraps and cashier stations
- Return area for carts and baskets in food markets and other high-volume stores
- Customer-operated electronic scanning equipment
- Support space requirements: how merchandise is brought into the department, how much stock will be on the selling floor, and how much will be concealed.

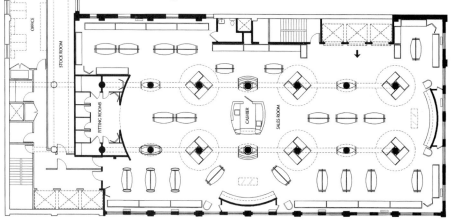

◀ ▲ *To be most effective, merchandise displays should be positioned in the plan to create a "pinball" effect to drive traffic from side to side and from the front to the back of the store. Moe Ginsburg men's store, New York City. Charles E. Broudy & Associates. (Photo courtesy Charles E. Broudy & Associates.)*

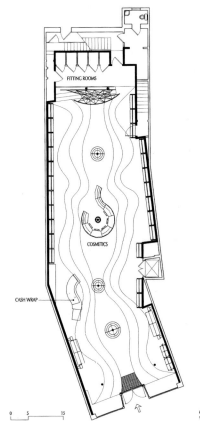

▶ A structural column at Dylan's Candy Bar, New York, becomes a giant spray of oversized plastic lollipops. J. Newbold & Associates. (Photo: Peter Paige.)

◀ ▼ Commander Salamander, Washington, D.C. Charles E. Broudy & Associates. (Courtesy Charles E. Broudy & Associates.)

FITTING ROOMS

COSMETICS

CASH WRAP

0   5   15

COMMANDER SALAMANDER
WASHINGTON D.C.

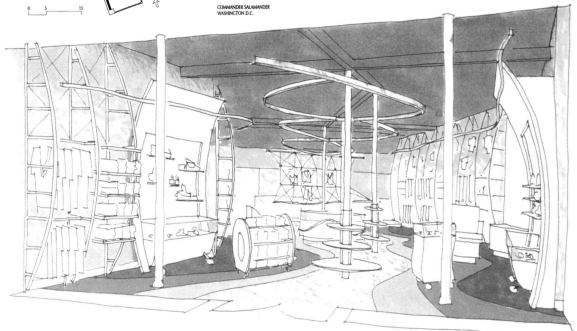

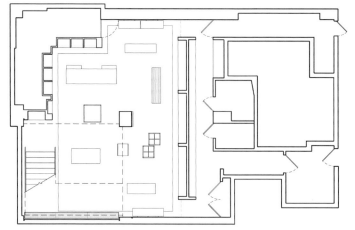

The plan for the three-level Coach leather products and apparel store on Madison Avenue, New York City, utilized a wide sculptural stairway to encourage customers to visit each floor. S. Russell Groves, PC.

▲ View of the lower level selling floor. (Photo © 2000 Sharon Riesedorph.)

◀ Lower level plan. (© 2000 S. Russell Groves.)

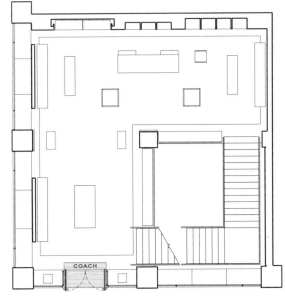

▲ View of the street-level selling floor. (Photo © 2000 Sharon Riesedorph.)

◄ Second level plan. (© 2000 S. Russell Groves.)

▲ View of the second-level selling floor. (Photo © 2000 Sharon Riesedorph.)

▶ Cashwrap. (Photo © 2000 Sharon Riesedorph.)

▶▶ Scuptural stairway is highlighted by photomurals. (Photo © 2000 Sharon Riesedorph.)

EXTERIOR AND STORE ENTRY DESIGN

Retailers can gain a competitive advantage when they capitalize on a store's exterior design to communicate their image to the marketplace. At the outset of the project, the merchant and the designer have to agree on answers to questions such as the following:

- Is the store purely a point of retail distribution, or a major flagship statement?
- Will the building be a mass-market box, or a showcase for a luxury brand?
- Is the building just a bland, utilitarian enclosure, or is it an icon, a signature statement for the brand and the retailer?

The answers to these questions will determine the overall design goals for the project. The retailer typically establishes the project budget, which has a tremendous impact on whether the design goals

can be achieved. The retailer's budget must correlate with the strategic value and importance of the storefront image as defined in the project goals.

Basic Design Considerations

For any project—freestanding store, big box, strip, street, or mall—to create the exterior design, designers have to consider these parameters:

- The type of store
- The context of the location
- Restrictions
- Styles and trends

Based on the type of store, the retailer has a strategy affecting the store's exterior design. The strategy includes both an investment philosophy and an experience philosophy. The investment philosophy is based on whether the store exterior is to be updated regularly or is to last the life

▼ ▶ *Section and exterior of the Toys "R" Us flagship store in Times Square, New York City. Architect: Gensler; interior design: J. Newbold Associates. (Photo courtesy Toys "R" Us.)*

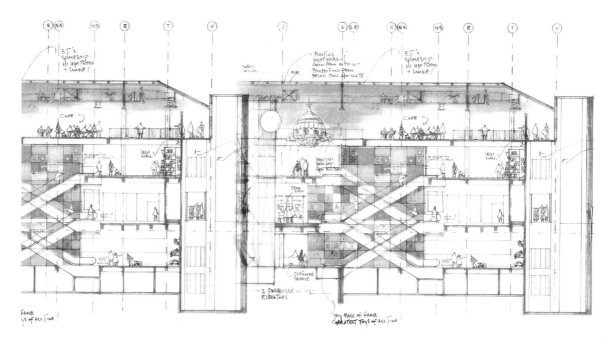

of the retailing concept. The experience philosophy is based on what the retailer desires in regard to consumer response to the exterior store design.

In designing a freestanding store or box, the approach depends on the end use—that is, the type of retailing to be carried out in the store. Is the store a distributor of multiple brands, such as Kohl's, Target, and Wal-Mart, rather than a single brand, such as a Nike store? Look at the nature of the box: Is it proprietary and single purpose? Or does the design need to be more flexible, because the store will carry a broad spectrum of items, from baby wear to electronics?

Storefront Design Strategies

A thorough understanding of the retailer's strategy is critical in developing a store-front design approach. The designer must understand whether the store's intended image is one of minimalism, abundance, value, tradition, or another concept. In designing a storefront, the designer should consider a number of factors:

The degree of separation or integration with the sidewalk or the mall walkway that best suits the retailer's positioning. Will the storefront be a welcome mat, a barrier, a filter, or a non-front?

Leveraging frontages. Smart retailers consider the exterior as alternative media. Others miss this opportunity, but at the same time spend millions of dollars on media and conventional advertising. Meanwhile, one of the store's most obvious assets—its frontages and display windows—may remain essentially unleveraged.

Sight lines. The storefront is a billboard that draws attention to itself when seen from a highway by those in vehicles, or

▶ *Stores appealing to an upscale clientele express their image by storefront design and materials. Bloomingdale's, Aventura, Florida. Robert Young Associates. (Photo: Paul Bielenberg.)*

by people on foot on a sidewalk or a mall walkway. The circulation patterns approaching the store and the sightlines provided need to be understood. Customers who are driving down the highway or walking along a street, coming from a shopping center parking lot, or going along the walkways, approach the store at an angle. Yet designers conventionally draw the "front elevation" without realizing that in many cases the side wall or window display is likely to be more visually critical than the storefront elevation itself.

The appropriate visibility to the interior. Some merchants consider the storefront as a frame, allowing people to see into the store. A merchant should see the storefront as an opportunity to make a statement about his or her image and particular own market position. These elements communicate the exterior message:

• The materials selected

• The architecture

• The signage

Enlightened merchants do not see the storefront as simply the veneer that goes over the face of the leased space or street frontage, but consider the first 10–15 ft into the store as part of the storefront zone. For stores that carry more moderate, popularly priced merchandise, the retailer typically wants the merchandise to have more visibility and customers to have greater accessibility to the product. The whole storefront may be a wide-open door or a front with a door in it that is entirely transparent.

The more exclusive the store's offerings, the more select its traffic may be. This type of store can afford to be much more closed up; it can have doors that a customer must open, acting like a filter. Elizabeth Arden's Red Door storefront creates a signature statement.

Integration of indoor and outdoor life. A trend toward more and larger transparent openings—windows, doors, even entire walls—is being felt in store design as well. Retail activity and fashion are exhibited from the inside out. An extreme ex-

▲ *Gucci, Fifth Avenue, New York City.*

◀ *Gucci, Rodeo Drive, Beverly Hills, California.
(Photos: Vilma Barr.)*

ample is the soaring glass storefront of the Hugo Boss store on Fifth Avenue in New York City. It was planned to function both as a display window for the Boss apparel and accessory collections, and as a stage where the store's staff and customers present a changing panorama on several levels that are connected by a dramatic staircase.

Context and Restraints

Retail stores that cater to pedestrians should be designed to reflect an awareness of the context around them. For example, at many of the stores in the Soho section of New York City, minimalism stands out because there is so much complexity around them. Many of the buildings have ornamental iron fronts dating from the mid to late 1800s. In a typical shopping center, the context is minimal, so a storefront may use higher-impact design to call attention to itself or communicate the image of the store. The maximum height of a storefront that will register visually with visitors to a shopping center is approximately 12 ft.

The most liberal development constraints are those of freestanding stores with parking lots. There may be con-

▲ Storefronts become billboards when viewed by vehicular or foot traffic. Pawsenclaws, Staten Island, New York, is a mall store with a wide entry to attract shoppers. JGA, Inc. (Laszlo Regos Photography.)

straints regarding the size of a sign or the style that can be used, such as for a red brick Colonial gas station. The next most liberal in respect to constraints is a community center that may be anchored by a bookstore or home improvement store. Such stores often use a generic approach to architecture. The landlord can dictate who gets an arch, a tower, or a vault. In the newer lifestyle centers, the landlord may decide that he or she wants more diversity in the architecture, that the anchor tenants should be more expressive, and the specialty tenant less so.

An example of a store type that expresses its character is the outdoor retailer. Galyan's stores utilize raw limestone and exposed steel outside; inside they are basi-

cally warehouses. Visitors to Cabela's are greeted with an enormous sculpture of sparring grizzly bears. A Bass Pro store looks like a rambling hunting lodge that seems to have been transported from a lakeside site in a secluded forest. REI renovated a century-old trolley terminal in Denver and made the most of the high ceiling and natural light to display its products in a classic setting.

Some shopping centers enforce very strict requirements: nonilluminated signs, all-glass front, and no rolling grilles, only doors. Other centers, such as lifestyle or thematic facilities, often require the same materials found in the center (wood or brick, for example) to be used on a tenant front. In the Desert Passage in the Al-

◀ A freestanding store can utilize architecture or oversized display elements as exterior identification in an open or built-up environment. FAO Schwarz, Orlando, Florida (Photo courtesy FAO Schwarz.)

▼ Bokoo Bikes, Chanhassen, Minnesota. Lampert Architects. (John J. Unrue Photography)

▲ *These open-back windows highlight the store's interior and the merchandise displays inside at Tempus Expeditions, Mall of America, Bloomington, Minnesota. Courtesy of FRCH Design Worldwide. (Photo: Dan Forer.)*

addin in Las Vegas, all the tenants had to incorporate a Moroccan or Casbah-type theme. For the Hollywood and Highland mixed-use center in Los Angeles, which contains the Academy Awards theater, tenant storefronts are designed in an updated version of the classic sets that represent vintage Hollywood.

In the least restrictive centers, the landlord generally has certain criteria for storefront designs. These include the distance over the lease line beyond which stores cannot go, or the maximum amount of glass that can be used on a storefront. Otherwise, the tenant is free to bring its own identity to the center.

Some chains use a prototype design for their outlets across the country. Others

regionalize the look: a white stucco storefront for Florida or stone for New York. The message should remain consistent, however, even if the client has multiple stores in various locales. The Gap and Banana Republic stores are the most urban-looking stores in the shopping centers in which they have branches. Their city stores are even more "urbanized," incorporating stainless steel, underlit glass floors, exposed ductwork, limestone, and marble, with details that evoke a sense of modernism and the machine age. The overall effect is the same, but the various stores reflect the settings within which they exist.

Styles and Trends

Storefronts go through design cycles, much like fashions in apparel. The retail industry went through "the mapleing of America" some years ago, a basic trend characterized by all-glass fronts, glass doors, maple floors, white walls, white ceilings, and maple display fixtures. Then the themed retailers entered the scene: children's theme stores and entertainment properties. Currently, more theatrical-looking retailers, including Restoration Hardware, Pottery Barn, and Williams-Sonoma, present a blended approach, classic but with attitude and character.

The "big box" stores that featured a concrete block building with a sign on the front now have developed atriums, styled entranceways, and landscaping to meet the more demanding expectations of today's customers.

For a street-front store, consider awnings to protect foot traffic from the rain. An awning can carry the firm's logo to extend the store's street presence and is also a decorative symbol of hospitality and welcome.

A downtown landmark in Pittsburgh, Pennsylvania, is the F. & R. Lazarus department store. The facades relate to the exteriors of the surrounding commercial structures. Cooper Carry Architects.

▶ Overhangs mounted at a 90-degree angle define entrances and windows. (Photo courtesy Cooper Carry, Inc., ©Gabriel Benzur Photography.)

▼ Elevation, Fifth Avenue facade. (Image courtesy Cooper Carry, Inc.)

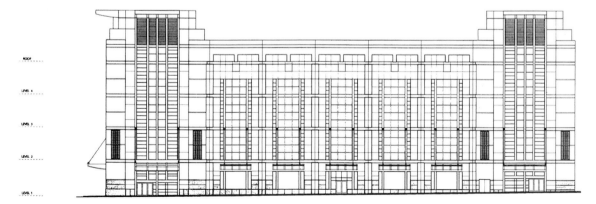

▶ *Traditional multiple pane.*

▲ *Contemporary multiple pane.*

▲ *Large single-pane glass panels.*

◀ *Butt-glazed storefront.*

◀ *Minimal base.*

▶ *Variable-height bulkhead.*

▲ *Landscape planter bulkhead.*

▶ *Recessed storefront plane.*

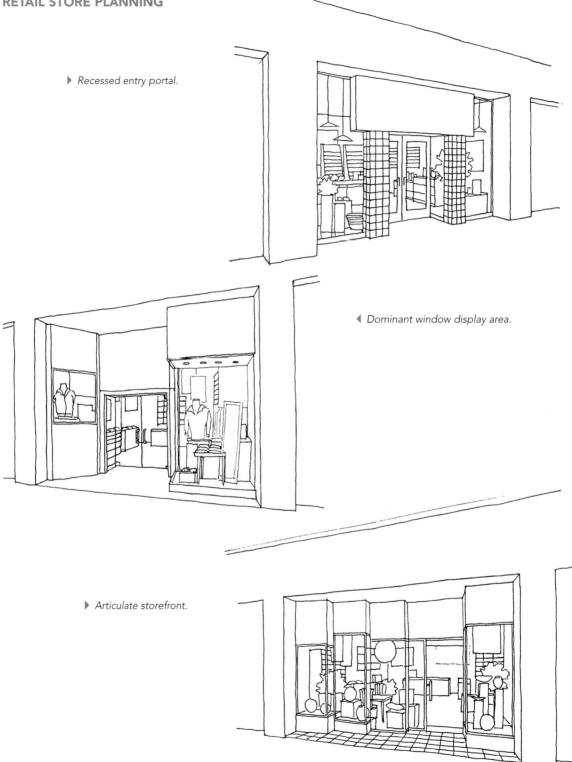

▶ *Recessed entry portal.*

◀ *Dominant window display area.*

▶ *Articulate storefront.*

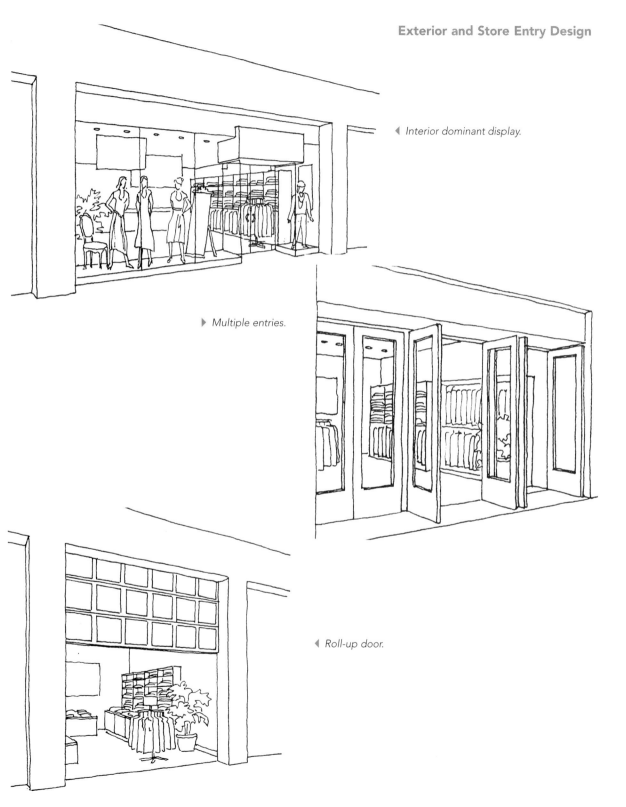

◀ *Interior dominant display.*

▶ *Multiple entries.*

◀ *Roll-up door.*

FlatIron Crossing, Broomfield, Colorado. Designed by Callison. (Photo by Chris Eden.)

▶ FlatIron Crossing, Broomfield, Colorado. Designed by Callison. (Photo by Chris Eden.)

◀ Canal City Hakata, Fukuoka, Japan. Designed by Jerde. (Photo by Hiroyuki Kawano.)

◀ Cingular Wireless Store, prototype design, multiple U.S. locations. Designed by Callison. (Photo by Chris Eden.)

◀ Denver Pavilion, Denver, Colorado. Designed by ELS Architects. (Photo by Timothy Hursley.)

▲ Totem, New York City. Designed by Nicholas Dine. (Photo by Vilma Barr.)

▶ Lazarus, Chicago.
Designed by
Cooper Carry.
(Photo courtesy
Cooper Carry, Inc.)

▶ Parfums Caron,
New York City.
Designed by Pascal
Bunaly. (Photo
courtesy Richter +
Ratner Contracting.)

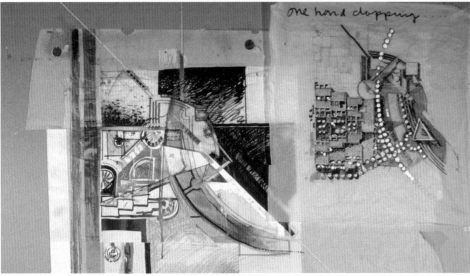

◀▲▼ Horton Plaza, San Diego, California. Designed by Jerde. (Conceptual sketch by Jon Jerde.) (Photo by Benny Chan.) (Photo by Stephen Simpson.)

▶ *Brian Bailey, Toronto, Canada. Designed by II BY IV. (Photo courtesy II BY IV Design.)*

▼ *Burdines at Florida Mall, Orlando, Florida. Designed by Pavlik Design. (Photo courtesy Pavlik Design.)*

▶▶ *Core Pacific City, Taipei, Taiwan. Designed by Jerde. (Photo courtesy of Jerde.)*

▶▶ BellWorld Flagship Store at Toronto Eaton Centre, Toronto, Canada. Designed by HOK Canada. (Photo courtesy HOK Canada; Ronald Ng, photographer.)

◀ ▼ REI, Seattle, Washington. Designed by Mithun. (Photos by Robert Pisano.)

▶▶ Mizner Park, Boca Raton, Florida. Designed by Cooper Carry. (Photo courtesy Cooper Carry, Inc., © Stephen Traves Photography.)

▶ Grand Gateway, Shanghai, China. Designed by Callison. (Photo by Chris Eden.)

 Qiora Store & Spa, New York. Designed by Architecture Research Office, New York in collaboration with Shiseido Cosmetics. (Photo © Shiseido Cosmetics America Ltd.)

◀ *Universal CityWalk, Los Angeles. Designed by Jerde. (Photo by Stephen Simpson.)*

◀ *The Block at Orange, Orange, California. Designed by D'Agostino Izzo Quirk Architects. (Photo by Erhard Pfeiffer.)*

▶▶ The Forum Shops at Caesar's Palace, Las Vegas, Nevada. Designed by Dougall Design Associates, Inc. (Photo © The Forum Shops.)

▶ The Spectrum, Irvine, California. Designed by RTKL. (Photo by Dave Whitcomb, © RTKL Associates, Inc.)

▶▶ Robina Town Centre, Queensland, Australia. Designed by Jerde. (Photo by Tim Griffith.)

▶ Lindt & Sprungli, Toronto, Canada.
Designed by II BY IV Design.
(Photo courtesy II BY IV Design.)

Pawsenclaws & Co. at Staten
Island Mall, Staten Island, New
York. Designed by JGA, Inc.
(Laszlo Regos Photography.)

▼ Namba Parks, Osaka, Japan.
Designed by Jerde. (Conceptual
sketch by Jon Jerde.)

◀ *Simply Books at Douglas International Airport, Charlotte, North Carolina. Designed by Chute Gerdeman.*

▼ *Essence du Papier, Toronto, Canada. Designed by II BY IV Design. (Photo courtesy II BY IV Design.)*

▶ *The North Face, Beverly Hills, California. Designed by JGA, Inc. (Laszlo Regos Photography.)*

▼ *Planetarium Store at the American Museum of Natural History, New York City. Designed by JGA, Inc. (Laszlo Regos Photography.)*

CHAPTER 5

RETAIL STORE DESIGN

COLORS, MATERIALS, AND FINISHES

The primary objective of store design is to create a unique environment specifically suited to the merchandise being presented for sale. In designing a retail store, the priorities of store design should be clearly understood.

A retail space is not designed to be complete without the product in place. If it looks finished without the product, it is probably overdone.

Store Design Priorities

1. Product presentation
2. Communication (graphics, media)
3. Lighting
4. Architecture

In developing a store design, be conscious of the materials and finishes that will be part of the final design. Do not make the mistake of thinking that colors, materials, and finishes are applied after the design is done.

The Primary Design Challenges in the Use of Materials

- Use materials in unexpected ways.
- Understand the realities of the materials.

Setting the Stage For Retail Selling

The store as environment
Stores are becoming more like habitats and less like buildings. The finishes are becoming more indigenous to the experience rather than something to fill up blank walls.

Create interest

A backdrop for a retail setting does not have to be bland or without its own character. For example, you can make both the floors and the walls the same bright color, such as red. The idea is that when you use this much of a strong color, it becomes a background color but has stronger visual appeal than a typical neutral tone.

Tools to create interesting backgrounds are not limited to paint, wall coverings, or wood veneers. Lighting is the catalyst that can turn texture and configuration into a finish.

Think of background in a macro sense. A zigzag wall can be considered a texture. Linen as a wall covering in a store is attractive when used as an accent to paint or other smooth finishes. Linen

▼ Successful store designs can contribute significantly to increased traffic and higher volume. Concepts relating to scale, pattern, and quantity can be applied to options for colors, materials, and finishes to produce an environment that adds to the sales appeal of the merchandise. The Museum Shop at New York City's American Museum of Natural History was a tall, awkward space that was part of a recent expansion. It became a trilevel mini-department store with the addition of selling balconies, a full-height wall that was cast from an actual mountainside, wood detailing, and the artful lighting plan that enlivens the entire space. JGA, Inc. (Laszlo Regos Photography.)

▶ Oversized checkerboard-pattern flooring, like the checkered flag seen at auto races, leads into a Pit Shop mall store. JGA, Inc. (Laszlo Regos Photography.)

applied to a 100,000 sq ft wall would have limited impact on a viewer. But imagine the texture of linen magnified 30 times so that it translates into a giant basket woven of 18-in.-wide wood pieces. That material then becomes an appropriate and dramatic finish for the space.

Living on the edges

In retail, successful designs that contribute to increased traffic and sales volume are typically those in which the designer has played with the "edges." These are spaces where the designer can exaggerate or understate—scale, color, pattern, quantity—to achieve a merchandise-enhancing setting. In contrast, when everything in a completed space is in just the right scale, the design typically draws fewer shoppers to the space and to product displays.

▶ At J. B. White (now Dillard's) in Augusta, Georgia, the flooring of the main aisle and side aisles is a pattern of squares within squares in contrasting colors. Overhead, a gently curved electrical grid with exposed lamps spans the space. Fitzpatrick Interiors Group. (Photo courtesy Fitzpatrick Interiors Group.)

The middle path is often too predictable for retail, particularly for stores that gain a competitive edge by promoting style and current trends. Most merchants who carry fashion goods, for apparel or items for the home, spend a good deal of time looking for a new and exciting assortment of products to ensure customers returning to their stores. A store design that reflects a middle-of-the-road approach throughout runs the risk of being out of step with the store's merchandising objective.

A designer can propose and explain concepts to the retailer that demonstrate how a creative and artistic utilization of an "edgier" design philosophy—where appropriate and within the bounds of good taste and strategic business thinking—can add drama and extra attraction to the merchandise on display.

It's just paint

For functional or lifestyle reasons, colors, materials, and finishes have different criteria: There are those that are permanent, versus those that are disposable or easily altered. A painted surface is an example of changing an interior by repainting with another color, a relatively quick and cost-effective technique.

Build the set to the story

The next step is to establish a vocabulary and create the storyboard. The designer's role is to build the set to the story.

Storyboarding and unorthodox materials

It may be useful to initially storyboard the retail environment, using a conventional design approach. In this way, you can end up with a more objective, consumer-oriented approach to design. A

◀ The Issey Miyake shop in the Soho section of New York is seen here from Hudson Street through open doors. The first floor is dominated by a hanging metal sculpture, the work of architect Frank Gehry, who is responsible for the overall store design. (Photo courtesy Vilma Barr.)

▼ Basic materials like metal and wood are transformed here into elements scaled to link the interior architecture with the displayed products.

Aston Martin Jaguar of Tampa, Florida, has hanging metal mesh panels on which stage lighting beams images. JGA, Inc. (Laszlo Regos Photography.)

▲ With careful matching of the color rendering index of the area's ambient and feature lighting, background colors that flatter the complexion can boost sales. At the cosmetics section of the Neiman Marcus branch in Tampa, Florida, the soft peach hue of the walls is repeated in the display fixtures. Robert Young Associates. (Courtesy RYA and Paul Bielenberg, Photographer).

mesh used for athletic outerwear, or automotive car paint can be examined with a fresh viewpoint as options for a planned store interior. Discovering a distinctive solution to a store interior design problem may come from considering the application of atypical materials from a new and original perspective.

Using display fixtures as design elements

Off-the-shelf retail display fixturing often has more to do with function than with style. It is up to the designer to give the store owner the most return for an investment in a merchandise display program. In planning a selling floor, basic display systems such as poles, slatwall, or gondolas combine function with a creative outlook in form, materials, finishes, or scale.

Fixturing is a key element in expressing a merchant's image. Many fixture suppliers have staff members who can help you to modify or customize existing products in their lines. They may also be able to manufacture fixtures to your specifications.

Blurry-eye test

A designer evaluating the palette of his or her project's colors, materials, and finishes should give it the "blurry-eye" test, because that is how a customer generally sees a store. Anything the designer cannot objectively judge to be meaningful in carrying out the project's objectives will not be meaningful to the customer either.

Customers in upscale stores are particularly aware of their surroundings. Yet that does not mean that the space must be done more expensively. It does mean that it has to be done more thoughtfully, with considerable attention paid to the details.

storyboard describes graphically what the store should feel like, what people should think of it, and their points of reference. A materials library may include samples of finishes that can be characterized as sleazy, cheap, and offensive. But one of them may just be the right thing needed for your project to express a merchandising point of view. For example, such common products as corrugated honeycomb packing materials, or the webbing

Pulling It All Together

Increasingly, retailers are coordinating the major elements of the store environment with other communications techniques to effectively emphasize their images to the customer. Background tones and accent colors used in store interiors, plus the texture of materials used on floors, walls, or fixtures, can be graphically adapted in two and three dimensions. This form of visual coordination is a critical part of the store experience for today's customer.

The following are examples of techniques and items used in retail brand positioning:

- In-store graphics, such as product information signs and decorative banners
- Electronic information boards, kiosks, and tabletop screens
- Collateral and print materials such as catalogs, brochures, and direct mail pieces
- Shopping bags and boxes
- Product hangtags

▼ *This Levi's shop-in-shop is set off from the surrounding departments by a blue wall behind the cashwrap, undulating bench, large-format text on the area rug, and pair of torso forms. (©2001 Morla Design. Photo: Cesar Rubio.)*

▲ Retail components of widely promoted brands often utilize in-store graphics such as these photo blowups in the Elizabeth Arden store on Fifth Avenue, New York City. JGA, Inc. (Laszlo Regos Photography.)

LIGHTING

A retail space lives and breathes by the success of its lighting plan. "Lighting is the most important decorative item in the store," said the former CEO of a major New York women's specialty store. "The quality of lighting can make or break merchandise. If the lighting is great, it doesn't make any difference if the merchandise is on mannequins, pinned up on a display, or presented as a still life."

Basic Principles of Retail Lighting

A store's lighting should make customers feel comfortable on the sales floor and create an irrepressible desire to own whatever merchandise they are looking at.

Great lighting enhances a store's design, which will in turn enhance the merchandise. Effective store lighting can be used as a creative tool to:

- Attract shoppers
- Move merchandise
- Dramatize ceilings, floors, and walls
- Flatter both merchandise and customers
- Provide visual comfort
- Use energy efficiently

Lighting, however, is technology and requires special skills to plan, design, and maintain.

Retain a lighting consultant to assist you with creating a functional, effective

lighting plan. A list of lighting designers who are experienced in retail design and are members of the International Association of Lighting Designers (IALD) can be obtained by contacting the International Association of Lighting Designers Merchandise Mart, Suite 9-104, 200 World Trade Center, Chicago, IL 60654; phone: 312-527-3677; fax: 312-527-3680; e-mail: iald@iald.org; website: www.iald.org.

The letters "LC" following a person's name represent "Lighting Certified," a credential earned by professionals who have passed examinations testing their knowledge of the lighting design specialty.

Attract shoppers
Light attracts. Light can be subtle or overt. It can divert and influence. It is the quickest and most direct form of nonverbal communication.

The quantity, quality, and effect of exterior and interior lighting are quickly evaluated by shoppers. People see vertical surfaces first, whether inside or outside a structure. They will let the light help guide them into and through the store, and into the next level of merchandise evaluation and selection.

There are very few "standard" retail lighting solutions, because nearly every store has a unique merchandise mix, trade area, customer profile, and image, all of which combine to give it the personality that the design, including the lighting, must communicate.

Move merchandise
Retail store lighting is not a space lighting problem; it is a merchandise lighting problem and should be conceived with a solid sales orientation.

▲ Store planners and designers bring lighting designers into the conceptual design process at an early stage to develop the lighting program along with the overall interior and, where applicable, exterior themes. Some firms have lighting specialists on staff; others opt to retain lighting consultants to suggest the latest advancements in illumination technology and product introductions to enhance the store's design. The London flagship of the venerable Liberty of London brand was given a total store design and visual presentation makeover. Displays on sculptural freestanding and wall-mounted fixtures are illuminated by recessed and flush-mounted fixtures, some fitted with color-changing lamps. 20/20 Limited. (Photo: Adrian Wilson.)

▶ Lighting plans for retail interiors can emphasize the architecture and floor plan, create a visually dynamic ceiling, and define wall surfaces. Circular, glass-enclosed upper showroom, Steuben, Madison Avenue, New York City. Ralph Appelbaum Associates. Lighting by Johnson Schwinghammer Lighting Consultants, Inc. (Photo: Peter Mauss/ESTO, courtesy Steuben.)

Lighting and merchandise presentation work in tandem to differentiate products. Merchandise on display is enhanced by compelling compositions and lighting techniques. The techniques by which the designer can add sales appeal to the merchandise with lighting effects, while still staying within the constraints of the project's budget and applicable energy codes, can provide the client with a noticeable competitive edge.

Dramatize ceilings, floors, walls

Lighting is an extremely malleable, as well as precise, design tool. A store planner can highlight, subdue, sculpt, signal, or wash walls—all within the frame of an overall plan.

Excellent retail architectural lighting plans can echo the floor plan, create a visually dynamic ceiling (overhead zone), and define wall surfaces (perimeter zone). Techniques that can be used include the following:

- Cove lighting
- Dropped ceiling outlined with lighting
- Neon accents
- Showcase lighting
- Lighting at mirrors
- Spot lighting above displays
- Wall washing
- Lighting under shelves

Flatter merchandise and customers

Light and color are interdependent. The choice of light source will control the appearance of color in objects and people. Because most stores use a variety of light sources, the designer's lighting plan should ensure a balanced color rendition to flatter both merchandise and customers.

Provide visual comfort

Brightness is the sensation produced either by light from a light source or by light reflected from a surface. When quantitatively measured, it is called "luminance." A balanced luminance ratio between the merchandise and the environment can make it easy for customers to identify and examine the merchandise in the selling area.

Glare distracts shoppers and fatigues employees. Caused by unduly bright light sources or reflected surfaces within the visual field, glare can be avoided by adjusting the luminance of lighting equipment, changing the angle between the source and the line of sight, or increasing the general brightness of the space.

Developing the Lighting Plan

The lighting plan can be developed after these factors have been determined:

- The type of merchandise to be carried in each section

- The size and shape of each department

- Ceiling height

- Colors and materials for walls, ceilings, floors, and fixtures

- Type of display windows (closed back or open back)

Even for chain stores, lighting experts advise that lighting design cannot be duplicated from one store to the next without making some adaptations. For example, two shops operated by the same company opened within a short time in the same city. The ceiling fixtures lit the merchandise in the wall racks perfectly in the first store. In the second store, however, designers did not take into account the fact that the ceiling was 4 ft higher; as

The use of a light-emitting diode (LED) to illuminate products in the Boucheron perfume line eliminates shadows and harsh reflections. (Photo courtesy Lucifer Lighting.)

a result, the fixtures illuminated the wall well above the merchandise.

Light the store

Determine the overall color impression when planning the general or ambient lighting for a store. The color temperature—quoted in degrees Kelvin (K)—of a light source is the yardstick. The higher the color temperature (4100°K being the highest for retail), the cooler the color impression will be, to create a crisp, no-nonsense feeling.

Lower color temperatures, 2700°–3000°K, give a warmer color impression, often specified for higher-end stores to create an intimate, more residential feeling. A color temperature of 3500°K, which is more neutral, is a popular specification for store interiors.

Light the merchandise

Visualize the lighting plan with the product displays in place, and then specify the lamps and fixtures where they will effectively light the merchandise. Do not give the same intensity to expanses of the walls or floors. If customers cannot easily examine the merchandise and read prod-

▲ *Supermarkets gain a competitive advantage with feature lighting combined with daylighting, resulting in cost-efficient, pleasing environments. Lunds, Plymouth, Minnesota. Robert Gorski Associates. (Photo: Paul Markert, © Lund Food Holdings, Inc. 2002. All rights reserved.)*

uct information, chances are they will not buy. The following questions can serve as guidelines.

Have all the feature areas been identified?

- Along the main and secondary aisles?
- On the perimeter zones?

Is the footcandle level at the back of the store high enough to draw customers without appearing garish?

Has the color rendition quality been checked for the range of products that will be carried in the department?

- Basic stock
- Seasonal merchandise

- Holiday items

Does the stock have a typical color quality?

- Men's business clothing is usually dark.
- Children's clothing, toys, and major appliances are usually bright, pastel, or white.

Does merchandise salability depend on glitter?

- Jewelry
- Crystal

Dazzle multifaceted reflector (MR) lamps beaming from above and in-the-case illumination are two basic and effective solutions. Other options include fluorescent lights, multifaceted reflectors, and special incandescent strips with lamps.

Will the lighting plan accommodate movable display items?

- Gondolas
- Racks
- Tables

Will prepackaged merchandise be stacked on the selling floor?

Will shadows created by packaging affect the readability of product information?

Divide up the merchandise area

Sculpt space with light. Pendant lights and other types of hanging fixtures can visually delineate a space Other techniques include cove lighting using wood or drywall enclosures, and integrating lighting with crown molding.

Direct the shopper to the merchandise

Lighting can influence traffic flow to specific displays or to sections of a store, particularly the back and perimeter walls. High-intensity lighting can highlight a specific area as a focal point or emphasize a feature wall. Merchants favor focal point and display lighting to draw the shopper to the newest and the best merchandise and to coordinated displays.

Create accent and supplemental lighting

Accent lighting emphasizes the shape, texture, finish, and color of merchandise relative to its surroundings, elevating specific product attributes. In addition to requiring ambient and feature lighting, cosmetics and jewelry benefit from task and examination fixtures to give additional emphasis to individual items.

Vary the accent factor in different sections of the store. The "accent factor" is the relationship between the brightness of an object and that of its surroundings. An accent factor of 2 means the accent is two times brighter than the surrounding area, an accent factor of 5 is five times brighter, and so forth. The higher the accent factor, the more dramatic the effect.

Merchandise price points can be supported by lighting. Sconces and hanging fixtures are effective in environments where higher-end merchandise is sold.

Provide accurate color rendition to enhance merchandise and flatter customers

The Color Rendering Index (CRI) indicates how colors will be perceived by the human eye. Daylight, which contains all the colors in the spectrum, has a value of 100 percent. The higher the CRI value, the more "natural" colors will appear under light. Values above CRI 80 indicate very good color rendering.

▼ Displays of glass, crystal, and other products shown on transparent shelving or reflective surfaces require light sources that minimize glare. Wall cases and circular black table inset with electronically programmed images, Steuben, Madison Avenue, New York City. Ralph Appelbaum Associates. Lighting by Johnson Schwinghammer Lighting Consultants, Inc. (Photo: Peter Mauss/ESTO, courtesy Steuben.)

▲ The gift shop at the Belvedere, Vienna, Austria. (Photo: Glenn Barr.)

Make shoppers and employees feel comfortable

Low-wattage and low-voltage lighting reduce the amount of heat transferred to the store environment and cut down on the cooling load to be handled by the mechanical system. For example, some 90-watt tungsten-halogen lamps are equal to a standard 150-watt incandescent lamp. To reduce glare, aim the luminaires so they are not in the direct line of vision of either employees or customers, or provide shields to deflect glare.

Louvers, glare shields, barn doors, and lenses prevent light from shining directly into customers' eyes. If such accessories are not included with the basic luminaires, they are available separately from the manufacturers.

Fitting room lighting techniques

To be most flattering to the customer, the primary source of light for fitting rooms should *not* be from above; rather, light should be soft and diffuse, from the side and front, to minimize wrinkles and skin imperfections.

High-color rendering triphosphor fluorescent lamps and halogen incandescents are well suited for mirror lighting. Neiman Marcus adds extra flair to fitting rooms with wall sconces mounted sideways.

Avoid boredom

An unrelieved expanse of a selling floor illuminated only by fluorescent lamps will give a flat look to the space and the merchandise. Diffused light from wide distribution downlights or large area light sources, such as fluorescent luminaires or indirect lighting systems, tends to reduce the variations that relate to form and texture. Three-dimensional merchandise benefits from directional lighting, so provide for enough diffusion to counteract harshness.

Contrast increases visibility. The more contrast, the more the shopper is encouraged to examine and evaluate the accented merchandise.

- Increase the contrast between objects in the foreground and those in the background.
- Provide luminance contrast. Increase the amount of light on an area to make it more visible.

Create proper aiming angles

Calculate the distances needed for proper vertical displays so that the illumination is on the face of the merchandise. For example, in lighting bulky items such as comforters, the lighting built into a valance should extend out 3 ft, not 2 ft, to wash down the front of the display and avoid being caught at the top level. Conversely, lighting for bins in a card shop requires light sources close to the cards for readability.

Focusing charts are helpful in calculating the angles for maximum effectiveness. A rule of thumb is nothing higher than a 45-degree tilt to prevent glare.

Minimize the number of lamp types used in the store

A store owner who attended a recent retail lighting workshop said he used *38* different lamp types. This number of lamps types is a likely source of problems for the maintenance staff. Lamp manufacturers suggest limiting the types of rated watt lamps used on the selling floor for both spot and flood luminaires to simplify maintenance.

Lamps of 35, 50, or 73 watts offer enough variety for most small stores and provide the owner with the choice of varying the light output with lenses, filters, and baffles. 45-watt and 90-watt PAR 38 lamps produce beam spreads that will handle many different end uses, such as feature and accent lighting.

Get your lighting fixtures on time

Allow enough lead time to get the fixtures in time to open a new store or renovated existing facility. Check on the current delivery estimated by the manufacturer.

Imported fixtures should be Underwriters Laboratories (UL) listed and not prewired. Lighting that is built into display fixtures should also be UL labeled. If not, the local building inspector cannot issue a certificate of occupancy and the store will be prevented from opening.

Lighting dos and don'ts

Dos

- Establish lighting budgets early. Get unit pricing on all fixtures to be used in the store. Avoid package deals.
- Facilitate safe passage of motorists and pedestrians on the store's grounds. Contribute to effective security and surveillance of people and property.
- Emphasize the store's character and image to communicate that it is a desirable place to shop.
- Create impressive entrance lobbies with lighting that complements the architecture and provides a safe and attractive transition from the exterior to the interior.

- To stimulate sales, reduce customer dissatisfaction, and minimize returns, ensure that merchandise is displayed under a lighting system that produces the illuminance and color customers will perceive during actual use.

- Light merchandise displayed on or near counters at three to five times the level of ambient and circulation area lighting.

- Invest in perimeter lighting to improve visibility and the visual impact of wall displays, so as to draw shoppers from the main aisle into the merchandise space.

- Consider dimming controls to compensate for the different illuminance levels required during day and evening business hours.

- Investigate demand-size management (DSM) programs to help minimize lighting energy waste and improve the efficiency of lighting systems.

Don'ts

- Where possible, avoid locating show windows on west facades, where late afternoon sun can cause visibility difficulties.

- Don't aim light sources into the eyes of customers or sales personnel.

- Avoid lighting over mirrors in fitting rooms or selling alcoves, as direct downlights call attention to skin imperfections and create unflattering shadows.

- To avoid ultraviolet (UV) damage or fading, do not leave uncovered merchandise close to light sources.

- Failure to consider periodic lighting equipment maintenance can quickly depreciate the illuminance level by

nearly 50 percent. Vertical and horizontal surfaces that are not clean can affect light reflectance levels.

- Don't aim light on the floor or the walls if you are not selling floor or wall coverings. Direct accent lighting with an appropriate beam spread at the merchandise, not above or below it.

Solve Unusual Space Problems

Expand or retract space

Some stores should appear to be larger; others, less cavernous. The designer can create these optical illusions through the use of colors and materials, through the lighting plan, or by a combination of colors, materials, and lighting.

To make a small space seem bigger, use bright, light colors. At the same time, emphasize the height of the ceiling with uplighting.

- Floor-mounted fixtures will direct bright light toward the ceiling without interfering with a person's line of vision.

- Ceiling-mounted fluorescent or cold cathode tubes contained in a cove project light upward and often make a distinctive architectural statement.

Lighting projected on wall areas will add to the expansive feeling of a space.

- Wallwashers can be recessed into the ceiling or surface mounted.

- Cove lights around the perimeter will conceal the source of the light while casting illumination on the wall surface.

To visually reduce the space, specify a dark color for the ceiling and walls.

- Spotlight the merchandise, and reduce ambient lighting.

Make low ceilings seem higher and high ceilings appear lower
To add height to a ceiling, use wallwashing up-lights on a light color surface.

- Pendant lights project illumination downward, making a ceiling appear lower to the viewer. Spaces also seem to be more intimate when pendant lights are introduced.

Make a narrow store seem wider and a wide store look narrower
Create the impression that there is more floor space between walls or partitions than actually exists.

- Specify a light color with a reflective surface.
- Wash the walls with light.
- Project light by specifying adjustable ceiling fixtures such as track lights.

Make a store seem less wide

- Use dark colors.
- Direct sources of light on merchandise with a narrow-beam pattern created by track lighting and spotlighting.

▼ *Coves illuminated by fluorescent or cold cathode tubes make a distinctive architectural statement. Circular ceiling design above main escalator well, F.& R. Lazarus, Pittsburgh. (Courtesy Cooper Carry, Inc. © Gabriel Benzor Photography.)*

▲ *Evening lighting for open-back windows dramatizes the products featured and the props, when used. Dylan's Candy Bar takes advantage of frontages on Lexington Avenue and Sixtieth Street on New York City's Upper East Side. Interior design by J. Newbold Associates, Inc. Architecture by Allen & Killcoyne Architects. Lighting by Focus Lighting, Inc. (Photo: Peter Paige.)*

Lighting Store Windows

Show windows are a panorama of messages about the store's image, its point of view, and the merchandise being featured. Store windows can:

- Impress
- Influence
- Inform
- Amuse
- Entertain

There are two basic types of display windows: closed back and open back. Store designers should work closely with their client's visual merchandisers to provide sufficient outlets, power supply, and structural supports, which are the basis for shopper-stopping windows.

Closed-back windows

Behind the glazing of a closed-back window, the display area is enclosed on three sides, focusing the viewer's attention on the staged scenario depicted in the window without any of the peripheral views presented by open-back or partially open-back windows.

Open-back windows

In an open-back window, the store interior is visible behind the mannequins, props, or other display elements, allowing the depth and selection of the merchandise within the store, as well as the movement, color, and illumination of the store's interior, to augment the window display.

Track lighting

Tracks can be mounted horizontally or vertically. The most frequently specified lamps are 150-watt spotlights and low-voltage pin spots. Overhead tracks can cause apparel to appear wrinkled. Footlights that shine upward can counterbalance down lighting. Tracks and individual floor-mounted lights that beam illumination upward toward mannequins create a subtle elegance.

Stage lighting

C-clamps, Kleig lights, and barn-door louvers add drama to store windows. They are integrally theatrical and help to rivet the viewer's attention on the setting.

Combination lighting

Windows that contain displays of many small items, such as calculators, tape recorders, or cameras, are best lit at an even, high-footcandle level. Fluorescent and incandescent lighting used in combination can measure 100–300 footcandles.

Pin spots

High-power, high-output pin spots can aim a circular beam measuring 6–12 in. at specific items of merchandise. Products such as jewelry or small art objects benefit from judicious pin spot lighting. Framing projectors create many shapes, including rectangles and squares.

Filters and colored lamps

Entire displays can take on a specific hue—warm or cool—when gel filters are placed over incandescent bulbs or white lamps are replaced with colored ones. This display technique adds allure to both the merchandise and the background setting.

SIGNS AND GRAPHICS

Effective retail graphics succeed when they (1) attract shoppers into the store, (2) create wayfinding elements that let customers know where to go and how to get there, and (3) provide product information customers need to make a buying decision.

Attracting Customers

- Bold color at the entry point gets attention.

- The size of the type, the type font, and the colors of the background and type should be designed to integrate with the existing architectural palette. Colors can be more saturated in graphics than those used in the interior, when kept within the same family of colors.

- Animated additions to a basic sign include movable elements, either wind-activated or mechanically driven, and illuminated projections, such as those created by gobos attached to the front of a light fixture. The image(s) projected can be verbal messages, products, or other visuals shown in one or more colors.

Wayfinding

- A store directory can show location by floor, or a map may indicate how to reach a desired area from the customer's starting point.

- Areas can be identified by prominently positioned signage, suspended or mounted overhead, that is visible to customers from other sections of the store.

- A number of signs are required by local ordinance, showing exits; locations of elevators, escalators, and stairs; and directions to public transportation and garage levels.

Displaying Product Information

Signs containing product-specific information—"silent salespersons"—should contain a maximum of three short messages that can be easily read and comprehended by shoppers. To help the customer read the messages, apply the following basic concepts:

▲ Neon tubing, filled with gas that turns colors when electrified, is a traditional sign material. The neon sign above the inside entrance to the Museum Store at the Franklin Institute, Philadelphia, grades from orange to light green, which enlivens the high-ceilinged corridor. Charles E. Broudy & Associates. (Photo courtesy Charles E. Broudy & Associates.)

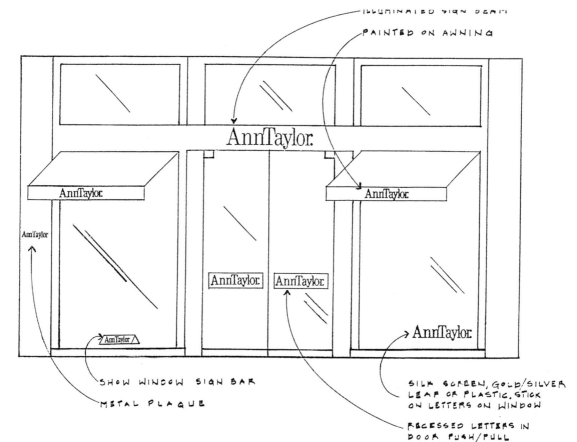

ILLUMINATED SIGN BEAM
PAINTED ON AWNING

AnnTaylor.

AnnTaylor

AnnTaylor

AnnTaylor

AnnTaylor

AnnTaylor

AnnTaylor

SHOW WINDOW SIGN BAR
METAL PLAQUE

SILK SCREEN, GOLD/SILVER LEAF OR PLASTIC. STICK ON LETTERS ON WINDOW
RECESSED LETTERS IN DOOR PUSH/PULL

▲ *Alternative techniques to "sign" a storefront:*
- *Show window sign bar*
- *Metal plaque*
- *Illuminated sign beam*
- *Painted on awning*
- *Letters in window can be silk screen, gold or silver leaf, or plastic stick-on*
- *Recessed letters in door's push/pull*
(Prepared by Charles E. Broudy & Associates.)

- Be consistent with colors and typography style throughout the entire store.
- Determine the hierarchy of information, and arrange the messages in order of importance to the customer. For example, a sign in a children's shoe department may read:

TODDLER SHOES
(large type, identify the product)

Sizes 6–12
(medium type, quantify the product)

$6.95 to $15.00
(smallest type, price)

Special Amenities

Two- and three-dimensional graphic elements can contribute to a store's ambience without directly linking to any particular display product:

- Benches
- Murals
- Sculpture
- Banners

CASE STUDIES

Stride Rite Children's Shoe Store

Stride Rite is an 85-year-old company that manufactures children's shoes, operates retail stores carrying its full line of footwear, and distributes its products through additional retail channels.

◀ ▼ *The Saugus, Massachusetts, Stride Rite children's shoe store was the prototype for "The Joy of Growing Up" theme applied to the new brand image campaign. Square display elements mounted on springlike bases are movable and adjustable for height. Elkus/Manfredi Architecture Ltd.; graphics by Selbert Perkins Design Collaborative. (Photos courtesy Selbert Perkins Design.)*

Feedback from Stride Rite's primary market of mid- to upper-income families indicated that Stride Rite stores rated high for value and selection, but were described as difficult to navigate and the product line confusing. To revitalize and update its brand, Stride Rite retained Grey Advertising, Elkus/Manfredi Architecture Ltd., and Selbert Perkins Design Collaborative to develop a brand repositioning program that included package design, an identity program, print communications, and catalogs, as well as an interior and exterior sign program for the company's new prototype store.

The brand image was refocused on the theme "The Joy of Growing Up." A bright new logo with playful cartoonlike faces reflects gender equality and multiculturalism. Stride Rite's brand categories were reorganized for easier consumer comprehension.

The basis for the Stride Rite graphics program is a system of modular units that can be mixed and matched to create a retail brand identity system. Its design menu incorporates a variety of design elements, ranging in size.

- Bright primary colors—red, blue, and deep yellow—and a bold typeface were employed for the graphic elements. Starting with the identifying sign above the store's front entrance and continuing through the store to the back wall, the graphics allow customers to quickly and easily find the section with products to fit their children's needs.

- Innovative graphics for sizes and categories were used throughout.

- Interactive sculpture, geared to children, was installed within the store.

- Flexible square-block display elements mounted, on springlike supports and carrying the new logo, can be adjusted for height for use in the store's windows or grouped effectively to present products.

Stride Rite tested the new concept in 10 stores. Based on a strong positive response from customers and employees, a full national rollout of 500 stores was implemented.

▸ ▸▸ *Wireless technology products from Omnipoint Communications are displayed in illuminated stainless steel shadow boxes in the company's sales showroom on Boston's upscale Newbury Street. Blue neon inside the shadow boxes is repeated in a hidden cove above the wood-covered feature wall. At the rear of the store is a full-height metal relief sculpture formed of squares that represent the evolution of the phone. Store design and graphics by Selbert Perkins Design Collaborative. (Photos courtesy Selbert Perkins Design, Environmental Graphics.)*

Omnipoint Communications

Omnipoint, a digital cellular service provider, operates its regional flagship retail store on Boston's fashionable Newbury Street, home to art galleries, jewelers, and high-end apparel and specialty stores.

Omnipoint wanted to create a showroom atmosphere to present its wireless technology image in a sophisticated architectural environment showcasing the products as individual sculptures. Against a background of blue neon with yellow accents, stainless steel shadow boxes appear to float, each containing a front-facing product mounted with hidden supports. Prices are posted directly beneath each sample.

Geometric forms, from floor to ceiling, help guide customers through the space. A wall-mounted relief sculpture placed at the rear of the store depicts the past, present, and future of communications via a time line of phone icons, from early models to those of the present.

GUIDELINES FOR RETAIL GRAPHIC DESIGN

- Be aware that a coordinated graphic design program can range between 1 and 2 percent of construction cost.

- Pay attention to details. Everything matters.

- Understand the merchant's concerns and the special requirements of the space to be occupied.

- Request qualifications and conduct interviews of suppliers.

- Full-scale models can help sell the project. Coordinate with fabricators regarding the time required to produce the items needed and assemble them.

- Allow for research time to evaluate electronic elements, such as LED (light-emitting diodes) technology, for programming requirements.
- Integrate the graphics within the project's multidisciplinary approach.

Exterior
Wall

- Pinned off—Pin mount; individual letters. Sophisticated, for quality store.
- Rear illuminated—Neon tube creates glow on wall; letters are in silhouette.
- Quality appearance—Background wall material should be receptive to light halo.
- Box sign—Fluorescent tubes behind plastic face in a metal box. Economical; easy to change sign face.
- Direct-mounted—Screw mount to wall. Easy installation.
- Direct-mounted plaque—Brass or stainless steel; nonilluminated.

Canopy

- Illuminated letter—Individual letter mount; metal, plastic. Surface-applied. Glowing letter is more elegant. Usually used in quality stores.
- Neon—Neon or fluorescent; behind plastic face. Individual, distinctive. Not applicable to all types of stores.

Pylon or tower

- Freestanding—Illuminated; heights vary. Flashing or blinking lights are usually not permitted. Used for highway recognition for shopping centers or larger stores. Sometimes lists tenants.

Hanging

- Wood—Carved wood often with gold leaf lettering. Used when a traditional, antique, or casual appearance is desired.
- Metal—Wrought iron, often with scrollwork. Identifies a craft shop or tradesperson.

Glass applied

- Glue-on or rub-on letters for show windows—Cutout letters of thin plastic or plaster.
- Changeable signage for show windows.

Awning

- Canvas or metal; graphics can be painted. A lightweight and semipermanent device to unite multifacade stores. Stripes, patterns, or solids are appropriate.

Banners

- Fabric or canvas. May have plain or patterned background. Can be temporary or long term.
- Can be changed seasonally.

Interior
Departmental and directional signs or graphics

- Can be suspended from ceiling or valance-mounted. Illuminated or nonilluminated, depending on the effect to be created. Directional arrows and signs should not confuse customers.
- In department stores or large stores, identification signs should be properly located for easy reading. A variety of surface backgrounds and types of letters create and extend the mood of the environment.

Name brand or product category

- Can be placed above merchandise on a valance or suspended from above. Designer logos can be used.
- Can be temporary or permanent, depending on the store's policy. Surface background is important if names will change. Letters can be cut out of any appropriate material.

Directories

- In large stores and department stores, directories are needed to help customers get to the proper merchandise or service areas quickly and easily.
- Directories can be wall- or floor-mounted or suspended from ceilings.

Maps may also be employed; most are rear-illuminated.

Photomurals

- Large photo enlargements (prints or transparencies) can be used to encourage patrons to buy toiletries, lingerie, jewelry, and the like.
- These photos may be black and white or color, front-illuminated or rear-screen color transparencies.

Point of purchase

- Tabletop graphics and displays play a large part in retailing. They range from TV monitors of fashion shows, to nameplates, to mirrors custom-fabricated with a trade name.

◀ *Reading Terminal Market, the venerable century-old market hall in downtown Philadelphia, upgraded its exterior signage. Mounted against the brick facade are black wrought iron brackets. Colorful pressed metal representations of the products sold by the Market's individual purveyors inside are mounted atop the brackets or hung from curved extensions from the main support. Dark red awnings define the entries and windows. Charles E. Broudy & Associates. (Photo courtesy Charles E. Broudy & Associates.)*

▲ Signs of various retailers in New York. Pinned-off Thomas Pink signs for the Madison Avenue and 53rd Street store. Sawicki Tarella Architecture + Design. (Photo: Joseph Weishar.)

▶ Signage for the Fossil chain; a sculptural direct-mounted plaque is accented by outlines and patterns formed by small white lamps. JGA, Inc. (Laszlo Regos Photography.)

▲ Jo Malone's white awnings protect product displays in the east-facing windows. The store is in the historic Flatiron Building located where Broadway, Fifth Avenue, and 23rd Street in New York City come together. (Photo: Vilma Barr)

◀ Contemporary Soho, New York City, home furnishings retailer Troy is identified by glass-applied signage near the base of its tall front windows. (Photo: Vilma Barr.)

DISPLAYING MERCHANDISE

The visual appearance, colors, textures, layout and sounds of a store affect customer response to the merchandise on display. A selling floor's layout can be designed to influence customer actions and encourage the desired response to purchase.

Careful attention to customer behavior and proper merchandise display can make the difference between sales success and sales failure. Important elements to consider include the following:

- Customer expectations and how they are formed
- Customer responses to a store environment
- Exterior influences
- A floor plan that customers can understand to help them locate the merchandise they seek
- Presentation techniques and freestanding and built-in display fixtures

Customer Expectations and How They Are Formed

Customers quickly evaluate what a store represents to them personally. From the moment they see the logo on the outside of the store, they begin to form an opinion about:

- The kind of service they can expect, ranging from self-service to the availability of numerous well-informed sales associates.
- The price range of the store's merchandise, ranging from popular-price to luxury.
- The merchandise categories carried by the store. Full-line department stores may offer selections ranging from furniture to children's clothing.

Shoppers can intuitively relate the quantity of merchandise displayed on the selling floor to the store's overall cubic space to establish the store's price points in their own minds. Tight aisles and closely spaced display fixtures loaded with merchandise typically indicate a popular-price or mass-merchandiser approach; wide aisles and artfully displayed products appeal to an upscale market.

There are eight factors that help customers to form an opinion about what they will find inside the store, which are supported by the store's three-dimensional physical aspects:

1. Location
2. Advertising and publicity
3. Exterior design
4. Signs, logo, and name
5. Word-of-mouth
6. Previous visits
7. Approach by car and/or on foot
8. Display windows

Customer Response to a Store Environment

The majority of shoppers, regardless of culture or geography, respond automatically to three basic aspects of a store's interior: height, light, and turning to the right. All three are to be considered throughout the design development process to create a store design that stimulates traffic and sales.

Typically, a person's eyes are drawn to a light source. Designers should provide lighting on the displays on the back wall of the store so that the shopper's eyes move to the back instead of concentrating only on the merchandise at the front of the store.

More than 90 percent of all customers

entering a store turn to the right unless they know that the item they want to purchase is on the left. Typically, customers scan a store visually from left to right.

Customers often pass by the first department to the right, off the main entrance, an area referred to as "the Bermuda Triangle" of store design. This reaction occurs because they would have to make a sharp 90-degree-angle turn upon entering, a direction that many shoppers avoid, opting instead to make the easier 45-degree-angle turn once they are farther into the store. One way to call attention to the first department is for the merchant to present three different looks—left, center, and right—so that as a shopper enters, the shopper's glance bounces from department to department. The floor plan should allow for flexible layouts that can be placed to entice the shopper.

Exterior Influences

Windows

The last piece of information about the store that is observed by the shopper before entry is the windows. Street or mall windows are typically built up on a platform to make the setting look like a stage. For example, Crate & Barrel has been consistent over the last three decades in its signature style of window presentation. Its windows, without back walls, look into the interior and carry an image that has made the firm a fashion leader in mid-price home furnishings and a major national player in this market. Crate & Barrel's merchandising strategies allow it to feature new home products and color palettes that are often in advance of the fashion colors promoted by apparel stores.

Small side windows can also draw shoppers' attention to the merchandise selection inside.

▲ The exterior design of a store contributes to the image it communicates to the marketplace, allowing the customer to develop an expectation of the shopping experience that will be found inside. An example is Cereal City, Battle Creek, Michigan, a themed shopping and entertainment venue. JGA, Inc. (Laszlo Regos Photography.)

▲ Crate & Barrel makes its store interiors serve as windows. The wide entry to this mall store is like an open window; for street-level stores, large glass windows look into product displays and the store interior beyond. (Photo: Joseph Weishar.)

▶ An entry that admits only one or two customers at a time communicates the store's exclusivity. The Elizabeth Arden signature Red Door salons and retail stores, such as this one on Fifth Avenue in New York City, are an expression of the cosmetics company's highly promoted brand. JGA, Inc. (Laszlo Regos Photography.)

Entries

For stores that depend on attracting heavy traffic to enter throughout its business hours, the wider the entry and the more people who can come in, the better. H&M stores have a very wide entrance in street-facing stores and mall shops. XOXO stores in Turkey have no front entrance at all, so that shoppers, in good weather, pass in one motion from the sidewalk to the store interior.

Upscale boutiques may limit the width of their entries to permit one or two customers to enter at a time, extending the store's image of exclusivity. Elizabeth Arden's well-known brand, "Red Door," was derived from the single entry/exit door, painted bright red.

Creating a Helpful Floor Plan

A floor plan should be developed that is easy for customers to understand and can help them to locate the merchandise they seek.

Subtle influences

- The deeper shoppers go into a department, the more they will purchase.
- Plan the store's layout to entice the shopper to leave the main aisles and shop farther into the departments. Merchandise placed off the main aisles often carries higher profit margins.
- Allow for visual points of reference approximately 20–30 ft apart so that the shopper is visually enticed and pulled through the store.
- Time spent in movement is added browsing time. A time-proven retailing axiom is "The longer a customer is in the store, the more he or she will buy."

Store layout guidelines

- The hard or main aisle of a store is established based on the architecture of the building. In a mall store that is a minimum of 30 ft wide, it is possible to plan a loop aisle for left, center, and right departments. The objective is to create a loop from the front to the back and back again to the front. With this configuration, the amount of merchandise shown on the aisle is doubled. Better vistas are created for the entire assortment.
- For mall stores of 1,200–3,000 sq ft, the cashwrap station and register can be positioned on the left side from the entrance, which makes it the right side on exit. In larger stores, of up to 20,000 sq ft, a central cashwrap is an option.
- Stores of more than 3,000 sq ft usually have columns. They are the highest points on the sales floor and should be recognized as potential prime selling areas. They can be used for feature presentations or to call attention to sale merchandise. A discount store often uses a column for full merchandise display impact.

▼ Columns can be used to direct traffic around the store, to the rear or to wall displays, or to give height and drama to a merchandise display. This Sephora cosmetics and fragrance store has boldly striped black-and-white columns that run the length of the store, from the horseshoe-shaped lipstick display at the front to personal care products at the back. (Photo: Vilma Barr.)

- The minimum space for a vendor's shop-in-shop is approximately 250 sq ft; the maximum is approximately 1,000 sq ft. Each vendor's shop is judged on customer response to the products and the planned dollar sales volume the collection is meeting.

- Aisle widths in supermarkets, drugstores, and discount stores should be planned so that shoppers with baby carriages will not bump into each other.

Visual and Textural Balance

A balanced layout is essential to successful retail presentation.

- The proper distance to the first visual point of encounter from the store entry should be no more than 25–30 ft, from the hard aisle to the farthest point.

- A path can lead customers to a point beyond 30 ft deep by 16 ft wide, a secondary loop or main aisle.

- Stores larger than 10,000 sq ft require a secondary main aisle of 8–10 ft. Smaller stores can have main aisles no less than 5 ft wide. A secondary aisle or an aisle inside a department can be 4 ft. (Macy's Manhattan store has a 16 ft wide first-floor aisle that creates a classic grand entry.)

Customers will react to a change in surface texture beneath their feet or to colors they see, whether they are in a large or small store. For example, if the hard aisle is all wood, the color can be changed to lead customers into the departments radiating from it. A change from hard surface to carpet signifies luxury and soft goods.

Boutiques, high-end fashion stores, discount stores, and warehouse clubs all follow the same rules. The elements of balance that change are the space, the merchandise, and the lighting.

▼ Merchandise display fixtures should be easy for the retailer to move or reconfigure. Fixture manufacturers will often customize the styles in their line to meet a designer's specifications for changes in dimensions, finishes, and structural features. The Pylon Collection from Alu is mounted on rigid freestanding supports. (Photo: Vilma Barr.)

Presentation Techniques

Freestanding and built-in display fixtures

Customers should see merchandise first, *not* the fixtures. Display fixtures serve as platforms for presenting merchandise. Designers should mock up the intended fixtures they are considering for a store or department, or shop the fixture market with the presentation of a collection, rather than disparate items, in mind.

Designers must recognize the merchant's requirements for low-capacity units for high-margin, high-fashion; for medium-capacity units for showing collections; and for high-capacity units for basic merchandise. A variety of fixtures are used for clearance merchandise, depending on the age and the unsold remainder of the stock.

Fixtures are planned by considering the number of units per sq ft (or square meter) and can range from 4 to 12–15 units per sq ft. The difference depends on the size and bulk of the merchandise. Displaying the basic merchandise in specific quantities is a key factor in fixturing each of a store's departments or sections. The chief issue is, How many items must be in stock to maintain a presence through the selling day? How much product is it necessary to have on display during the day so that it will not be totally depleted at the end of the day and look unappealing to the customer? For example, how many drinking glasses? At a store like Crate & Barrel, how many glasses do customers buy at one time? Sufficient shelving should be planned to house the supply for a day's selling.

Seasonal versus year-round staple items

Underwear and lingerie are sold year-round, usually in the same place in a multiline specialty store. Ski wear, beach wear, and holiday items are seasonal. The store designer should discuss with the merchant how much space will be allotted to permit the swing (seasonal) department to operate smoothly.

Hung or folded merchandise

Folded merchandise takes up less space than hung merchandise and permits the display of more items per cu ft. Nordstrom's provides an example of how to display best-selling basic items that are folded. Men's shirts are artistically presented and maintained by the sales associates on a moment-to-moment basis. Whenever the merchandise is examined by customers, it is quickly rearranged by the sales associates so that it looks perfect again.

To avoid a "warehouse" look on the selling floor, display walls at Zara, the international women's, men's, and children's apparel chain based in Spain, displays one or two items per size or SKU (stock keeping units). When these are sold, they are immediately replaced from the stockroom to maintain a full range of selections. As a result, Zara creates an "urgency" to buy.

Radical Change

Today's consumer is translating our current speed of communications to a sense of fashion. For many, the faster you follow apparel and accessory trends, the more fashionable you are perceived to be.

Most other commercial or institutional interiors may undergo minor changes in a period of a year or two. Retailers, however, need to change several times a year. To facilitate rapid and ongoing changes, consider the following factors.

Lighting

Store designers apply theatrical lighting techniques to cost-efficiently change the way a selling space or a merchandise display is perceived by the shopper. For example, programmable controls for light-emitting diodes (LEDs) can wash walls or ceilings with color as an all-over wash or in overlapping patterns. Up-lights, behind wall cases or in coves, can be designed as a soft background element in a space, or, fitted with brighter lamps, can visually draw the shopper to the merchandise displays.

Flexible departments

Departments can be separated by partial walls on wheels, or panels can be ceiling hung. Many manufacturers offer merchandise display fixtures of sufficient height that are constructed to be moved. These can also change the way a department appears to keep it fresh-looking in the shopper's eye.

Mobile fixtures

Display fixtures outfitted with wheels on casters offer flexibility, but the added wheels can raise the cost of a fixture. In most departments, 10 percent flexibility is sufficient for the merchandiser's needs.

Incorporating wall systems

The exterior walls constitute the only fixed perimeter. The ability to change the back wall with signage, graphics, or merchandise—hanging, folded, or boxed—should be built into the system.

▼ A prototype Red Wing Shoe Company factory-owned store in the Mall of America, Bloomington, Minnesota, has an up-front glass-enclosed walk-in section that provides information about the product, the craftsmanship, and the history of the company's line of boots and outdoor footwear. SteinDesign. (Photo © 1999 George Heinrich.)

◀ At Mindworks in Tampa, Florida, displays are mounted on poles and a pedestal. Along with the change in the flooring color and the curve of the niche behind, the units provide a graceful visual change of pace from the high-density wall displays to the right. Chute Gerdeman. (Michael Houghton Photography.)

▲ Fashion mannequins help to tell a story in store windows. This fanciful setting in Macy's San Francisco store, with a mannequin in profile, promotes a charity event, the Black & White Ball. Mannequins are available in a wide range of styles and materials. (Photo: Vilma Barr.)

◀ Part of the collection on view at the New York City showroom of Bay Area Design of San Francisco. (Photo: Vilma Barr.)

◀ Fashion mannequin dressed to reflect a biker theme in the window of a shop on Melrose Avenue, Los Angeles. (Photo: Vilma Barr.)

Mannequins

To incorporate mannequins into a store design, the designer must consider the following:

- Types of mannequins—full forms, with or without heads; torso forms without heads; special mannequins available for sports, group presentations, children's wear, and so forth.

- Number of mannequins necessary to show the current lines.

- The style of fashion image presented by the mannequins and their relationship to the design of the store interior.

Each of the two elements should reinforce the message of the other.

- Women's departments should have four to five times the amount of mannequin presentation than men's sections.

- Men's displays often use torso forms to show structured merchandise (suits, jackets), ranging from casual to formal merchandise.

- Mannequins are also available with "look panels" or T-stands attached. The merchandise on the form carries a panel or stand in the back, holding the same merchandise for examination by shoppers.

The Language of Merchandise

- Everything in retail is about merchandise. It is the first consideration for all decision making.
- In-store presentation is the most powerful selling tool for that merchandise.

Customers today want to be in a shopping environment that relates to them. Successful store designers grasp the importance of the store's layout and design on the ultimate decision to purchase.

Thoughtful planning of the store interior—along a constantly evolving, always alluring merchandise display program—provides the competitive edge.

THE PLACEMENT OF AISLES AND DISPLAYS FOR MAXIMUM MERCHANDISE VISIBILITY

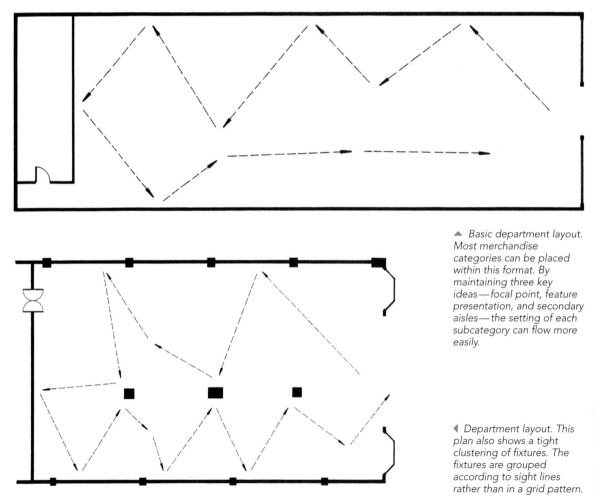

▲ Basic department layout. Most merchandise categories can be placed within this format. By maintaining three key ideas—focal point, feature presentation, and secondary aisles—the setting of each subcategory can flow more easily.

◀ Department layout. This plan also shows a tight clustering of fixtures. The fixtures are grouped according to sight lines rather than in a grid pattern.

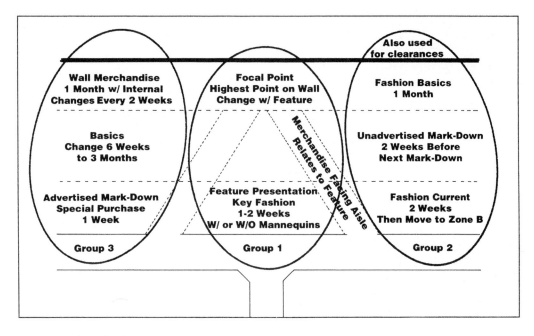

Bounce plans direct customers to product display locations. The eye movement plan, or bounce plan, can show where to position the best-selling departments.

Even without columns, aisles can be created to make islands.

(All drawings: Joseph Weishar.)

◀ *Plan: columns and aisles for a specialty store. The aisles are placed by using the columns as center points of island departments. This technique benefits smaller spaces because it can highlight specialized merchandise.*

▼ *Plan: columns and aisles in a large store. The same basic column-and-aisle principle holds for larger spaces.*

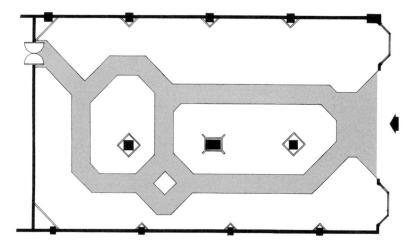

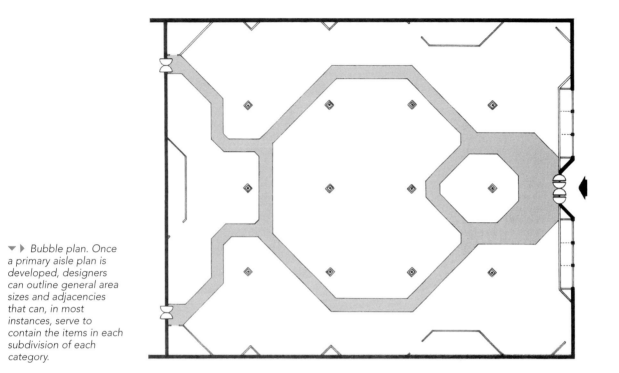

▼ ▶ Bubble plan. Once a primary aisle plan is developed, designers can outline general area sizes and adjacencies that can, in most instances, serve to contain the items in each subdivision of each category.

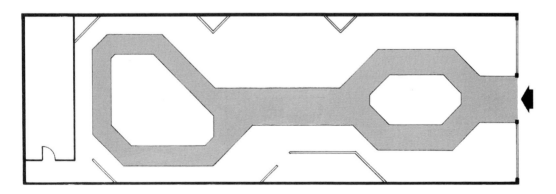

CHAPTER 6

PLANNING FOR RETAIL AND MIXED-USE CENTERS

THE DEVELOPMENT PROCESS
Shopping center developers are becoming increasingly sophisticated, seeking more opportunities for mixed uses by including media and entertainment, community services, cultural institutions, residences, and office space.

Today investors and financial backers often require that the bulk of the tenant space in a retail center be precommitted by bankable or creditworthy tenants. To ensure a bankable tenant mix, developers are more often turning to large national chain tenants with firm financial resources rather than single-unit independent retailers. As a result, the traditional small ma-and-pa shops are, in many cases, overlooked; small independent operators, such as toy stores, record shops, candy stores, shoe stores, and bookstores, have become almost extinct.

Retailing Trends
The saturation of the market with retail projects and the consolidation of stores and developers in the 1990s have drastically changed the development environment. Large, open sites are no longer easy to find; expansion and renovation of existing projects are becoming more common. To successfully compete, retail centers must have a solid foundation based on accurate market research, appropriate tenant mix, and good design. Projects

---

SAMPLING OF CURRENT RETAIL TRENDS

Demographic and Psychographic Changes

Aging population

More working women

Focus on leisure

Demand for value

Dilution of traditional family unit

Less discretionary time

More eating out

Demand for personal services

Grocery Industry Changes

Data capture and self-scanning technology

Restaurant/fast food growth

Rise in health/fitness products

Major food operations opened by national discounters

Operating Issues

Limited labor

Technological changes

   In-store electronic capabilities

   Competition

Capital-intensive requirements

Growth of non-store shopping modes

   Internet, catalogs, TV, telemarketing

Concept Changes

Niche retailers, catering to age groups or product specialties

Changes to traditional department store

New Retailing Formats

Urban revitalization and redevelopment

Airport redevelopment

Entertainment retail formats

Additional Issues

Product manufacturers operating their own retail facilities, bypassing traditional retailer

Consolidation of retailing organizations

Rising costs

Inadequate labor supply for construction

---

that are anchored, well tenanted, properly located, and optimally designed are, for the most part, all that will be built.

THE ARCHITECT-DEVELOPER RELATIONSHIP

The design of shopping centers and mixed-use complexes, unlike that of many other building types, is highly influenced by third parties to the architect-developer relationship. It is not uncommon to begin the design process when none of the major tenants is known. As major tenants are identified, their particular requirements frequently alter the design and, in many instances, the fundamental plan of a project.

The four fundamental steps in the development process are as follows:

1. Define the market.
2. Create the tenant mix.
3. Confirm the project's economic viability.
4. Implement the project.

WORK PROGRAM OUTLINE

Data Assembly

Project definition

Regulatory requirements

Community framework

Program/market analysis by owner

Physical conditions

Program Coordination

Program review/evaluation

Market analysis review

Conceptual Design

Alternative design preparation (including waterways)

Area allocation summary

Construction budget review

Design coordination with owner

Alternative selection

Schematic Design

Schematic design preparation

Develop selected alternative

Prepare codes and regulation summary

Initiate consultant work on schematic design

Prepare project manual

Design presentation

Prepare presentation drawings

Provide design data for cost estimation

Cost estimate

Prepare construction cost estimate

Confirm official construction budget

Approval by owner

Design Development

Design development investigation

Consultants' design coordination

Detail code review

Drawing layout

Specification development

Cost estimate

Design development approval by owner

Document Production

Consultant coordination

Construction drawings

Specifications

Construction estimate update

Final checking

Approvals

District

State

Federal

Bidding

Construction Overview

Project Management

Contractual arrangements

Budgets and schedules

Team selection

Review meetings

Client relations

Financial management

Project records

Quality control

Managing changes

WORK PROGRAM SCHEDULE

	2002								2003												2004					
	May	Jun	Jul	Aug	Sep	Oct	Nov	Dec	Jan	Feb	Mar	Apr	May	Jun	Jul	Aug	Sep	Oct	Nov	Dec	Jan	Feb	Mar	Apr	May	Jun

Buildings

- Data assembly
- Program coordination
- Conceptual design
- Schematic design
- Design development
- Construction documents
- Agency approvals
- Plan check
- Bidding
- Building construction
- Tenant furnishings
- Amenity construction

Site

- Engineering design
- Agency approvals
- Engineering construction

○ Client approval

BASIC SHOPPING CENTER CONFIGURATIONS AND TYPES							
Type	Concept	Total Sq Ft	Acreage	Number of Anchors	Typical Anchors	Anchor Ratio (%)*	Primary Trade Area (miles)**
Neighborhood center	Convenience	30,000–150,000	3–15	1 or more	Supermarkets	30–50	3
Community center	General merchandise; convenience	100,000–350,000	10–40	2 or more	Discount department store; supermarket; drugstore; home improvement; large specialty/discount apparel	40–60	3–6
Regional center	General merchandise; fashion (mall, typically enclosed)	400,000–800,000	40–100	2 or more	Full-line department store; jr. department store; mass merchandise; discount department store; fashion apparel	50–70	5–15
Superregional center	Similar to regional center but has more variety and assortment	800,000+	60–120	3 or more	Full-line department store; jr. department store; mass merchant; fashion apparel	50–70	5–25
Fashion/specialty center	Higher end; fashion oriented	80,000–250,000	5–25	N/A	Fashion	N/A	5–15
Power center	Category-dominant anchors; few small tenants	250,000–600,000	25–80	3 or more	Category killer; home improvement; discount department store; warehouse club; off-price	75–90	5–10
Theme/festival center	Leisure; tourist oriented; retail and service	80,000–250,000	5–20	N/A	Restaurants; entertainment	N/A	N/A
Outlet center	Manufacturers' outlet stores	50,000–400,000	10–50	N/A	Manufacturers' outlet stores	N/A	25–75

*The share of a center's total square footage that is attributable to its anchors

**The area from which 60–80% of the center's sales originate

Source: Copyright ©1999 by International Council of Shopping Centers.

DEFINING THE MARKET

"Fail to plan, plan to fail." Nowhere is this truism better applied than in the development industry today. The development landscape is littered with retail centers that have not met with market success and have fallen into a state of mediocrity and poor economic return. To be sure, retailing is a highly competitive and fluid industry with shoppers who are mobile and discriminating in the search for the best shopping environment and offerings. For every successful development, there are many more underperforming centers or "stressed assets." The fundamental difference lies in the appropriate and proper predevelopment planning.

To minimize the inherent risks in retail development and to ensure the correct market positioning of a proposed center, a logical and rigorous sequence of investigative steps must be undertaken by the development team or a qualified consulting group. This critical process is depicted in the schematic flowchart below.

▼ *Market positioning flowchart. (Courtesy Thomas Consultants.)*

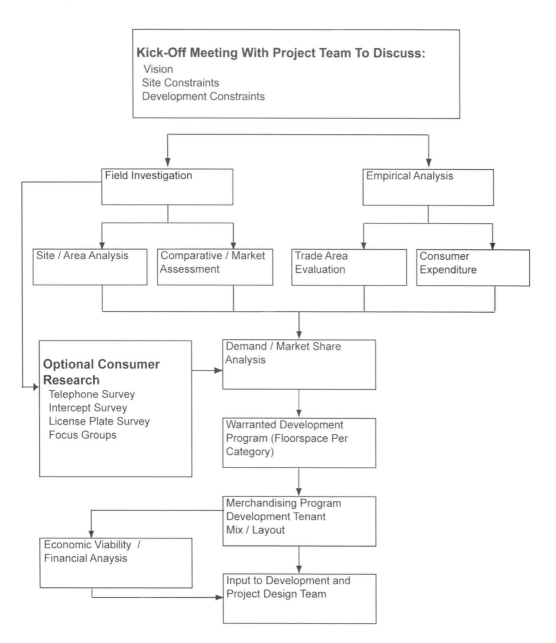

Kick-Off Meeting With Project Team To Discuss:
Vision
Site Constraints
Development Constraints

Field Investigation

Empirical Analysis

Site / Area Analysis

Comparative / Market Assessment

Trade Area Evaluation

Consumer Expenditure

Optional Consumer Research
Telephone Survey
Intercept Survey
License Plate Survey
Focus Groups

Demand / Market Share Analysis

Warranted Development Program (Floorspace Per Category)

Merchandising Program Development Tenant Mix / Layout

Economic Viability / Financial Anaysis

Input to Development and Project Design Team

Market Positioning

To enhance the ability of a retail center to best match the demands of local and regional consumers, a detailed market positioning exercise must be conducted. Far more than traditional market research, this rigorous approach critically evaluates the potential market from the qualitative and quantitative perspectives, thus ensuring that no stones are unturned in the understanding of the market opportunities and consumer needs. The resultant findings play a vital role in the following areas:

- Development strategy (size and category/tenant mix)
- Marketing
- Leasing
- Operating plan

To commence the market positioning process, the client and the project development team engage in a kickoff workshop. The objective of this workshop is to ensure that all team members share the overall vision and philosophy and understand the challenges. Upon completion of the workshop, the process generally takes the following steps:

Field investigation (qualitative)

Site/area analysis

The attributes of the site are examined in detail to assess their importance in the overall development scheme. In particular, elements such as site coverage, the regional and local relationship of the site to the market it serves, the compatibility of surrounding land uses, the transportation linkages, and the proximity of competitive centers must be studied to truly recognize the attributes of the site so that the development can best benefit from its inherent strengths and mitigate its weaknesses.

▼ *Elements such as site coverage, compatibility of surrounding land uses, and transportation linkages must be studied to develop a project that benefits from the inherent strengths of the site and mitigates its weaknesses, as shown in a 1998 diagram produced for The Gateway in Salt Lake City, Utah. (Illustration: Thomas Consultants.)*

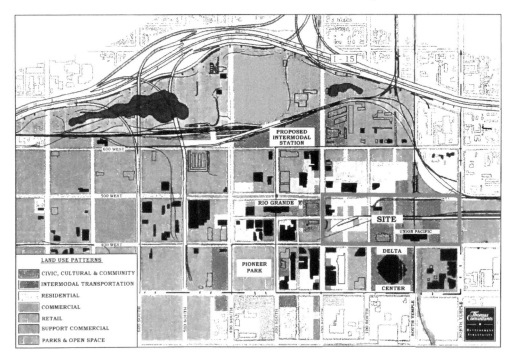

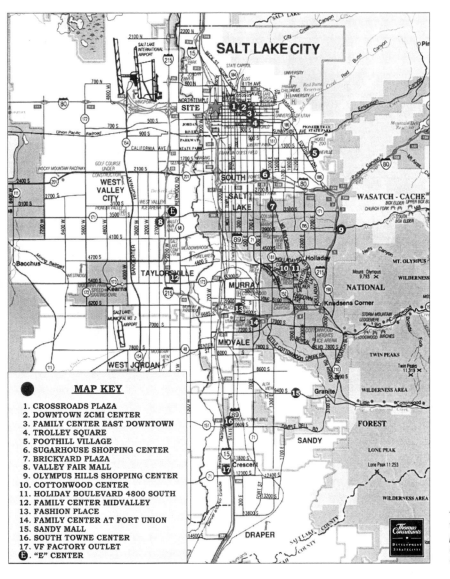

MAP KEY

1. CROSSROADS PLAZA
2. DOWNTOWN ZCMI CENTER
3. FAMILY CENTER EAST DOWNTOWN
4. TROLLEY SQUARE
5. FOOTHILL VILLAGE
6. SUGARHOUSE SHOPPING CENTER
7. BRICKYARD PLAZA
8. VALLEY FAIR MALL
9. OLYMPUS HILLS SHOPPING CENTER
10. COTTONWOOD CENTER
11. HOLIDAY BOULEVARD 4800 SOUTH
12. FAMILY CENTER MIDVALLEY
13. FASHION PLACE
14. FAMILY CENTER AT FORT UNION
15. SANDY MALL
16. SOUTH TOWNE CENTER
17. VF FACTORY OUTLET
Ⓔ. "E" CENTER

◀ Competitive retail projects were mapped to show proximity to The Gateway. (Illustration: Thomas Consultants.)

Competitive/market assessment

An assessment should be carried out in terms of the retail infrastructure within the surrounding region. In this process, the critical operating characteristics, strengths, and weaknesses of the competitors of the subject development should be analyzed. This assessment is undertaken to avoid po-tential duplication of merchandise offerings and to critically define the inherent market opportunities for the subject center.

Empirical analysis (quantitative)

Trade area evaluation

Based on the site assessment and the na-ture of the competitive infrastructure,

▶ *The primary and secondary trade areas were mapped to indicate The Gateway's potential market reach. (Illustration: Thomas Consultants).*

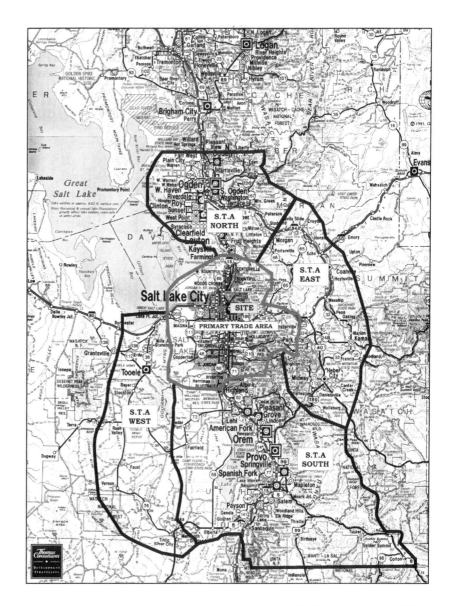

the appropriate trade area for the proposed development should be delineated. This process should determine the current and potential scope of influence the development would have in the surrounding regions.

The success of the project is critically dependent on the consumers it intends to serve. As individual regions may differ significantly, a detailed understanding of the population base of the various trade area regions and their associated characteristics will greatly enhance the proper merchandising and future marketing of the center. Accordingly, the critical parameters, such as, but not limited to, popu-

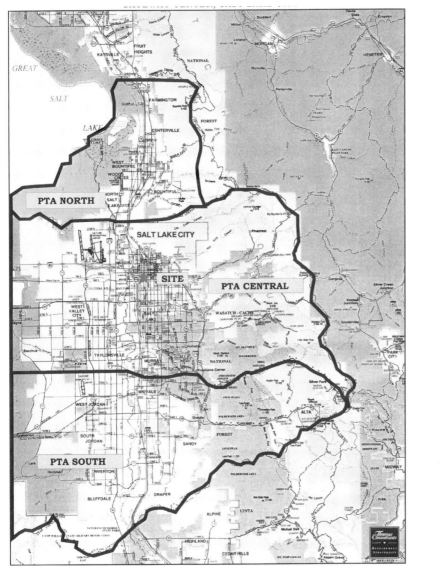

◀ The primary trade area was further broken down into individual regions, which were critically analyzed to provide a detailed understanding of the respective population bases. (Illustration: Thomas Consultants).

lation, income, household profile, and so on, should be assessed in detail for each trade area subregion.

Consumer expenditure

With the proper study of consumer demographic variables, all relevant expenditure patterns in each retail, service, restaurant, and entertainment category should be defined. This is of utmost importance in that it can indicate the market potential that is, in fact, available in the trade area and can play a crucial role in the allocation of the proper amount of floor space for each expenditure category.

TRADE AREA POPULATION							
			POPULATION				
	1990	**1996**	**Annual Growth 1990–96 (%)**	**1998**	**2001**	**2005**	**2010**	**Projected Annual Growth (%)**
Primary Trade Area								
North	76,380	89,453	2.6	93,432	99,130	108,146	120,577	2.2
Central	485,293	548,334	2.0	570,487	603,513	653,262	728,353	2.0
South	242,873	285,151	2.6	297,836	316,300	345,066	384,731	2.2
PTA subtotal	804,546	922,938	2.2	961,755	1,018,943	1,106,474	1,233,661	
Secondary Trade Area								
North	268,559	310,916	2.4	325,383	346,038	378,989	424,624	2.3
West	23,009	25,848	1.9	26,577	28,037	29,640	31,774	1.4
East	26,593	36,310	5.1	38,521	41,882	47,322	55,126	3.1
South	263,590	309,819	2.6	326,775	355,403	395,369	451,705	2.7
STA subtotal	581,751	682,893	2.6	717,256	771,360	851,320	963,229	
Total Trade Area	1,386,297	1,605,831	2.4	1,679,010	1,790,303	1,957,794	2,196,890	
Utah State Total	1,722,850	2,000,630	2.4	2,085,539	2,224,988	2,417,857	2,682,621	2.1
Trade Area as % of State	80.5%	80.3%						

Source: *Thomas Consultants Inc., 1998.*

Positioning and market share analysis

After a detailed understanding of the trade area and the consumers residing within it, an appropriate niche should be identified that would put the subject center in the best possible position to benefit from the demands and aspirations of the marketplace. Specifically, the target market/consumer segments should be identified. Based on the existing and planned competitive infrastructure, the optimal market positioning can then be determined.

With the market positioning direction established, market share in each retail, service, restaurant, and entertainment category should be projected, based on the anticipated strength of this development and its effectiveness within the targeted market. Utilizing the latest retail sales forecasting methodologies, the probable levels of sales (turnover) for a predefined period (generally five or ten years) of operation is then projected. This information can allow a subsequent detailed financial analysis to be performed.

Consumer Research

In many cases, the market positioning strategy can also benefit significantly from a well-designed consumer research program. In general, four major avenues of research can be conducted, based on the particular need and circumstance. Specifically, telephone surveys, direct intercept surveys, focus groups, and license plate surveys can enhance the overall understanding of the marketplace. The results can play a critical role in the evaluation of

TRADE AREA DEMOGRAPHIC PROFILE

	PTA North		PTA Central		PTA South		Total PTA		BENCHMARK, STATE OF UTAH	
			PRIMARY TRADE AREA							
Age Distribution										
0–4	7,657	8.6%	45,783	8.3%	26,042	9.1%	79,482	8.6%	173,994	8.7%
5–17	25,762	28.8	121,480	22.2	87,004	30.5	234,246	25.4	533,529	26.7
18–24	9,144	10.2	63,773	11.6	27,997	9.8	100,914	10.9	249,423	12.5
25–34	11,331	12.7	87,996	16.0	39,930	14.0	139,257	15.1	282,057	14.1
35–44	11,466	12.8	86,210	15.7	50,004	17.5	147,680	16.0	288,084	14.4
45–54	10,040	11.2	52,378	9.6	30,125	10.6	92,543	10.0	185,398	9.3
55–64	6,468	7.2	33,932	6.2	11,982	4.2	52,382	5.7	114,750	5.7
65–74	4,532	5.1	30,530	5.6	7,131	2.5	42,193	4.6	94,465	4.7
75+	3,053	3.4	26,252	4.8	4,936	1.7	34,241	3.7	78,930	3.9
Average Age	31.0		32.7		28.1		30.6		30.6	
Marital Status										
Single	11,689	23.2	90,956	25.7	37,901	23.8	140,546	24.9	299,784	25.3
Married	33,724	66.9	205,199	58.0	106,225	66.7	345,148	61.3	740,672	62.4
Widowed	2,126	4.2	21,017	5.9	4,188	2.6	27,331	4.9	57,914	4.9
Divorced	2,877	5.7	36,564	10.3	10,866	6.8	50,307	8.9	87,678	7.4
Household Income										
(1996 Estimate)	$58,810		$48,969		$56,580		$54,786		$47,250	
(1998 Estimate)	$66,170		$55,554		$62,883		$61,519		$52,612	
(2110 Estimate)	$77,085		$65,432		$72,337		$71,618		$60,655	
Index to State Average	126		106		120		117			
Household Income Distribution										
Under $15,000	2,423	9.2	37,263	18.3	8,226	10.3	47,912	15.5	109,322	17.2
$15,000–25,000	2,882	10.9	34,806	17.1	9,501	11.9	47,189	15.2	102,920	16.2
$25,000–35,000	3,522	13.3	30,821	15.2	11,292	14.1	45,635	14.7	100,177	15.7
$35,000–50,000	5,226	19.8	35,613	17.5	17,248	21.5	58,087	18.8	122,460	19.2
$50,000–75,000	7,244	27.5	33,382	16.4	18,527	23.1	59,153	19.1	115,629	18.2
$75,000–100,000	2,164	8.2	12,540	6.2	6,848	8.6	21,552	7.0	37,374	5.9
$100,000–150,000	1,553	5.9	9,276	4.6	4,568	5.7	15,397	5.0	25,542	4.0
$150,000+	1,373	5.2	9,592	4.7	3,869	4.8	14,834	4.8	23,005	3.6
Total Number of Households	26,387		203,293		80,079		309,759		636,429	

Source: U.S. Bureau of the Census, Thomas Consultants Inc., April 1998.

	RETAIL EXPENDITURE POTENTIAL BY CATEGORY					
	1998			**2001**		
Category	**Total Households**	**Household Expenditures ($)**	**Category Potential ($)**	**Total Households**	**Household Expenditures ($)**	**Category Potential ($)**
Apparel/ accessories	322,708	3,451	1,113,665,308	348,261	3,995	1,391,302,695
Furniture/ household goods	322,708	1,421	458,568,068	348,261	1,645	572,889,345
Home electronics	322,708	1,740	561,511,920	348,261	2,014	701,397,654
Sports/toys/ hobbies	322,708	1,387	447,595,996	348,261	1,606	559,307,166
Specialty retail	322,708	1,401	452,113,908	348,261	1,622	564,879,342
Food/super market	322,708	5,146	1,660,655,368	348,261	5,958	2,074,939,038
Alcohol/ tobacco	322,708	1,478	476,962,424	348,261	1,711	595,874,571
Personal care/ services	322,708	1,205	388,863,140	348,261	1,395	485,824,095
Cinema	322,708	51	16,458,108	348,261	59	20,547,399
Attractions/ games	322,708	30	9,681,240	348,261	35	12,189,135
Restaurants	322,708	2,651	855,498,908	348,261	3,069	1,068,813,009
Total	322,708	19,961	6,441,574,388	348,261	23,109	8,047,963,449

Source: *Thomas Consultants Inc., 1998.*

the potential market share and the appropriate merchandising mix for both new developments and the repositioning of existing properties.

CREATING THE TENANT MIX

After the sales potential of a site is determined, the physical development program for the project can be initiated. Based on the projected level of sales (turnover) in each retail category analyzed, an appropriate productivity factor (sales per sq ft) can be applied to determine the retail size warranted for each merchandise category.

A development program for multitenant retail centers is likely to be a mix of destination or anchor tenants, complemented by ancillary tenants that depend more on impulse purchases. Destination or anchor tenants are those tenants initiating a customer trip, such as a grocery store (I need food) or a cinema (I want to see a movie). Ancillary tenants are those retail-

(TOTAL PRIMARY TRADE AREA)					
	2005			**2010**	
Total Households	**Household Expenditures ($)**	**Category Potential ($)**	**Total Households**	**Household Expenditures ($)**	**Category Potential ($)**
378,000	4,819	1,821,582,000	418,777	6,091	2,550,770,707
378,000	1,984	749,952,000	418,777	2,508	1,050,292,716
378,000	2,430	918,540,000	418,777	3,071	1,286,064,167
378,000	1,937	732,186,000	418,777	2,449	1,025,584,873
378,000	1,957	739,746,000	418,777	2,474	1,036,054,298
378,000	7,186	2,716,308,000	418,777	9,085	3,804,589,045
378,000	2,064	780,192,000	418,777	2,609	1,092,589,193
378,000	1,683	636,174,000	418,777	2,128	891,157,456
378,000	71	26,838,000	418,777	89	37,271,153
378,000	42	15,876,000	418,777	53	22,195,181
378,000	3,702	1,399,356,000	418,777	4,679	1,959,457,583
378,000	27,875	10,536,750,000	418,777	35,236	14,756,026,372

ers that rely on large numbers of customers passing by who will make an impulse or complementary purchase. Such tenants include purveyors of focused lines of fashion, clothing accessories, shoes, crafts, and novelties.

Although the analytical method of creating a development program is important, it tends to limit the development to existing or known potential populations. This type of analysis may not consider or be able to predict the impact that a unique project, such as Universal CityWalk, Los Angeles, may have in creating its own market demand.

With the initial tenant mix defined, input is provided for the production of a master plan layout diagram. The master plan, based on the identified strategic recommendations, addresses the following factors:

- Strategic positioning of retail/ restaurant/entertainment anchors and components

FACTORS AFFECTING TRADE AREA DEFINITION	
Access Attributes	Controlled-access highways will generally expand the trade area farther than if major access routes are four-lane, unrestricted-access roads.
Physical Barriers	Freeways, rivers, railroads, mountains, and other barriers inhibit movement across the trade area.
Competition	William J. Reilly's *The Law of Retail Gravitation* (1931) still holds true: "The customer will shop at the closest facility where comparable products can be obtained."
Areas of Dramatic Use Change	Industrial areas, airports, floodplains, and undeveloped areas inhibit movement and can pose psychological barriers that customers may choose to avoid.
Location in Relation to Workplace	If a retailer is located between a residential area and a major employment center, the trade area will be expanded in the direction opposite of the workplace.
Travel Time	Different retailers and project types will attract customers from different distances. The amount of perceived time spent in travel will often influence the consumer's decision to visit a retailer.
Mass Transit Facilities	A location convenient to a mass transit station will expand the trade area in proportion to the "drawing power" of the traffic station.

WARRANTED FLOOR SPACE	
Type of Space	**Area (sq ft)**
Comparison goods	
Apparel/accessories	86,523
Furniture/household goods	68,759
Home electronics	30,320
Sports/toys/hobbies	104,803
Specialty retail	95,881
Food convenience and services	
Food	39,403
Alcohol/tobacco	3,960
Personal care/services	31,472
Entertainment	
Cinema	79,062
Attractions/games	45,094
Restaurants, bar, impulse food, and café	
Restaurants/fast foods	96,472
Total	681,749
Source: Thomas Consultants Inc., 1998.	

▼ *Tenant mix diagram similar to this partial Gateway tenant breakdown enables more refined market positioning analysis to be conducted on a shop-by-shop revenue basis. (Illustration: Thomas Consultants.)*

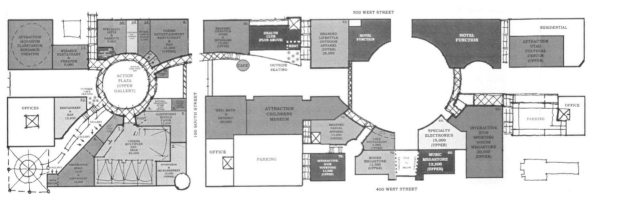

- Optimal circulation and flow
- Integration with other adjacent uses
- Indication of strategic catalytic activities to achieve project success

A tenant mix diagram, based on the development master plan created by the project architects, is then produced. This detailed tenant breakdown can allow for the subsequent revenue analysis to be conducted on a shop-by-shop basis.

Factors Affecting Retail Sales

Determining an effective tenant mix requires more than a statistical analysis of demographic data. A thorough understanding of a tenant's customers' buying habits must be combined with the statistical data to arrive at a successful tenant mix. A good location for one retailer may be bad for another.

For example, a home improvement warehouse store on a regional freeway, removed from the neighborhood population, may succeed because of its ability to draw, from large areas, customers willing to make destination trips. But that location may not be profitable for a large grocery store that lacks the same drawing power and needs to be more convenient to the population it serves. The following are the four primary factors that drive retailers' ability to generate sales.

Tenant mix

Retailers relying on impulse or complementary purchases require a tenant mix that draws large numbers of shoppers with complementary purchasing habits. Examples of types of tenants relying heavily on such a mix are sellers of clothing accessories, focused lines of fashion, crafts/novelties, and other retail lines that do not do well if freestanding and that rely heavily on other tenants to create the needed traffic volume.

Site attributes

Tenants that rely heavily on convenience, impulse, and accessibility (usually selling less distinguishable products) need optimal site attributes, such as convenient curb cuts, sign visibility, high traffic counts, and locations on the going-home or going-to-work side of the street. Retailers that rely heavily on site attributes include gas stations, donut shops, and fast-food restaurants.

Demographics

If high concentrations of a certain type of customer are needed, the demographics of the trade area—the concentration of large numbers of target customers—are crucial. The more focused or niche oriented the product, the greater the importance of finding large trade areas, that is, areas with the highest percentage and highest number of target customers. Products such as high-price fashion (upper-income customers), office supplies (business concentrations), and toys (younger, single-family households) fall into this category.

Competition

Some merchants, such as fast-food restaurants, like to be as close to their competition as possible. But the level of competition will also have a bearing if the amount of existing space dedicated to a certain product type has reached the point beyond which additional competition will not be profitable. Startup companies in a new market segment (i.e., Barnes & Noble and Borders in the book segment) look for areas where they can capture market share without having to take it from one of their major competitors.

When a concept is in its prototype stages, competing retailers are inclined to avoid competition if there are adequate opportunities to expand their operations without forcing price competition. Other retailers, such as car dealers, furniture stores, and movie theaters, prefer to cluster their stores to create zones that are identified by the consumer as providing a high concentration of a certain product.

CONFIRMING THE PROJECT'S ECONOMIC VIABILITY

Once the development program for a project is defined, the economic viability is confirmed. To do this, a physical plan and construction budget must be prepared. The plan and construction budget be-

come key components of the developer's overall financial analysis, or pro forma. The developer's pro forma represents the reconciliation of capital expenditure, operation expense, and income, that is, the financial feasibility of the project. Capital expenditure is the total project cost, which includes actual construction (hard) costs and development (soft) costs such as architectural/engineering fees, leasing commissions, governmental fees, and permits.

When the initial site planning studies begin, anticipated major tenants are identified. Major tenants will have a strong impact on the physical design of a retail project. Such tenants may have defined prototypes with specific requirements for size, proportion, location of

---

TYPICAL DEVELOPMENT COSTS

Land Costs
Site
Closing costs

Direct Construction Costs
Site Preparations
  Demolition
  On-site preparation
  Off-site work
  Signalization
Building costs
  Buildings
  Tenant improvements

Indirect Construction Costs
Permits, fees, etc.
  Traffic mitigation
  Water connection fee
  Irrigation tap fee
  Sewer connection fee
  Planning permits
  Engineering permits

School fees
Grading permit
Building permit
Architectural consulting costs
  Preliminary
  Design/approvals
  Exterior elevations
  Tenant coordination
  Site landscape
  Site working drawings
  Sign program
  Construction supervision
Testing/Inspections
Engineering/consulting costs
  Survey
  Soil test/certification
  Toxic investigation
  Traffic survey
  Acoustic survey
  Parcel map
  Civil engineering

Leasing Costs
Shops
Marketing promotion

Project Overhead
Legal/accounting fees
Property taxes (18 months)
Overhead/supv.

Contingency Financing Costs
Capitalization required
Equity provided
Initial land carry
Net land carry
Const. interest less land
Const. loan fee
Perm. loan fee
Mortgage brokerage fee
Loan closing costs

Source: *Urban Land Institute.*

SAMPLE INCOME PRO FORMA

Tenant	Credit (%)	Area (sq ft)	Cost/Sq Ft ($)	Year 1	Year 2	Year 3	Year 4	Year 5	Year 6
Major A	100	23,000	18	$414,000	$414,000	$414,000	$414,000	$414,000	$455,400
Major B	100	55,255	14	773,570	773,570	773,570	773,570	773,570	850,927
PAD 1	100	5,000	SALE	0	0	0	0	0	0
PAD 2	100	6,000	SALE	0	0	0	0	0	0
PAD 3	50	7,000	25	175,000	175,000	178,500	182,070	185,711	189,426
Stores A	0	2,500	23	57,500	57,500	58,650	59,823	61,019	62,240
Stores B	0	5,000	27	135,000	135,000	137,300	140,454	142,263	146,128
Stores C	0	3,000	23	69,000	69,000	70,830	71,788	73,223	74,668
Total Minimum Rental		106,755		1,624,070	1,624,070	1,632,800	1,641,705	1,650,787	1,778,809
Percentage Rental				0	0	0	0	0	0

Land Coverage 24.51%

Expense Reimbursements

				Year 1	Year 2	Year 3	Year 4	Year 5	Year 6
Cam inc. fee @ 5.00%				196,162	201,066	206,093	211,245	216,526	221,940
Ins/tax fee @ 5.00%				159,981	163,256	166,599	170,010	173,491	177,045
Total Reimbursements				356,144	364,323	372,692	381,255	390,018	398,984
Total Operating Income				1,980,214	1,988,393	2,005,492	2,022,960	2,040,805	2,177,793

(total minimum rental + total reimbursements)

Operating Expenses

Total credit income 64.39% $1,275,070
Total noncredit income 35.61% $705,144

				Year 1	Year 2	Year 3	Year 4	Year 5	Year 6
Credit vacancy @ 1.00%				12,751	12,751	12,768	12,786	12,804	14,010
Noncredit vacancy @ 5.00%				35,257	35,666	36,434	37,218	38,019	38,838
Management @ 4.00%				77,288	77,599	78,252	78,918	79,599	84,998
Cam @ $1.75/sq ft/yr				186,821	191,492	196,279	201,186	206,216	211,371
Insurance @ $0.15/sq ft/yr				14,363	14,722	15,090	15,468	15,854	16,251
Property taxes @ 1.150% $12,000,000				138,000	140,760	143,575	146,447	149,376	152,363
Unreimbursed owners expense				15,000	15,375	15,759	16,153	16,557	16,971
Total Operating Expenses				(479,481)	(488,365)	(498,157)	(508,176)	(518,425)	(534,802)
Net Operating Income				1,500,733	1,500,028	1,507,334	1,514,784	1,522,380	1,642,991

(total operating income – total operating expenses)

Unleveraged Return on Total Development Costs				9.99%	9.99%	10.04%	10.09%	10.14%	10.94%

Debt Service

Loan amount Rate Term Coverage

$12,500,000 8.25% 30 1.33				(1,126,900)	(1,126,900)	(1,126,900)	(1,126,900)	(1,126,900)	(1,126,900)
Net Cash Flow from Operations				373,833	373,128	380,435	387,884	395,480	516,091

(net operating income – debt service-loan amount)

Equity Cash Return

				Year 1	Year 2	Year 3	Year 4	Year 5	Year 6
Equity/pref return $2,516,658/9.00%				226,499	226,499	226,499	226,499	226,499	226,499
Accrual				0	0	0	0	0	0
Total preferred cash flow				226,499	226,499	226,499	226,499	226,499	226,499
Split balance @ 60.00%				88,400	87,977	92,361	96,831	101,388	173,755
Total Cash Return to Equity				314,899	314,476	318,860	323,330	327,887	400,254
Percent Return to Equity				12.51%	12.50%	12.67%	12.85%	13.03%	15.90%
Balance to Manager (40.00%)				$58,934	$58,651	$61,574	$64,554	$67,592	$115,837

Projected cpi 1.025
Projected shop rent escalation 1.020

Source: Urban Land Institute

public entries, service areas, and other items. If the tenant prototype cannot be reasonably accommodated within the site, negotiations with the tenant will typically be required.

The initial designs and layouts allow for a preliminary feasibility analysis in which the development program and site are evaluated against the development pro forma. Accurate projected construction costs are a key element in this evaluation.

IMPLEMENTING THE PROJECT

Once a project is designed and prior to the start of construction, a major effort may be needed to obtain discretionary governmental approvals, to negotiate operating agreements for multitenant projects, and to qualify for construction loans.

Governmental Approvals and Entitlement

As a result of legislation dating back to the late 1960s, the right to develop land is no longer an inherent right vested in the property owner, but is more commonly a negotiated process with governmental agencies. In 1969 the federal government passed the National Environmental Policy Act, which included the Clean Air Act, requiring local governmental agencies to become more responsible for the impact on air quality caused by development and the resulting traffic generation. In California, the California Environmental Quality Act (CEQA) requires the developer to quantify the potential impact of a development project and provide for mitigation to acceptable levels.

The negotiation and review process includes public participation and hearings, which may politicize the process, as opposed to technical reviews that quantify impact in numeric fashion. Although the review process is typically administered and approved by professional planning staffs, any decision is normally subject to a final appeal by an elected body, such as a city council.

Zoning changes in areas that are built out with adjacent residential uses are becoming especially difficult to obtain. Home owners are becoming better organized and more effective in determining the outcome of zoning changes. Even minor changes within a commercially zoned area for variances or special use permits may be very elusive.

Working with home owner and other community groups is becoming a common part of the development process. It is important to understand that the developer is in a serious negotiation process, which may have a major aesthetic and economic impact on the design of the project. The ability to be flexible and adjust the design in response to public concerns is vital, as the community will be more supportive of a project in which its concerns are accommodated.

The outcome of the entitlement process is never guaranteed, and public relations in handling the review and approval process is often the most critical aspect of the effort.

Development Agreements

Multitenant projects frequently have master agreements that set the operational standards for both the developer and the tenants. Agreements of this type are sometimes known as reciprocal easement agreements (REAs) or easements, covenants, and restrictions (ECR) agreements.

Development agreements address many of the operational issues, such as hours and days during the week when a tenant is open; ability of customers to cross over different parcels when major anchors own the land for their stores, including the parking; paying for common area expenses, such as parking lot lighting, and maintenance operations, such as maintaining site landscaping.

Tenant leases

Construction loan sources for U.S. retail projects frequently require that a significant portion, sometimes 50 percent or more of the project, be precommitted prior to the start of construction. This provides the lender with an additional level of security beyond normal market research projections, as it confirms a level of rental income and tenant mix commensurate with the developer's pro forma. In addition to requiring the precommitment of a percentage of tenant area, lenders also review the actual tenants to determine whether they are considered bankable or credit worthy. Larger national tenants with firm financial resources are typically desired over single-unit independent retailers.

SUMMARY

All successful retail developments have a specific commonality. That is, a center has been well conceived with its development rationale/strategy well established and supported by market realities. The utilization of a carefully formulated market positioning program, supplemented by the necessary consumer research and financial analysis, will go a long way in establishing and entrenching a retail development over the long term in an ever-competitive marketplace.

SITE PLANNING

Site Selection

Fundamental to the development process for a new shopping center or mixed-use project is site selection. The site may be owned by the developer, in which case the process is focused on defining what the site can support. Or the developer may seek to locate or purchase a site to fit a desired project type.

The right site is critical to the economic success of a retail project, and suitable sites for shopping centers are hard to find. Tenants that rely heavily on convenience, impulse, and accessibility—gas stations, donut shops, and fast-food restaurants—will need optimal site attributes, such as convenient curb cuts, sign visibility, high traffic counts, and locations on the "going-home" or "going-to-work" side of the street. In selecting and/or evaluating a site, whether for a small neighborhood center or for a power center, the developer looks for the best possible combination of the following characteristics:

- Demographics
- Location and distances
- Shape
- Access
- Visibility
- Size
- Topography
- Utilities
- Surroundings
- Environmental impacts
- Zoning
- Financial benefits to the community

Each of these factors affects tenants' sales, which translates into gross rent, the cost of developing the project, and the cost of operating it. When considered together, the result is the project's free and clear return on investment.

Demographics

- The daytime and nighttime population within the determined trade area indicates the sales potential for the retailers, restaurants, service providers, and offices, that operate within a shopping center.

- The income levels of that population, as well as its age, ethnicity, and psychographic profile, will dictate the tenant mix within a project.

- Growth of the population is important for adding more stores and services to the center and generating higher income.

Location and distances

An analysis of existing and future competition is part of every site selection process.

Neighborhood centers draw from a distance of approximately 1½ miles, depending on the density and character of the residential area. Generally, walking distance is not a valid criterion in suburban locations, but in built-up areas where high-density multifamily housing and mixed uses are part of the general development pattern, walking distances must be considered. The site's location in relation to other commercial areas and mass transit facilities is also a factor.

Community centers, including power centers, draw from an area within 3–5 miles of the site.

Regional centers draw from a distance of 8 miles or more, but driving time better determines the area of influence for a regional center.

Access

If a site is not easy to enter and safe to leave, it must have the potential to be made so.

Neighborhood centers should have access from collector streets and should not have minor residential service streets as their principal means of access.

Community centers should be located for access from major thoroughfares. Because they have a broader array of stores than neighborhood centers, community centers should be accessible to an extended trade area via freeways.

Regional centers are customarily located on sites that are easily accessible from interchange points between expressways and freeways. If a center is easily reached, travel distances will likely be long. Access routes will allow customers, employees, and service vehicles to travel comfortably and easily to and from the centers.

Visibility

Good visibility improves a center's accessibility. Shoppers driving at local traffic speeds (35 miles per hour) can easily overshoot the parking area entrance if they have not seen the center from the road. Overpasses, hills, curves in the road, and heavy vegetation all impede visibility.

Heavy traffic also prevents potential shoppers from easily seeing tenant signage and points of access. Even though traffic flow is conducive to retail business, a site that fronts on a highway with visual distractions (including signs) is less accessible.

Shape

- The site should be regular in shape and unified, undivided by highways or dedicated streets. Very few successful centers exist on divided sites.

- Many of the traditional strip commercial areas of the past are inappropriate for today's commercial developments. To accommodate parking and traffic circulation, shopping centers require much greater depth than did the old strip patterns.

- A site with a regular shape—no acute angles, odd projections, or indentations—is most amenable to an efficient layout. If an irregularly shaped site is used, it still needs adequate frontage so that the center is visible from thoroughfares.

- Portions of an oddly shaped site may be unusable. However, oddly shaped parcels may accommodate freestanding facilities. For example, odd parcels could may auto service centers, drive-in restaurants, convenience facilities, dry cleaners, or financial institutions.

Size

As a rule of thumb, there will be a 1:4 ratio of building to site area (or as stipulated by local zoning regulations); that is, each acre (43,560 sq ft) will have roughly 10,000 sq ft of building area to 33,560 sq ft of surface parking area and sidewalks (including landscaping, circulation space, delivery area, etc.).

Many cities are becoming conscious of excessive parking requirements and are working with developers to downsize their projects' parking lots. Requirements for landscaping are increasing, and there is a growing need for storm water detention, both of which take additional land.

Topography

Topography is an important factor in the selection and layout of a site and in the design and construction of buildings.

- The ideal site has minimal subsoil complications, neither solid rock nor a high water table, and a slope of less than 3 percent.

- Ground that is fairly level or gently sloping to the street is easily adaptable to shopping centers.

- A steeply sloping site is more expensive to design and construct. With skill, it can be adapted to provide customer access at different levels. Such sites can also be used to separate retail uses from office uses.

TYPICAL STORE SIZES FOR MAJOR RETAIL CATEGORIES	
Store Type	**Size Range (sq ft)**
Warehouse clubs	110,000–135,000
General merchandise and discounters	100,000–130,000
Home improvement stores	100,000–130,000
Supercenters	125,000–180,000
Supermarkets and combo stores	55,000–200,000
Sporting goods stores	50,000–60,000
Catalog showrooms	50,000
Toy stores	45,000
White goods stores	35,000–50,000
Furniture stores	35,000–40,000
Baby goods stores	35,000
Home electronics stores	32,000–58,000
Bookstores	25,000–45,000
Apparel stores	25,000–45,000
Super pet stores	20,000–35,000
Computer stores	25,000–45,000
Office supply stores	20,000–45,000
Athletic shoe stores	20,000
Music stores	15,000
Drugstores	8,600–15,000

Utilities

Off-site improvements are a critical part of capital costs. Easy access to water, sewers, gas, and electricity will keep down the project's costs.

Surroundings

The public is not well versed in shopping center design. Whether the land is raw or developed, the local political climate may be opposed to any, or any further, development, especially that of an "intrusive" shopping center.

If the site, particularly one for a proposed neighborhood center, is adjacent to residential areas, any adverse impact on the livability of the houses nearby must be offset. The shopping center must be a "good neighbor," enhancing the quality of the physical environment through carefully designed landscaping, walls, and walkways.

The project must not create visual, noise, or traffic pollution. If the only site access provided is local residential streets, or if commercial uses are not clearly separated from single-family detached residences, the development proposal may well be killed.

Local objection can be overcome by explaining that the shopping center will be an architecturally harmonious unit that

- Uses less energy than freestanding stores and produces minimal air pollution
- Offers integrated parking for public benefit
- Controls truck delivery, signs, lighting, and landscaping
- Will have walls, solid fences, landscaped berms, or dense plantings of evergreens to buffer the center's sound and illumination levels

Environmental impacts

If a site is in an environmentally sensitive area, the cost and difficulty to develop it must be considered carefully.

Zoning

Zoning changes sought in areas that are built out with any residential uses are especially difficult. Home owners are becoming better organized and more effective in determining the outcome of zoning changes. Even minor changes within a proposed-zoned site, such as variances or special use permits, could be very difficult.

Financial benefits to the community

- Commercial developments also produce a sizable return in real estate and sales taxes. The total cost of public services (police and fire protection, schools, streets, and utilities) is much less for commercial facilities than for residential developments.

- A site adjacent to high-density apartment developments also benefits from greater walk-in trade. Development of apartments or offices adjacent to a shopping center site makes an excellent transition between a shopping center and a single-family residential area.

Optimizing Coverage

A reasonable goal for ratio of building area to total land area is 1:4, or 25 percent coverage.

In larger new centers with a number of "category killers," a "warehouse club," a multiscreen cinema, and some restaurants, 21–22 percent coverage is a reasonable expectation.

In older centers, particularly those in dense urban areas and possibly with some two-story space, coverage is frequently as much as 30 percent. If required green areas can be grouped together into larger blocks of space, there is less impact on the plan and the coverage than if they are spread out into the parking lot.

Use new pad sites in existing centers efficiently to fill "gaps" in the parking fields. Avoid creating small interrupted segments of parking around pad sites. Consider pad site parking an extension of the long, efficient parking aisles radiating out from the main shopping center buildings.

For renovated projects, where property depth permits, build out old shallow-depth shop space to larger depths, both to improve coverage and to serve the anchor tenants. In selected high-visibility locations, it is often practical to slope

some 40 ft depth lease space on the exposed side of major anchors, with no rear service, but with greater exposure to the side street.

Understanding the most common store sizes can facilitate efficient planning and increase the likelihood that multiple anchors can be marketed in the same slot within a center.

There are few mini-anchors of 8,000–15,000 sq ft being leased today. Drugstores have grown larger to become "combo stores" or "super-drugstores."

Parking

A successful shopping center must address two fundamental aspects of parking design:

1. Quantity (there must be enough)

2. Distribution (it must be in the right places)

Most zoning ordinances in the United States require 5 parking spaces per 1,000 sq ft of retail space. In the past several years, however, the warehouse clubs and big box stores have been asking for 6–7 spaces per 1,000 sq ft. These anchors, as well as restaurants (10–15 cars per 1,000 sq ft) and multiscreen cinemas (1 car per three to four seats or 25 cars per 1,000 sq ft) force land coverage down and can choke off other tenants by dominating the parking lot at peak hours. Of the total required parking, however, approximately 10 percent can be located at the rear of the stores to serve employees.

Peak hours

Recognizing that retail, restaurant, office, and cinema parking peak at different times, progressive municipalities have adopted shared parking tables for mixed-use projects, allowing the same parking

▼ *The parking lot at FlatIron Crossing orients parking spaces at an acute angle, whereas an early plan for Bella Terra oriented parking spaces at a 90-degree angle. Each is laid out so that customers do not have to cross through parked cars or walk too far to get to the center.*

FlatIron Crossing, Broomfield, Colorado. (Image: Callison.)

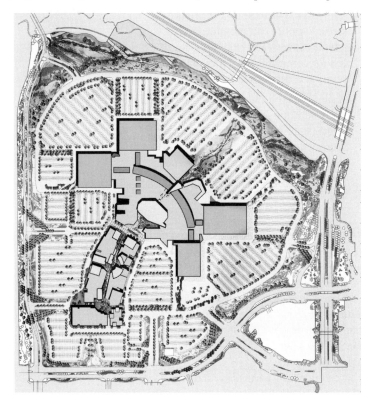

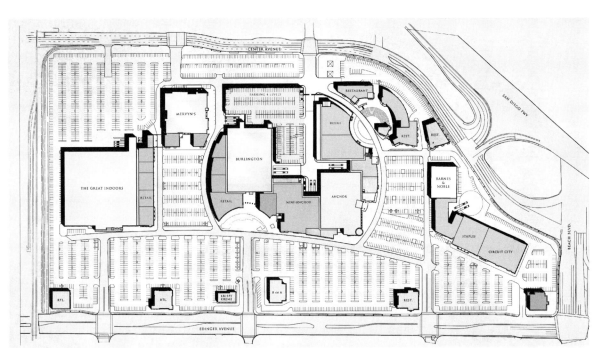

space to be counted for office uses between 8:00 A.M. and 5:00 P.M., and for cinema or restaurant use from 5:00 P.M. to midnight, for instance. This reduction in required parking also recognizes multiple stops on a single trip to a mixed-use development.

Average size
The average size of a parking space is 9 ft × 18 ft, whether angled or in a 90-degree configuration. Typically, municipalities allow or require that 20–25 percent of all spaces be for compact vehicles (7 ft 6 in. or 8 ft × 16 ft) and that 2–5 percent of spaces be set aside for disabled persons (12–13 ft wide).

Two-way aisles
The configuration that parks the greatest number of cars on a given amount of land is the use of 90-degree parking stalls

on 24-ft-wide two-way aisles. This arrangement accommodates approximately 10 percent more cars than a 60-degree-angle configuration, although customers and retailers prefer the ease of maneuvering offered by the angled space.

One-way aisles
Using one-way drive aisles rather than two-way aisles results in no increase in yield, even in large lots, and circulation is made more complicated in one-way systems. A good rule of thumb is to figure one parking space for each 400 sq ft of land area, exclusive of building area, service zones, and perimeter landscape buffers.

Another land-efficient concept for a a parking lot layout is to group compact cars on both sides of one drive aisle, thereby saving width for an entire double row of cars and the drive aisle. Such a compact

▲ Bella Terra, Huntington Beach, California. (Image: Jerde.)

135

bay is typically 50–52 ft wide rather than the normal 60 ft, and it is less likely to be used by standard autos. Aisles must be oriented perpendicular to the main driveway and storefront line. This allows customers to circulate up and back, in front of their destination store. It also increases safety, because customers use the open drive aisles to walk from their cars to the store, thereby avoiding the dangers of passing between parked cars.

Ideal slope
The ideal slope in a parking lot is 3 percent. This allows for sufficient drainage but helps to prevent runaway shopping carts and avoids difficulties with heavy, hard-to-open car doors. A slope of 7–8 percent is allowable in limited areas—at entry drives, for instance. In areas of steep slopes, a parking lot can effectively be broken into terraced pads, separated by landscaped strips running perpendicular to the storefronts.

Surface parking for single-level retail projects
Site coverage
Surface parking for single-level retail developments will occupy approximately 25 percent of the total site area. For projects with more intensive parking demands, such as multiplex cinemas and restaurants, site coverage may be closer to 20 percent.

Distance
The distance customers are required to walk after parking their cars may be described as a "level of service" or "level of convenience" issue.

Traffic aisle orientation
Generally, traffic aisles should be oriented perpendicular to the primary building facade. This allows customers to walk down the driving aisle toward the stores, as opposed to crossing the area through the parked cars.

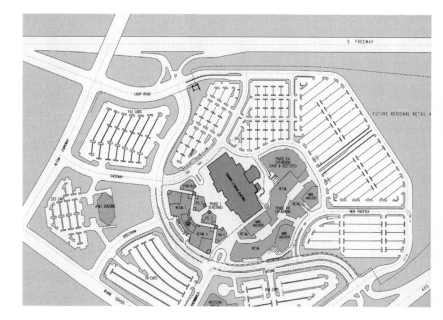

▶ Located at the intersection of two major freeways in Irvine, California, the site for the Irvine Spectrum Center is highly visible and easily accessible. (Illustration: RTKL.)

Entries

Easy and smooth access to and from adjacent roads is important for ease of customer use. Entry areas that are free of other traffic, with sufficient stacking space, are essential. For larger projects, turn lanes for both right and left turns are desirable.

Fire lanes

The driving lanes immediately adjacent to the building generally have no parking. This area is typically designated as a fire lane to allow fire engine access along the sidewalk in front of the retail buildings.

Typical parking requirements for various uses are provided in the table below. These will vary from city to city and must be verified by a review of the applicable zoning ordinances.

Typical parking standards listed in the table below will also vary from city to city and must be verified by a review of the applicable zoning ordinance.

A 7'6" × 15'0" stall is common in cities that allow "compact" parking spaces. The percentage of required compact parking spaces will vary by city.

Anchor parking needs

Major anchors may require that compact spaces be located at the perimeter of the project to ensure the spaces most frequently used are full size for maximum customer convenience. In some instances, major anchors have required that compact spaces be the full depth of a standard stall in the event that a full-size car parking in a compact space will not reduce the available aisle width.

Angled parking

Angled parking is typically easier for customers to use, as compared with 90-degree parking. One-way 60-degree parking is the most convenient, as the aisle movement is one-way without opposing traffic. This simplifies the backing-out maneuver. However, the use of 90-degree parking with two-way aisles tends to provide approximately 10 percent more spaces.

Restricted-user parking

Restricted-user parking spaces for physically disabled people is typically required. Spaces must generally be located so that a person in a wheelchair does not have to travel behind the backs of other parking spaces to access the building. This is a dangerous situation, as a person in a wheelchair does not have a tall enough profile to be easily seen by someone backing a car out of a parking space.

Additional vertical clearance requirements (8 ft 2 in.) also apply for such spaces to allow for the use of specially equipped vans.

TYPICAL PARKING REQUIREMENTS	
Use	**Parking Spaces Required**
Retail	1 per 200 sq ft of gross leasable area (GLA)
Restaurant	1 per 100 sq ft of GLA
Cinema	1 per 3 seats
Office	1 per 300 sq ft of GLA

TYPICAL PARKING SPACE SIZES	
Parking Space Style	**Range of Typical Sizes (ft)**
Stall	9 × 18
Double-loaded bay	60 × 64
Single-loaded bay	42 × 46
Loading bay	10 × 45

MAXIMUM SLOPES FOR DRIVEWAYS AND RAMPS	
Incline	**Maximum Slope (%)***
Driveway or ramp	20
Cross-slope of driveway or ramp	10
Parking stall (any direction)	5

Transition slope required when slope of driveway or ramp exceeds 12 percent

Structured parking

Spans

For structured parking, long-span structures (18' × 55') are considered most efficient in terms of area as compared with short-span structures (30' × 30') because there are no columns located between parking spaces.

Vertical circulation

Vertical circulation between levels may be by either driving ramps or sloped parking floors. Sloped parking floor structures tend to be more efficient in total built area, but the sloped floors make level identification difficult. Sloped floors limit pedestrian circulation, especially if the sloped floors are parallel to the main building facade.

Surface parking for large centers

For larger projects such as regional or super-regional shopping centers, the surface parking is sloped to provide direct access to multiple levels. This concept was first utilized in the Southdale Mall in Edina, Minneapolis, designed by Victor Gruen & Associates, which opened in 1956. Structured parking may also be used to provide direct access to elevated levels if the site area is insufficient for surface parking.

CHAPTER 7

DESIGN OF RETAIL AND MIXED-USE CENTERS

ARCHITECTURAL DESIGN

The design of shopping centers and mixed-use complexes is a multidiscipline, "co-creative" process. It not only involves a wide array of engineering and design consultants, but is also influenced greatly by city officials, major tenants, significant investors, and, often, neighborhood groups.

By nature, a retail project is a modeled facsimile of the main street experience. It is also a product of its context and, at its best, can be the defining "there" that symbolizes the heart and character of a community.

In the constantly evolving world of retail, each project is different from the last. For every rule of thumb, there is an exception; for every prescriptive formula, there are successful projects that defy the norm. For the last 25 years, in fact, The Jerde Partnership has made a business of redefining retail design by breaking the rules—in some cases, doing the opposite of what would be considered industry standard. But in order to successfully think outside the box of retail design, one must understand what shaped the box. This book shows what we have found to work in the design of shopping centers and mixed-use complexes.

▼ *Design and development involve many stakeholders with individual interests, as illustrated in this cartoon. (Courtesy Development Design Group, Inc.)*

TENANT

CUSTOMER

ENVIRONMENTALIST

CITY OFFICIALS

DEVELOPER

ARCHITECT

This chapter describes the design process and what to look for to influence the outcome of a project. It then describes the contributions of some of the key design consultants—lighting, environmental graphics, and landscape designers—who directly affect the overall look, character, and function of a typical shopping complex.

In addition to specialty designers, many other consultants play significant roles:

- Engineers, structural, mechanical, electrical, audio/acoustic, environmental, curtain-wall, traffic, civil, etc., as described in other chapters
- Client-side consultants, economic, leasing, marketing, operations, event

programming, construction management, cost estimating, etc.

- For larger projects, water feature consultants, show consultants, information technology (IT) infrastructure specialists, and digital programming and display designers, etc.

Each designer, engineer, or other consultant contributes in many ways to a successful project; like a great jazz band made up of many talented soloists, they are guided by the compelling beat or melody of the design. It is up to the architect to define that music. This is what we call the co-creative process.

▼ *Fashion Island in Newport Beach, California, designed by The Jerde Partnership. (Photo: Tom Lamb.)*

Getting Started—Clients, Program, and Site

Clients

Almost every project comes with a client or client group, a site, and an initial program. A critical prelude to a fruitful design process is to know the background, experiences, and aspirations of the client. Although a close architect-client relationship is always fundamental, in the design of shopping center and mixed-use complexes, the experiences and expectations of the client greatly affect the degree of flexibility and creativity, as well as the implementation, of the design.

The following questions are helpful in understanding a client's goals:

- Is the client a corporation (publicly traded) or an individual?

- Is the project a "build to own and operate" or "build to sell"?

- Is the project intended to reinforce the "brand" awareness of the client?

- Can the project serve other revenue streams beyond development?

- What other projects has the client built, or what other projects does the client aspire to?

For many reasons, corporate clients have different agendas than individual owners. For instance, Steve Wynn's Bellagio in Las Vegas would probably never been built by Hilton or Marriott.

Recently, many large retail-based developers, such as Simon and Westfield, have begun to establish regional and international brand awareness. These developers are using unique identities, consistent quality, a mix of tenants, and even architecture, throughout their portfolios to differentiate themselves among their key audiences of investors, tenants, and shoppers.

As retail projects continue to evolve into more mixed-use environments, some retail-oriented clients having little or no experience in housing or office facilities may want to include these or other components in their projects. To develop mixed-use projects, clients may need to compromise one use (e.g., housing) to benefit another (e.g., retail); therefore, it is important for the architect to understand the client's priorities early in the process.

Clients who are looking to sell their properties for a profit shortly after completion may be less likely to spend money on first-cost amenities or sustainable design/technologies that reduce long-term operating costs.

All of these of factors are important in knowing the client.

Program

As discussed in the preceding chapter, on planning, the program for a project is usually established early on and then vetted by marketing/pro forma analysis. The program is often adjusted during the design process, however, to better match the opportunities of the site and the emerging layout of the project. For instance, an additional anchor or feature restaurant may present itself in the course of the design. Moreover, because many large mixed-use projects take years to realize, different retailing opportunities may be substituted over time.

The strength of the initial concept diagram will be tested by its resiliency in light of such changes. Lead designers should review any changes in the program and continue to propose refinements that will add value to the project and/or expand the client's vision. For example, other uses or tenant categories may be included on the site that can make the project more interesting, increase the size of the project's market, or lengthen the time spent per visit to the project.

Site

As discussed in Chapter 6, the site — its shape, context, and physical characteristics — is a key factor influencing the architectural success of a project. To evaluate the impact of the site's characteristics, it is best to start with an opportunity-and-constraints diagram highlighting likely points of arrival, adjacent uses, views, wind, sun and shadow, noise, and so forth. High and low points are indicated on the diagram, as well as utilities,

easements, and other factors that will influence the design.

For larger projects, it is a good idea to inventory the area surrounding the site to identify additional retail opportunities or districts that might influence the design. In many cases, in designing a shopping center or mixed-use project confined to a single block, there may be an opportunity to revitalize an entire neighborhood, downtown, or section of a city. The stronger the integration of the project with adjacent uses, circulation patterns, and other features of the surrounding area, the more successfully the project performs both as an independent structure and as a catalyst for economic impact on neighboring uses.

▼ *The program diagram, which identifies potential anchors, retail anchors, and other uses, may be continually refined throughout the lengthy design and development process to add increased value or expand the vision for the project. The program for The Gateway in Salt Lake City mixed a number of complementary uses to create a vibrant, 24-hour district in the downtown core. (Image: Jerde)*

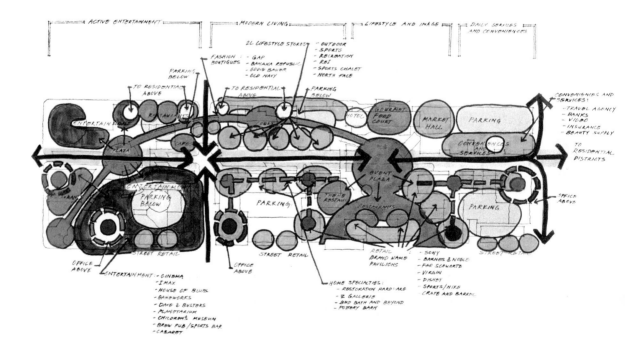

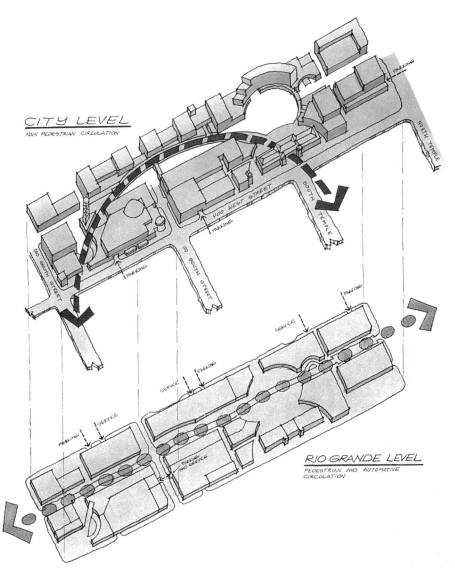

CITY LEVEL
MAIN PEDESTRIAN CIRCULATION

400 WEST STREET

SOUTH TEMPLE

NORTH TEMPLE

PARKING

200 SOUTH STREET

100 SOUTH STREET

PARKING

SERVICE

RIO GRANDE LEVEL
PEDESTRIAN AND AUTOMOTIVE
CIRCULATION

Concept Design—Placemaking and Experience Architecture

A vital but complex aspect of retail architecture is the creation of a focused and functional framework for merchandise and the exchange of goods and services. Indeed, one of the purest forms of retail architecture is the open-air bazaar, fixtured with only an overhead canopy for shade. In such environments, the buyer enjoys unimpeded access to the goods and the seller can freely beckon the buyer with the special of the day. In the open-air bazaar, the architecture plays a secondary role to the act of exchange, or the *experience*.

It is axiomatic in the design of successful environments for exchange to focus on the experience rather than the "object" or building that contains the experience.

▲ To take advantage of The Gateway's naturally sloping site, Jerde connected to existing circulation patterns on both levels of retail, effectively creating two "first levels" and generating strong pedestrian flow on each. (Image: Jerde.)

This realization yields a design philosophy of "placemaking," which is prevalent in today's shopping centers and mixed-use projects.

Placemaking has as its primary design intention the "space between" buildings, using the buildings themselves, the architecture, as a backdrop to the "place." Indeed, such an experience-oriented approach should apply not only to retail, but to any environment where human interaction and memorable experiences are key to the project's vitality. When properly executed, experience-oriented design attracts millions of people, creating for the user or customer the subtle or overt excitement of contact and feeling of belonging, and for the community a new or strengthened identity. Experiential projects often generate huge social and economic value.

Armature diagram

It is good practice to begin by determining the front door or the primary entry (where does the experience begin?) and choreographing the sequence of experiences—in the form of exploratory circulation patterns, water features, details, and so forth—that occur throughout the project. This approach parallels that of the city, which has multiple entry points and numerous sequences of experiences. (After all, what city other than medieval walled cities has had a single front door?)

◀ *When the spaces between the architecture— the spaces where social interactions occur— are compelling, huge numbers of people are attracted and the project exceeds revenue goals. At Horton Plaza in San Diego, California, the interior spaces connected to the street, creating a natural extension of the city, and more than 100 colors were used to contrast the dreary and decaying downtown. Nearly 18 years later, Horton Plaza leads the area's sales per square foot. (Photo: Stephen Simpson.)*

▲ *Canal City Hakata in Fukuoka, Japan, established a new mixed-use district that helped make Fukoka an international city. Designed as a series of districts that line an animated canal, the project attracted more than 46 million people in its first two years and increased citywide movie attendance by 50 percent. The increased pedestrian activity helped reverse declining revenues in the adjacent historic shopping arcade. (Photo: FJUD.)*

Although retail architects and developers have traditionally opted for circulation systems that are simple to navigate, Jerde creates armatures that combine a sense of clarity with mystery and discovery, ultimately resulting in an experiential sequence of differentiated spaces. Jerde uses the armature diagram to communicate to the client how customers will arrive, what they will experience, and where potential connections to adjacent properties and the heart of the project are located.

▼ *The Power & Light District in Kansas City, Missouri, used a curved entertainment promenade to link the hotel/convention district with the city's government district.*

To illustrate the sequence of experience, create an armature diagram. The term *armature* is borrowed from sculptors who first make a wire armature on which to add the body mass and features when sculpting a human figure. An armature diagram differs from what some architects call a *circulation diagram* because it is the primary structure for the experience and is intentionally designed, whereas many circulation diagrams merely represent the leftover, negative space between structures. An armature diagram indicates points of arrival, primary and secondary spaces, or thematic districts as they occur in the plan.

Armature diagrams can be simple or complex, taking the shape of bidirectional dumbbells, gridirons, racetracks, straight or serpentine forms, spirals, and so on. Conventionally, retail architects and de-

velopers have opted for simple diagrams that prevent customers from losing their way. The Jerde Partnership favors diagrams that combine clarity with a sense of mystery and discovery. These are designed to create a sequence of experiences and a hierarchical array of differentiated spaces. Use an armature diagram to communicate to the client how customers arrive, what they experience, and where potential connections to adjacent properties and the heart of the project are located.

Heartmaking

Most architects working on retail shopping centers seek to provide a sense of identity and "place" for their projects, which is usually manifest in the "heart" of the project. Following the belief that one of the best metaphors or parallels for

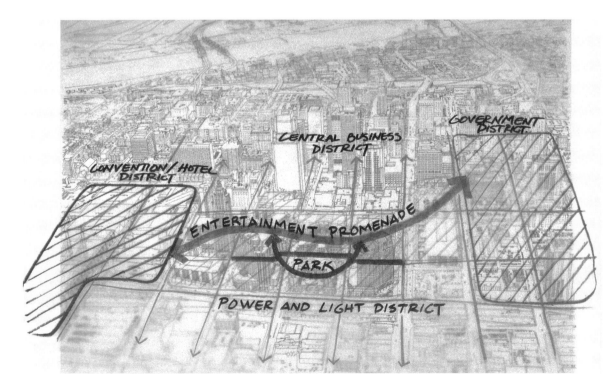

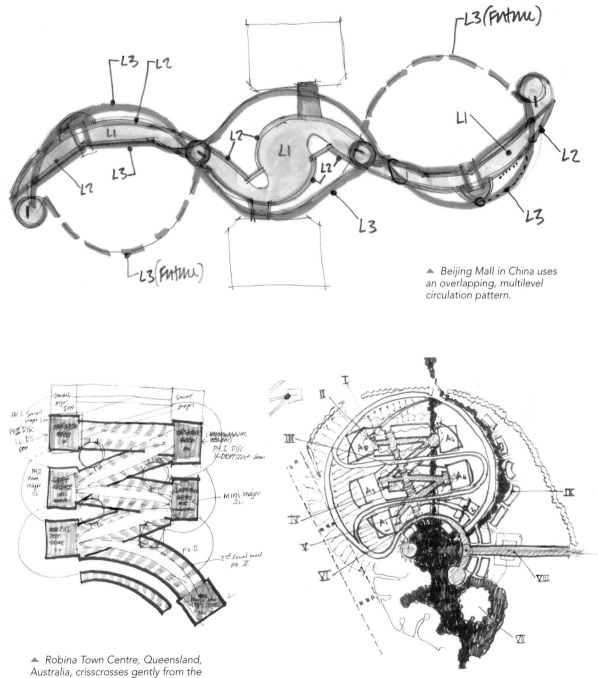

L3(FUTURE)

L3 L2

L1

L3

L2

L2

L1

L2

L1

L2

L3

L2

L3

L3

L3(FUTURE)

▲ Beijing Mall in China uses an overlapping, multilevel circulation pattern.

▲ Robina Town Centre, Queensland, Australia, crisscrosses gently from the waterfront up a sloping site, in a pattern similar to a folding ruler. (Images: Jerde.)

▲ To create a successful project that is embraced by the local community over time, it is important to design a main gathering spot where most of the activity will occur. Such spaces are often located at the center court or main plaza; some projects have more than one heart, but one clear and premier focal point is recommended. Here, shoppers pause to enjoy the dancing water in Palladium Plaza Fountains at CityPlace in West Palm Beach, Florida. (Courtesy CityPlace Partners and Elkus/Manfredi Architects, CJ Walker Photography.)

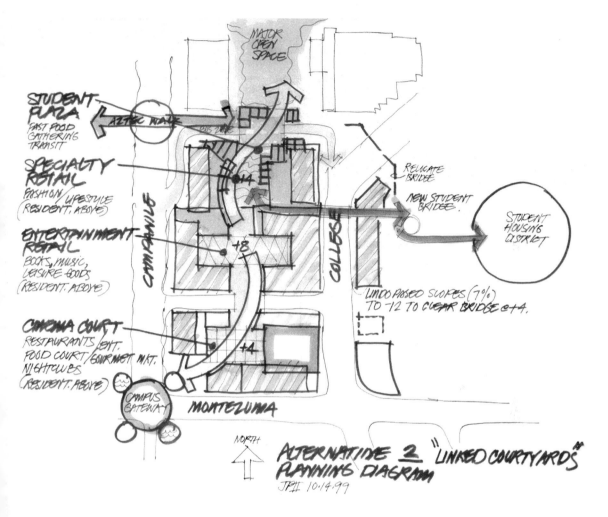

STUDENT PLAZA
FAST FOOD
GATHERING
TRANSIT

SPECIALTY RETAIL
FASHION/LIFESTYLE
(RESIDENT. ABOVE)

ENTERTAINMENT RETAIL
BOOKS, MUSIC,
LEISURE GOODS
(RESIDENT. ABOVE)

CINEMA COURT
RESTAURANTS/ENT.
FOOD COURT/GOURMET MKT.
NIGHTCLUBS
(RESIDENT. ABOVE)

MAJOR OPEN SPACE

AZTEC WALK

RELOCATE BRIDGE

NEW STUDENT BRIDGE

STUDENT HOUSING DISTRICT

LINDO PASEO SLOPES (7%)
TO 12 TO CLEAR BRIDGE @ +4.

CAMPANILE

COLLEGE

CAMPUS GATEWAY

MONTEZUMA

NORTH

ALTERNATIVE 2 "LINKED COURTYARDS"
PLANNING DIAGRAM
JPI 10.14.99

▲ An early armature concept for *The Paseo at San Diego State University* in San Diego, California, employs specialty retail and entertainment uses, capped by student housing, to create a connection between the university and the town. (Image: Jerde.)

shopping center and mixed-use design is the city, or main street, Jerde thinks that it is important for each project to have a main gathering spot or a town square, the "corner of Main and Main." This hub of activity forms the heart of the project; it is the spot where people would naturally meet, where the speeches are made, where bands play or performers perform, where the Fourth of July picnic and other events are held. Often these spaces are located at the center court, or main plaza; some pro-jects have more than one heart, but one clear and premier focal point is best.

District making

For shopping center and mixed-use pro-jects larger than 100,000 sq ft, Jerde sug-gests dividing the project into a series of *districts*. This approach follows the design metaphor of the city. Every great city or town is composed of a collection of smaller neighborhoods; in the best cities, each of these neighborhoods has its

New Urbanist Town Squares

The trend toward recreating the traditional town square for retail projects has grown and become more literal in the past few years. Neotraditional or new urbanist design retail centers have supplanted the indoor department-store-anchored regional mall. These types of pseudo–town squares are filling a void left in the wake of the suburbanization of the United States. Because much of the suburbs has a mass-produced, sometimes soulless quality, people are seeking a sense of connection to their community; some are finding it in these commercial developments. When these projects begin to include additional uses, such as housing, community uses like libraries, city council chambers, office space, heath care facilities, and the like, they truly become the town squares they aspire to be.

unique character and sense of place. Two advantages of creating districts for retail projects are clear:

1. Dividing a large project into smaller districts helps customers navigate their way through the project (and, more important, back to their cars).

2. Districts can organize the leasing into series where similar tenants or tenants with similar markets may prefer to gather.

In addition to providing several focal points throughout the project, districting creates desirable neighborhoods that help increase foot traffic along storefronts located in areas outside the hub at "Main and Main." Well-districted plans often create opportunity for a greater variety of tenants, thereby increasing the overall project's market penetration. There are several ways to create the distinction between districts, as discussed in the following paragraphs.

Architecture

A district's natural boundaries can be designed by shaping the plan and reinforced though paving patterns, wall materials, skylights, gateways, and other features. The Mall of America's enormous plan was divided into four distinct streets, each with its own architectural character, which were, at the time of design, dubbed Garden Street, Grand Avenue, Market Street, and Electric Street. The mall operator has indicated that the distinct character of each street has helped customers find their way around the project.

Leasing

The ideal district plan is not only differentiated by architectural character, but also by the stores within a district. Consider using the city's collection of varied retail neighborhoods as a reference: Antique, furniture, arts, nightclub, fashion, and other retail types—each has its own

distinctive district in a city. Sophisticated leasing plans suggest the layout for such districting.

Adjacent uses

Many districted plans are informed by the mix of uses on the site or adjacent to the site. For instance, the inclusion of a hotel may create opportunities for up-scale fashion or tourist amenities; office space nearby may offer an opportunity to a restaurant district for lunchtime and after-work crowds; an on-site cinema will attract tenants who can take advantage of before- and after-movie activities, such as browsing in book and record stores, dining in restaurants, or enjoying a nightclub.

Design concepts

One of the significant challenges in designing large scale, multitenant, mixed-use projects is the difference in the goals undertaken by both developers and archi-

▲ To help visitors navigate easily through the immense Mall of America, Blooming-ton, Minnesota, a series of districts were created, each with a different character and architectural statement, such as Market Street, shown on page 152. (Images: Jerde.)

tects to create a project that is both unique and distinctive, as well as one that complies with all of the tried-and-true, formulaic "rules" of the industry. With so much at stake, how can we design our projects so that they both stand out from or above the norm and can be readily leased by tenants who are drawn to the familiar? Much of what makes a project distinctive lies in the basic design concept or the main *idea* behind the project. Look for a key idea or story that will help you shape the design and thereby give the project its own character. If concept design is compelling and evocative enough, it can inform most of the key design decisions for the project, from the smallest architectural details to overall layout and leasing.

Begin by looking at the context of the site as the starting point for your concept design. If a designer wants to create the quintessential "there" of a place, it is best to start with what is unique about the site, its history, geography, culture, scale, and so forth—its essence. For instance, if a location is known for its brick architecture, try to make use of the material in the new project, which may be realized in a contemporary interpretation of a historic style. Sometimes there is no physical or historical feature of a site to use as the basic concept. Then it is best to create a sense of character.

> There is no way to separate form from meaning; one cannot exist without the other.
>
> —*Vincent Scully*

▼ *RiverWalk Kitakyushu in Kitakyushu, Japan, is designed to create a new identity for the emerging city. The project uses architecture in the form of five distinct icons to connect the city's five varied districts. (Image: Jerde.)*

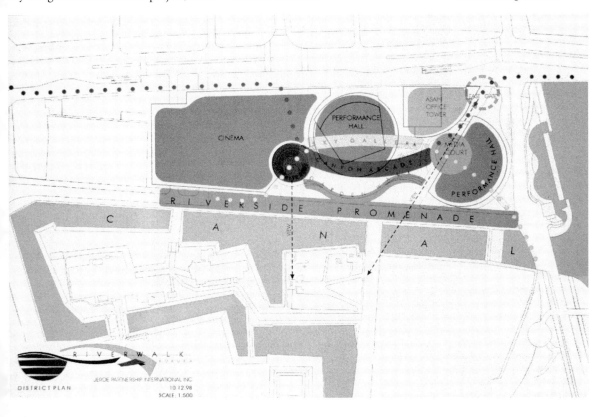

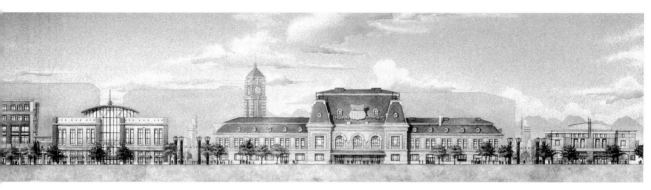

▲ *The Gateway uses brick and other materials familiar to downtown Salt Lake City, Utah. Starting with the existing Union Pacific depot, materials were selected that would match, complement, and expand the city's historic architecture. (Image: Jerde.)*

These design concepts can be categorized by two types: formative and transformative.

Formative design concepts

Projects are often sited in greenfield areas of new or very recent habitation and development. Many retail architects have used an agrarian design vocabulary to recall the early use of such sites. In some cases The Jerde Partnership has tried concepts that create a new local town center. Usually it tries to incorporate additional uses to make the town center concept authentic. For instance, Jerde's plan for the Robina Town Centre project in Australia included space for city council chambers, a library, and a town square (a church that was planned for the site was not realized). This project was sited at the heart of a massive residential development and became the commercial, cultural, and social gathering spot of the community.

Nature is also an important informing concept. Jerde often tries to bring as much of the indigenous landscape, locally quarried stone as well as the basic color of the soil and surrounding terrain, into a project. For instance, for a particular project, Park Place Oita, Japan, the concept was "Landscape is number one, buildings are number two." This simple design goal

set up the primacy of the landscape features and the integration of the project into a terraced hillside. The focal point of the project is the park at its center, connecting each of three levels with an outdoor landscape amenity with fountains, a waterfall, and generous planting. Even the parking lot was conceived as an orchard to relate to the site's original wooded character.

Sometimes formative concepts come from other sources of inspiration. The Mall of America, for instance, within its hard airport development context, had a totally internalized concept. Although not completely realized, the notion was that the project was a microcosm of the earth—of all of the best that the world, particularly the Americas, has to offer.

Many other architects have imported, whole cloth, a design concept from an entirely foreign culture. These projects have a thematic character that may be entirely appropriate for a resort-oriented project whose goal is to "transport" the users to an exotic experience. One of the most renowned and successful of this genre is Country Club Plaza, Kansas City, Missouri, designed and developed in the 1920s and 1930s. Developer J. C. Nichols's scheme used elaborate Andalusian architecture, including statuary, tile

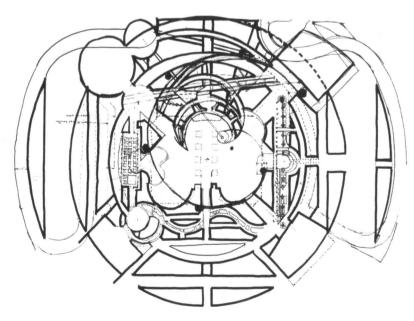

▲ The central feature of
Park Place Oita, Oita, Japan,
is a park area that connects
each of the project's three
levels with natural amenities,
consisting of fountains, a
waterfall, and generous
landscaping. (Photo: Jerde.)

◀ A conceptual sketch of the
Mall of America in
Bloomington, Minnesota,
shows the project as a
metaphorical Earth.
(Image: Jerde.)

mosaics, and fountains, some imported from Spain. Though having nothing to do with the local Kansas architecture, this fantasy environment is, to this day, one of the most successful and prestigious suburban town centers in America.

Transformative design concepts

Retail and mixed-use architecture reaches its highest and best purpose when used to transform dilapidated, underused, or economically depressed urban areas. Architects look forward to working on these types of projects because they can reanimate a vacant and derelict downtown into a vital center of social and commercial interaction. With a city as context,

there is usually a wealth of inspiration for a transformative design concept. (Sometimes what is called for is a reaction against context by providing an oasis or a respite from the city. This can be achieved in a number of ways, for example, by breaking away from a relentless grid or creating a new architectural typology, such as by establishing a dominant focal point where none exists or a great open space in a context where dense buildings dominate.)

In trying to revitalize a city with a retail mixed-use project, take the best of what the city has to offer and weave it into the project. The Jerde Partnership tries to make physical connections to adjacent

◀ *Country Club Plaza in Kansas City, Missouri, shows an Andalusian-influenced architecture. (Photo: Special Collections, Kansas City Public Library, Kansas City, Missouri.)*

▼ *A Moroccan design theme is evident in every aspect of the design of the Irvine Spectrum Center in Irvine, California. (Photo courtesy RTKL Associates Inc., Dave Whitcomb.)*

Inclusion and Allusion

Some architectural criticisms claim that some retail architecture, particularly that which has a thematic design, is unauthentic and manipulative. Typically, the critique includes the suspicion that corporations are using sophisticated marketing ploys, such as elaborate architectural fantasy environments, to lure an unsuspecting public into buying their products. Perhaps the public is not so naive as these critics posit. Robert Venturi, in both of his seminal books, *Complexity and Contradiction in Architecture* and *Learning from Las Vegas*, challenged this critique by pointing out the historical precedent and value of architecture of "inclusion and allusion":

"There are didactic images more important than the image of recreation for us to take home to New Jersey and Iowa: one is the Avis with Venus; another, Jack Benny under a classical pediment with Shell Oil beside him, or the gas station beside the multi-million dollar casino. These show a vitality that may be achieved by architecture of inclusion or, by contrast, the deadness that results from too great a preoccupation with tastefulness and total design. The Strip shows the value of symbolism and allusion in an architecture of vast space and speed and proves that people, even architects, have fun with architecture that reminds them of something else, perhaps harems or the Wild West in Las Vegas, perhaps of the nation's New England forebears in New Jersey. Allusion and comment on the past or present or on our great commonplaces or old clichés, and inclusion of the everyday in the environment, sacred and profane—these are what are lacking in Modern architecture. We can learn about them from Las Vegas, as have other artists from their own profane and stylistic sources." (Venturi 1972)

uses and districts and endeavors to tap into a public consciousness as well. When successful, these projects can achieve a transcendent value worth exponentially more than the on-site investment.

Jerde has accomplished several transformative design projects. Here the design concepts are simple, but the key to their success is their integration into the surrounding urban fabric. For instance, the goal for The Gateway in Salt Lake City, Utah, was to create a new 24-hour district in the form of a street lined by two levels of retail, as well as office, residential, cultural, and entertainment uses.

The Gateway's plan connects to the heart of the city. The concept for the master plan extended beyond the project site to anticipate growth patterns and trigger infill development in the downtown core, thus creating an active two-mile loop among existing attractions.

Taking advantage of the site's natural grade change, The Gateway connects to existing circulation patterns on both retail levels, resulting in strong pedestrian traffic on the ground and second levels.

The plan for The Gateway included preserving the site's only existing building, the historic Union Pacific depot, which forms the project's formal entry and serves as a space for exhibits and oth-er public events. It will also house the Virgin Megastore, which is new to Salt Lake City.

Throughout The Gateway, the architectural detailing is intended to be an extension of the city's early building stock from the turn of the twentieth century. The project also includes a water feature inspired by a creek that formerly ran through the site.

▲ The Gateway was designed to fit within Salt Lake City's existing context. The plan for the project preserved the site's only existing building, the historic Union Pacific depot, which has enormous stained glass windows depicting the history of the city. (Photo: Michael McRae.)

Namba Parks, a new transformative project currently under construction in Osaka, Japan, is an example of a design concept that reacts against the existing context. Located adjacent to the Namba Parks train station, this is a nine-level retail and entertainment project placed at the base of high-rise offices and future residential towers. The goal for Namba was to provide a respite from the dense, urban context in the form of a rooftop park that ascends from the grade level to the top of the podium. Bisecting the park is an eight-story canyon that opens the project's interior to natural light and fresh air.

Namba Park's architectural vocabulary recalls nature with horizontal banding reminiscent of sedimentary rock, the organic sinuous plan, the lush planting, and water features.

Telling the Story

Several types of drawings, diagrams, image boards, sketches, and renderings are used to communicate the concept design's ideas. The complexity of retail and mixed-use projects can be decoded and simplified with a well-thought-out diagram or illustration. These tools are very important in telling the story.

There have been great advances in graphic presentation in recent years, particularly in computer-generated three-dimensional images. The advantages of desktop publishing have also made the assembling of compelling presentation materials faster, cheaper, and with much higher quality.

◀ *The Gateway's water feature in the main plaza recalls a creek that was diverted from the site long ago. (Photo: Jerde.)*

▲ Renderings and a section of Namba Parks in Osaka, Japan, show the layers of retail and entertainment uses beneath the rooftop park. (Images: Jerde.)

THE CO-CREATIVE PROCESS

As discussed earlier in this chapter, the primary focus in designing an experiential place is the "space between" buildings, where visitors to the project wander, mingle, meditate—where they experience the project. The space between gives visitors a reason to visit the project that is not task-oriented, such as the need to make a specific purchase. The more interesting and enjoyable the space between, the more frequently people will come, or the longer they will stay, which may result in higher sales.

In designing the space between, develop a distinct story or main idea behind the project. Once the story has has been approved by the client, the co-creative process is initiated. During the co-creative process, designers specializing in lighting, environmental graphics, landscape design, and so forth, are brought in to make the story compelling through the overall look, character, and function of the shopping complex.

Landscape Architecture

The earth's landscape is the connection we share with things that are larger than ourselves—and with each other. We can design projects not as buildings, but as natural and organic forms that work in tandem with the natural context and the earth's landscape.

We can use landscape as a unifying canvas on which to place the pieces of a project. Because landscape influences every aspect of a project, we may take a holistic approach to landscape design. More than simply planting or adding greenery around the edges of buildings, landscape design is a framework for the experience.

Landscaped elements can create a deliberate path of discovery that unfolds throughout a project. This path of discovery is composed of a sequence of experiences, where plant materials can cause dramatic changes in atmosphere. A visitor may pass from a formal *allée* of trees into a maze, then out through a threshold that opens onto a grand lawn. In this way, landscape can serve as a wayfinding strategy; visitors can use various landscape elements as points of reference in navigating complex commercial spaces.

In addition to providing visual coherency, landscape touches the senses to provide sight, sound, touch, and smell experiences. Because plants, trees, shrubs, and other landscape elements are growing, alive, and animated materials, they are always evolving and changing to provide different experiences in each season.

Landscaping and natural features are critical to helping the architect establish the quintessential "there" of a place by extending an area's existing natural character (indigenous plants, trees, etc.) into the project or, in the case of sites on which previous developments removed the landscape, using the project as a way to reintroduce the natural character into a site.

Landscape design bridges the surrounding natural context with the building forms and interiors to contribute to the overall design character and distinctiveness of a shopping center or mixed-use development. Natural elements enhance the architecture by producing a pleasant, inspiring environment that attracts potential customers.

In addition to countering the frenzied pace that can be associated with shopping and running errands, natural elements provide a memorable environment of discovery versus one of predictability. People meander through plant-lined walkways and enjoy water features. Landscape elements significantly increase the amount of time customers spend inside a project, patronizing restaurants and checking out a few more stores.

Responsibilities of landscape designers

The landscape architect typically joins the project team in the schematic design phase when the architect has identified the zones in which the landscape architect will work.

After the architect outlines the project's functional and aesthetic framework, the landscape designer analyzes the relationship of the structure and its surroundings and establishes a logic for differentiating spaces that may be on the perimeter of the project.

In general, landscape designers are responsible for the following:

- Specifying plant materials, exterior paving materials, and the site furniture (benches, tables, chairs, trash cans, and urns) within an integrated plan that works with the site's climatic and soil conditions and meets the design objectives of the owner and the architect

- Creating water features or collaborating with a water features specialist

- Coordinating landscape lighting with the lighting designer

- Working with the environmental graphics designer to determine how landscaping can be used to enhance signage

- Aligning issues and costs relative to sustainability and ongoing

maintenance with the project's budget and performance objectives

Creating the landscape design

Design criteria

The design criteria evolve from the client's objectives for the project. The landscape architect meets with the client to discuss the site plan and describe the proposed landscape applications.

Budget

With the architect's approval of the landscape architect's concept, the landscape architect prepares the budget, which can range from 2 to 10 percent of the project cost.

Bid documents

Bid documents are prepared, and the landscape architect receives and evaluates estimates for materials and installation costs.

Codes and regulations

The landscape architect researches specific municipal code regulations that apply to the proposed landscaping program. Building permits are applied for.

Design development

During design development, the landscape architect completes details of planters, hardscape details, identification of tree types, and an irrigation plan where required.

Construction documentation

Construction documents are prepared for the contractor. During construction, the landscape architect's role is to observe the site in regard to such aspects as hardscape installation and the correct installation of large-specimen trees.

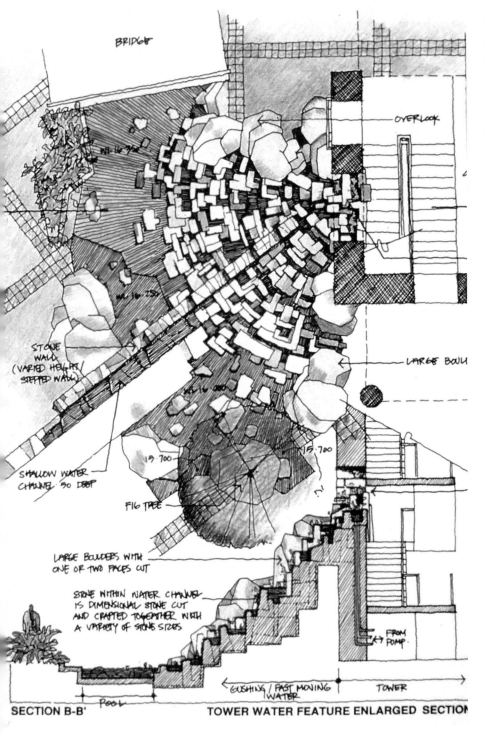

BRIDGE

OVERLOOK

STONE
WALL
(VARIED HEIGHT
STEPPED WALL)

LARGE BOU

SHALLOW WATER
CHANNEL 50 DEEP

15.700

15.700

FIG TREE

LARGE BOULDERS WITH
ONE OR TWO FACES CUT

STONE WITHIN WATER CHANNEL
IS DIMENSIONAL STONE CUT
AND CRAFTED TOGETHER WITH
A VARIETY OF STONE SIZES

FROM
PUMP.

GUSHING / FAST MOVING
WATER

TOWER

SECTION B-B'   POOL   **TOWER WATER FEATURE ENLARGED SECTION**

◀◀ ◀ *Robina Town Centre, Queensland, Australia, was designed as an organic and lush complex to complement its natural site on Australia's Gold Coast. Landscaping and the use of natural materials played a key role in establishing the project's natural character. Landscape designer EDAW. (Photo: by Dixi Carrillo; image: EDAW.)*

Jacaranda Tree.

North Formosa Cafe Elevation

Philodendrum selloum.

Transplanted Banana
Palm Trees.

Topiary Hedge.

Potted Chinese Juniper
Topiaries.

Undulating Hedge.

Passiflora caerulea
Blue Crown Passion Flower.

Accent Planting In
Decorative Pots.

Scale: 1" = 4'

City light fixture with
green vine cage.

Reflective water
Feature.

King Palm in Shrub
Planting.

18" Concrete Seat Wall.

Bus Shelter.

Ornamental
Chorisia Tree
With Shrub Planting.

Bus Shelter Garden.

Enhanced Paving.

King Palm.

Outdoor Dining With
Tables and Chairs.

Drake Elm Tree
with accent shrubs.

Bus Stop Shelter Plan

Scale: 1" = 10'

166

Interior landscaping

The interior landscape design may include permanent plant material, seasonal plants that will be changed periodically, or a combination of both.

When large plants or trees are used in the project's interior, request that the grower house them in a greenhouse for a year while the project is under construction to get them accustomed to a controlled environment before they are replanted in the building.

Creating an indoor ecology with suffi-cient sunlight, air, and water for plant-ings to flourish is challenging. A creative combination of natural lighting and arti-ficial illumination is needed to produce light of sufficient footcandles. Equip-ment that recycles air and water is used to provide ongoing systems. The use of self-watering planters that use a wick sys-tem that works like siphon, drawing from standing water on the bottom, is an alternative to running pipes through the floor or the ground and allows the pots to be moved.

◄◄ ▲ *One of the design goals of West Hollywood Gateway in West Hollywood, California, is to convert a brownfield site into a pedestrian-friendly urban environment that will influence future developments in the area. The landscape design uses lush landscaping and water features to create comfortable outdoor spaces at the locally famous Formosa Café, a bus shelter, and throughout the project. Landscape designer EDAW. (Images: Jerde; EDAW, Los Angeles.)*

▶ *Lighting is used to further animate a fountain at Robina Town Centre in Queensland, Australia. Lighting designer Kaplan Partners Architectural Lighting. (Photo: Dixi Carrillo.)*

▼ *The Lighting Practice designed the exterior lighting of Burdines at Florida Mall in Orlando, accentuating the white building's textured facade and emphasizing the two-story palm tree structures flanking the main entrance.*

Lighting Design

Visibility is critical to the success of shopping center and mixed-use complexes, and lighting has an integral role in enhancing a project's visibility. Over the past decade, developers have come to recognize lighting as more than a technical function. The creative use of lighting as spectacle or attraction and the effective lighting of nighttime facades can help to give projects a competitive edge, entice shoppers, and build sales volume.

Exterior lighting can turn a project and its identifying signage into an inviting billboard. Interior lighting can enhance

the three-dimensional quality of interior spaces. Applied lighting defines spaces and lends character and sparkle; it emphasizes scale and texture, gives the viewer perspective, and dramatizes foliage, water features, project signage, tenant signage, columns, and internally illuminated windows.

As lighting has become more important to the overall character of a project, lighting design has become more specialized and complex, combining the expertise of electrical engineers, who have historically executed lighting implementation, with that of specialized lighting consultants.

The lighting designer's role on the project team

- In the early planning stages, recommend the proper balance of integral and applied lighting to achieve the objectives and primary design intent agreed upon by the owner and the architect.

- Collaborate with other design specialties, including the architect, interior designer, graphic designer, and landscape architect. For example, in the planning stages the lighting and graphics consultants can identify the techniques best suited for external or internal illumination of informational and identify signs.

- Bring in subconsultants as needed. The lighting designer may need to retain a theatrical lighting specialist to recommend lighting fixtures and control devices to accommodate staged events and integrate with the architectural lighting design.

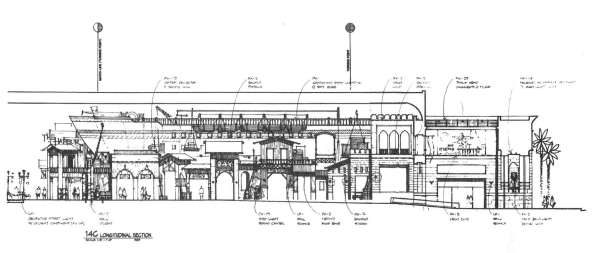

14C LONGITUDINAL SECTION
SCALE 1/8" = 1'-0"   REF.

• Establish a budget. The lighting designer works with the owner to clearly establish the goals of lighting and the relevant costs.

Guidelines for shopping center lighting
Three kinds of lighting

1. *Seeing light* falls on the horizontal surface, enabling people to see and perform tasks.

2. *Looking light* falls on the vertical surface and influences perceived light levels.

3. *Decorative lighting* is emitted by sconces, table lamps, and other accent luminaires.

Four kinds of lighting instruments

1. *Floodlights* illuminate large areas.

2. *Spotlights* illuminate very specific areas.

3. *Linear sources* create horizons.

4. *Point sources* emanate from decorative fixtures.

Deal separately with horizontal and vertical planes. Design in layers so that when budget cuts are required, the light layers can be eliminated in inverse order of importance; that is, the least critical layer is dispensed with first. Recognize the point in the lighting program when further cuts cannot be made without slighting the project.

Lighting basics
The color properties of light
There are two primary reference standards for lamps:

1. Kelvins measure color temperature, referred to as degrees K (for example, 3500°K). Most often, for retail, lamps having warm color ratings are used for ambient light and those with cooler ratings for illuminating feature products on display. Lower Kelvin temperatures are warmer, and higher Kelvin temperatures are cooler.

2. The Color Rendering Index (CRI) rates the color rendering properties of light. To the human eye, objects viewed under different types of lamps will vary in color: darker, lighter, sometimes appearing to be a totally different color. The maximum CRI is 100, the rating for natural light. Various lamp types have different CRI values.

◀ ▲ *Arabian-inspired Desert Passage in Las Vegas uses lighting to recreate the journey through ancient spice routes of Africa from Morocco to India, which includes hourly sunrise-to-sunset elapses. A plan shows the types of standard, theatrical, and special effects lighting used. Lighting designer: Kaplan Partners Architectural Lighting. (Images courtesy Kaplan Partners Architectural Lighting.)*

▲ Theatrical lighting, fire, water, smoke, and other special effects are incorporated into the Race for Atlantis show at The Forum Shops in Caesar's Palace, Las Vegas. (Photo courtesy The Forum Shops.)

Economics of luminaires

Three factors are considered in the selection of light fixtures:

1. Initial cost of purchase and installation

2. Maintenance costs to clean and replace the luminaire

3. Energy cost to operate the luminaire. Efficacy is the measure of how efficiently the lamp converts energy (watts) into lumens to produce light output.

Parking areas

• Lighting in parking areas should provide approximately 1.5 footcandles (fc) at the pavement surface.

• Poles should be placed in islands at the ends of parking bays.

• The height of the standards and the direction of the lighting should be specified to avoid spillover to adjacent properties.

• In parking structures, 5 fc is recommended for safety.

• Lighting that will diminish, to an extent, the colors of the automobiles should be specified. Lower CRI lights make the colors of cars appear less vibrant, and the project thus becomes a major focal point by appearing more brilliant.

Tenant lighting

For consistent lighting in a retail center, each tenant must adhere to storefront lighting standards to eliminate wide variations in lighting that may be distracting

◀ Theatrical lighting and billowing translucent fabric make Breeze Court, Hurst, Texas, one of the North East Mall's most unusual spaces. Lighting designer: The Lighting Practice.

BASIC CHARACTERISTICS OF LAMP TYPES

LAMP TYPE	COLOR CHARACTERISTICS			Light Control/ Distribution		OPERATIONAL CHARACTERISTICS				
	Color Temperature/ Appearance	Object Color Enhanced	Object Color Dulled	Beam Type/ Spread	Projection Range	Wattage	Efficacy	Lumens	Average Life (hours)	Relight Characteristics
Incandescent										
General service	2,700–3,200°K/ yellowish white	Red, orange, yellow	Blue	Broad	S–M	8–1,500	4–25	44–35,000	750–2,500	*Immediate*
Parabolic reflector				Spot, flood	S–L	30–1,000	5–15	150–18,9000	2,000	
Tungsten/halogen				Linear, spot, flood	M–L	200–1,500	5–25	1,600–35,800	4,000	Immediate
Fluorescent				Linear	S	4–200	20–85	85–16,000	7,500–12,000	
Daylight	6,250°K/ bluish white	Green, blue	Red							
Cool white	4,250°K/ white	Orange, yellow, blue	Red							
Deluxe cool white	4,050°K White	All colors	Minimal for all colors							
White	3,450°K Pale yellowish white	Orange, yellow	Red, green, blue							
Warm white	3,020°K/ yellowish white	Orange, yellow	Red, green, blue							
Deluxe warm white	2,940°K Pinkish white	Red, orange	Green, blue							
High-Intensity Discharge, Mercury				Broad	S–L	40–1,000	30–65	580–63,000	12,000–24,000	3–5 minutes
Clear	5,700°K/ greenish-bluish white	Yellow, green, blue	Red, orange							
Color-improved	4,430°K/ yellowish white	Orange, yellow	Blue							
High-Intensity Discharge, Metal Halide	3,720–4,200°K/ greenish white	Yellow, green, blue	Red	Broad	S–L	100–15,00	70–125	8,300–210,000	2,000–20,000	Up to 15 minutes
High-Intensity Discharge, Sodium				Broad	S–L					
High pressure	2,100°K/ yellowish white	Orange, yellow	Red, blue			70–1,000	60–140	2,150–140,000	16,000–24,000	Up to 15 minutes
Low pressure	1,740°K Yellow-orange	Yellow	All except yellow			18–180	Up to 180	1,800–33,000	10,000–20,000	Up to 15 minutes

Source: *The Jerde Partnership*

to customers. The developer's leasing staff should participate in early design meetings to achieve overall uniformity.

General criteria for tenant lighting

- Shield recessed fixtures; low-voltage strips and socket channels should be with a minimum cut-off of 45°.
- Do not aim fixtures forward of glass storefronts.
- Exposed lamps, including decorative fixtures, generally require the owner's written approval.
- Flashing lighting or signage generally requires the owner's written approval.
- Lighting should be a minimum of 80 CRI and a maximum of 3500°K.

Specific criteria for storefronts (includes first 10 ft from storefront inward)

- Lighting (illuminance) levels should not exceed 100 fc (1000 lux) for storefronts.
- Lighting (illuminance) levels should be at least 60 fc (600 lux) for storefronts.
- Contrast (luminance) ratios between any part of the store and the adjacent public surfaces and/or adjacent storefronts should not exceed 15:1.

For questions and further clarification regarding these criteria, consult with a lighting designer.

Environmental Graphic Design

Environmental graphic design extends the overall design concept into pedestrian-scaled features to create a compelling and immersive environment that embodies the idea of place. Environmental graphic design helps create the visual aspects of

Graphic designers who serve the developers and architects responsible for shopping centers and mixed-use projects must contribute to the energy, excitement, and activity of these places. We have to care deeply about people's lives getting enriched by the interaction of the marketplace. Retailing is more than just the bottom line. Graphic designers can go beyond creating identifying signs and wayfinding to add to the enjoyment of the experience for the users.
—*Deborah Sussman*

the shopping center or mixed-use complex, including exterior signage, wayfinding systems, sculptures, and packaging.

Environmental graphic design begins with the story and design objectives established by the owner and architect and develops a holistic design for the visual messages; it is not a series of separate elements applied to the architecture at the end.

Basic graphic design programs
Amenities
Special effects may include:

- Water and light features
- Vending kiosks
- Gazebos
- Banners, flags, and pennants

The graphic designer provides the overall design theme, flexible and/or expandable parts, and lighting and furniture details and designs.

▲ Tenant storefront lighting at FlatIron Crossing in Broomfield, Colorado, creates a consistent feel throughout the retail promenade. (Photo: © Callison; by Chris Eden.)

Signage and wayfinding

The signing system may include:

- Retail/tenant criteria guidelines
- Project and major facilities identification at site entries
- Regulatory and directional vehicular signing
- Street and building identification
- Informational and directional pedestrian signing
- Site directories and orientation maps
- Parking level and area identification signing
- Elevator identification and fire/life safety signing
- Office tenant identification signing
- Electronic marquee
- Bus and taxi loading and unloading information
- Restaurant, bar, cafeteria, and concession identification
- Restroom and telephone identification

- Changeable menu information signing

Temporary signing and graphics program

For new or renovated projects, consider a temporary graphic and signing program for use during the construction phase. The objective is to present a positive image of the project by providing a preview of things to come. Components of the program can include:

- Temporary project information and directional signing, such as identification of the building site and temporary entries and gateways

- Construction barricades and graphics

- Promotional on-site graphics

▲ At Universal CityWalk in Los Angeles, lighting is used to create eclectic and inconsistent storefronts. (Photo: Stephen Simpson.)

Considerations for shopping and mixed-use centers

Determine the needs of the retail tenants early in the planning process. Their requirements are weighed against the aesthetic outlines of the project established by the project architects.

Wayfinding is part of a center's image. Every two- and three-dimensional sign that is mounted, hung, or applied to a surface has a role in communicating the project's distinctiveness.

Seven basic phases of graphic design

1. Initial project analysis and proposal generation

    Strategic planning

    Information gathering

2. Communication

    Client/owner

    Other consultants

    The community

    State, city, and county governments

3. Programming

    Site research

    Photographic documentation

    Study plans

4. Schematic design

    Production

    Presentation

    Completion, with design direction

5. Design development

    Fabrication estimates prepared

    Presentation

    Production, including tenant criteria

    Completion, with final design chosen

6. Contract documents

    Production

    Compilation, including specs

    Completion, with approvals given

7. Contract administration

    Bidding

    Award of bid

    Production management

    Installation management

    Punch list management

    Final walk-through with client/owner

◀◀ *Communication Arts's signage and identity design for The Block at Orange in Orange, California, includes 90 ft high internally lit stylons with graphics that are easily changed. (Photo: Erhard Pfeiffer.)*

◀ *The image program for Oviedo Marketplace in Orlando, Florida, was inspired by its wetlands site. Oviedo integrates lush landscaping into an open, natural, gardenlike environment with graphic elements relating as garden sculptures. (Photo courtesy Sussman/Prejza.)*

Because Portland, Oregon, is the "City of Roses," Sussman/Prejza chose the rose as the icon for the city's Pioneer Place. The signage program incorporates various graphic and physical interpretations of the rose. At the center of the project's atrium, a sculpture/ fountain amenity is formed by metal rose stems reaching as high as 32 ft; the stems are etched with rose-related information that visitors can read and touch. Open petals at the top of the sculpture form a shadow rose on the polished marble floor. (Images courtesy Sussman/Prejza.)

Sussman/Prejza based the identity and wayfinding system of Hollywood & Highland, Los Angeles, on cinematic concepts not specific to any film industry era. The black-and-white system incorporates classic film icons, such as spotlights, cropped images, and extreme perspectives producing deep shadows. (Images courtesy Sussman/Prejza.)

Co-Creativity Case Study: Canal City Hakata, Fukuoka, Japan

Project Design Team

Design architect: The Jerde Partnership

Landscape architect:: EDAW, Irvine, California

Water features design: WET Design, Universal City, California

Environmental, merchandise design: Selbert Perkins Design Collaborative, Santa Monica, California

Lighting design: Kaplan Partners Architectural Lighting, Los Angeles, California

Conceptual design

Anticipating that Canal City Hakata would draw large numbers of people, The Jerde Partnership designed the project as a series of special districts primed for the gatherings of its guests. To connect to the site's location on the Naka River, Jerde established a canal as the armature of the project, the main element that links the project's areas.

Jerde proposed nature as a contrast to the surrounding city grid. Inspired by the universal forces of sun, stars, moon, sea, and earth, Canal City Hakata's districts were designed as places for users to discover and celebrate the mysteries of the universe and the natural wonders of the world.

Having established the design concept, a collaborative team of urban, landscape, graphic, and lighting designers and architects created Canal City Hakata as a walk through the universe.

▶ *To connect to the location of Canal City Hakata along the Naka River, Jerde established a canal as the project's armature. Surrounding the canal are a series of new districts, which both extend existing pedestrian paths and create new pedestrian connections with adjacent uses. (Image: Jerde.)*

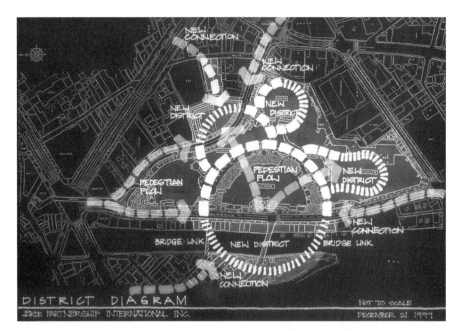

Architecture

The architecture of Canal City Hakata, which makes reference to time and nature, is indebted to Japan's high level of craftsmanship and construction. The building bases are stone. Their vertical faces rise from the canal, in a reference to the erosion of land by a river, forming a canyon over the centuries. As the buildings rise, the layers become more refined, lighter, and more modern. The color system is a traditional rich Japanese palette evolving out of the earth and often used as accent colors, providing local users with a familiar feel.

Landscape

The landscape is expressed through a vibrant color palette and the fragrances of nature. The perimeter landscape helps to establish Canal City Hakata as the new heart of the surrounding commercial district, with trees extending the shaded pedestrian environment to nearby streets. Providing a human-scale canopy, the trees create a distinctive landscape edge for the new buildings and establish the prototype for future enhancement of surrounding streets.

The interior landscape connects the project together along the richly planted canal and its five districts. The paving within the project's interior, designed to allow easy movement, is created in a series of patterns that integrate the distinct districts.

Water features

Water communicates the basic design concept of Canal City Hakata and allows visitors to experience a biosphere of humankind's natural world. Water features mark the timeless elements encountered throughout the project—sun, moon, sea, and stars—in one-of-a-kind innovations, including:

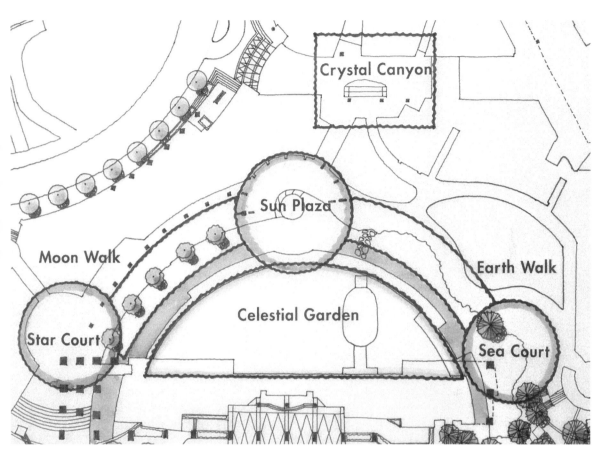

- Star Streamers, located in the Star Court, blend spiritual, mythological, and historical icons in a seven-pointed pattern composed of small, fast-acting, computer-programmed impulses called NanoShooters.

- The Banner Symphony is a series of illuminated kinetic water columns (MiniShooters) positioned in the middle of the canal and programmed to reflect the joyous life of the city.

Environmental graphic design
The graphics help to integrate Canal City Hakata. The logo represents three elements—earth, moon, and water. These elements form a universal, timeless concept of our environment, which has been applied to every graphic design detail.

Lighting
The lighting plan supports the sense of movement—the movement of water through the canal, the animated water features, people moving through the various spaces, and the movement of clouds, sun, moon, and stars in the sky above.

▲ To establish a contrast with its urban context, Canal City Hakata was designed as a place to discover and celebrate the natural wonders of the universe. This concept inspired its five districts: Star Court, Moon Walk, Sun Plaza, Earth Walk, and Sea Court. (Image: EDAW, Irvine, California.)

▲ *Reflecting Canal City Hakata's goal to create a place inspired by nature, generous landscaping was used along the canal and throughout the project's districts. Within the interior, several different varieties of ivy were planted along the upper levels. (Photo: Hiroyuki Kawano.)*

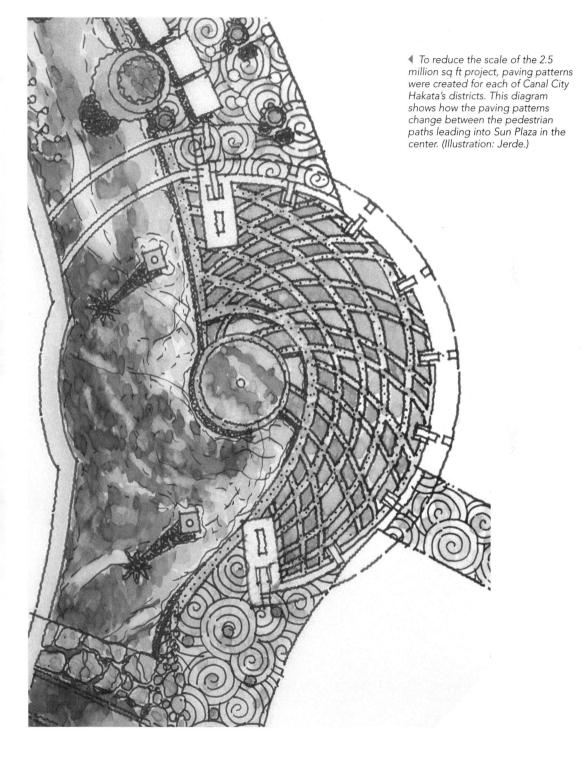

◀ To reduce the scale of the 2.5 million sq ft project, paving patterns were created for each of Canal City Hakata's districts. This diagram shows how the paving patterns change between the pedestrian paths leading into Sun Plaza in the center. (Illustration: Jerde.)

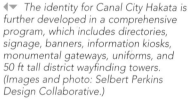 The identity for Canal City Hakata is further developed in a comprehensive program, which includes directories, signage, banners, information kiosks, monumental gateways, uniforms, and 50 ft tall district wayfinding towers. (Images and photo: Selbert Perkins Design Collaborative.)

◀ As the main natural feature of Canal City Hakata, water is animated both in the canal and along the pedestrian passages. (Illustration: Jerde.)

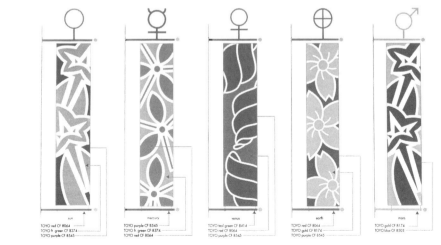

▲ Inspired by the movement or passage of time referenced by Canal City Hakata's universal districts, lighting throughout the project was designed to convey a sense of movement. (Photo: FJUD.)

CHAPTER 8
BUILDING SYSTEMS FOR RETAIL STORES AND MIXED-USE CENTERS

STRUCTURE

Structure, along with mechanical, electrical, and plumbing, is one of the four categories of building systems. Four basic types of materials are typically used in the construction of shopping facilities: wood, masonry, concrete, and steel. Material selection is governed both by the economics of construction and what is allowed by the local building code for the proposed size and use of a project. Refer to local building codes for the minimum requirements concerning what materials are allowed. The economics of construction are influenced by the cost of materials and labor and the time required for construction, which includes lead time prior to on-site work and on-site time itself.

Basic Building Materials
Wood

Wood, a renewable resource, may be used for small projects, but the limitations on allowable occupancy groups, area, and/or number of stories typically exclude it from larger projects.

Dimension lumber

Dimension lumber, the most readily accessible form, is precut into standard sizes. The sizes are nominal dimensions and are given in inches, such as a 2×4, which originally meant that the wood actually measured 2 in. by 4 in. in cross section. Today, a 2×4 is smaller in actual size.

Glu-lam/fabricated

Glu-laminated beams were an early form of fabricated wood, composed of multiple layers of wood held together with adhesives. This technique allowed for the fabrication of larger pieces of wood that would be difficult to obtain in a single piece.

Small pieces of wood, such as shavings, may be formed into sheets and combined with additional wood components to create wooden beams that are more dimensionally stable than natural wood. Other forms of fabricated wood include trusses and panelized wall or roof systems.

Masonry

Masonry may be used as an exterior wall with structural load-bearing capacity. In some instances it can be used as a shear wall when properly reinforced with steel and having the open cells filled with concrete.

Concrete

Concrete has a special application in utilitarian structures, such as parking structures, where the structural material can also serve as the finish material. When used in commercial buildings that require a rated construction, concrete provides the additional benefit of fireproofing with no additional treatment required.

Poured-in-place

With the use of poured-in place concrete, work can begin almost immediately after the foundations are in place, although the erection time for multilevel structures may be longer than that required for steel or precast concrete. The reason is the extra time required to form the reinforcing steel, to assemble the formwork, and to pour the concrete and let it set sufficiently to allow for the next level above to be cast. Concrete is traditionally poured or cast in place.

Precast

Precast concrete is typically provided in the form of columns, beams, and, sometimes, floor sections. The precast systems are often proprietary to a given manufacturer, and the exact method and dimension of the structural frame may vary from one manufacturer to another.

Steel

Steel, as a structural material, is especially relevant to larger structures. Because it is shop-fabricated, it may be ordered in a wide variety of shapes and sizes. This is often an advantage if a design has extensive unique conditions whereby the economics of using a concrete form multiple times is lost. Steel can also be designed to span large distances through the use of tapered girders or trusses.

▼ The relative efficiency of water-cooled and air-cooled systems. (Image: Building Officials and Code Administrators International, Inc.)

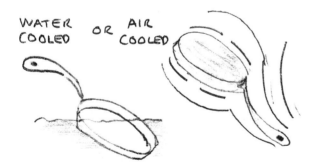

WATER OR AIR
COOLED COOLED

● WATER COOLED SYSTEMS ARE MOST EFFICIENT AND USE LESS ENERGY. THINK ABOUT IT! TO COOL A HOT FRYING PAN DO YOU WAVE IT IN THE AIR?

For larger structures, the basic structural system is typically steel or concrete. The selection of the material will take into consideration several issues:

- Span/structural depth/penetrations
- Fabrication time for site delivery
- Erection time on-site
- Relative cost factor
- Flexibility for future modifications
- Finish requirements

Where lateral resistance, seismic or wind, is required, there are three primary systems: moment frames, braced frames, and shear walls. The moment frame is typically the most expensive, but also the most flexible as there are no additional elements restricting leasing layouts. Braced frames and shear walls are less expensive, but require additional structural elements that may restrict leasing options.

To minimize the impact on leasing flexibility, braced frames and shear walls are typically located at the perimeter of the building shell. Often, interior locations for such elements must be provided. To minimize any leasing impact, it is best to locate such elements in areas where permanent walls are required for other reasons, for example, in exit corridors required in large, multitenant projects to satisfy requirements for egress from public common areas or tenant spaces.

Structural Considerations for Parking Structures

Structured parking is typically provided in retail developments only when the cost of land exceeds the cost of building a parking structure or there is insufficient land available for surface parking. As the cost per parking space in a structure may be three to four times the cost of providing a parking space on grade, the economic efficiency of the parking structure is a major issue.

A parking structure is essentially a structural platform without extensive exterior wall finishes or interior finishes. The major cost component is the building structure itself, and, accordingly, a primary goal in parking structure design is to provide the most efficient building possible. This efficiency is commonly determined by the number of square feet of building construction required for each parking space. Typical ratios for parking structures range from 325 to 375 sq ft per parking space.

The most efficient structural system for a parking structure is commonly referred to as a long-span structure. This type of system has columns spaced in an approximately 18' × 55' bay. This places the columns between the rows of cars and minimizes the impact of the structure on the parking layout. The long-span system is designed specifically for parking and is not always practical, especially where retail uses may be located either above or below the parking, as the long-span bay dimensions are generally not suited to retail layouts.

Where there is an interface with retail uses, more rectangular structural bays with approximate dimensions of 30' × 30' are used. The smaller bays are commonly referred to as short-span structures. These systems are less efficient than long-span structures, as the columns occur between parking spaces. The area occupied by a column between parking spaces is unusable for parking and increases the overall square footage of building structure required for each space. With short-span structures, it is also critical to ensure that the actual spacing of columns will conform with local parking standards for clear parking space and driving aisle dimensions.

MECHANICAL

Thermal Comfort

The design, installation, and operation of the mechanical system in a retail facility are critical to its commercial viability. Thermal comfort is the thermal balance of a person's body as a whole when neither a cooler nor warmer environment is desired. Thermal comfort is influenced by many variables, including the number and proximity of occupants within an environment; the level of physical activity; the type of clothing; and environmental parameters such as air temperature, mean radiant temperature, air velocity, and relative air humidity.

Thermal comfort is measured by three metrics:

1. Dry-bulb temperature: the measure of sensible heat in air, such as that provided by a common glass thermometer.

2. Wet-bulb temperature: the measure of air temperature with moisture, such as that provided by a common glass thermometer, with wet cloth wicking over its glass bulb, waved in the air. The difference between the dry-bulb and wet-bulb temperatures is related to the level of humidity in the air.

3. Mean radiant temperature: the weighted average of the floor, walls, and ceiling temperatures.

The amount of water vapor that can be absorbed by dry air depends on the air temperature: The higher the temperature, the more water vapor can be absorbed. Relative humidity is the amount of water vapor present at a given air temperature as compared with the maximum amount that could be absorbed at that temperature.

Design parameters for heating, ventilating, and air-conditioning (HVAC) systems are typically expressed as a combination of air temperature and relative air humidity, for example, maintaining 75° Fahrenheit and 50 percent relative humidity. A lower relative humidity can cause discomfort, drying the skin and mucous membranes and increasing static electricity. Too much humidity is uncomfortable, harms building materials through moisture absorption or condensation, and spurs the growth of mildew and mold.

The cooling capacity of HVAC systems is commonly measured in British thermal units (Btu). The cooling load consists of the latent heat removed to dehumidify the air and the sensible heat removed to lower the air temperature. The total cooling load is the sum of these two components. A common term for describing cooling loads is *ton,* which represents 12,000 Btu of heat energy. One thousand Btu is the amount of energy required to vaporize 1 lb of water.

In addition to thermal comfort, air quality has become a vital aspect of HVAC systems. *Sick building syndrome* is now commonly used to describe conditions in which a significant portion of a building's occupants suffer headaches, eye and/or throat irritation, fatigue, and other symptoms that subside upon their leaving the building. Legionnaire's disease, on the other hand, often results from a medical or biological cause.

Adequate ventilation is perhaps the most critical element in promoting air quality. The introduction of outside or recirculated air in sufficient quantities can dilute many potential irritants or other undesirable attributes as the stale air is removed. It is critical that incoming air be suitably filtered to ensure air quality. Ease of access to the HVAC system is also important to allow for periodic cleaning and maintenance.

Basic system types

All HVAC systems function according to the principle of heat exchange. Heat is exchanged through the differential of temperature between two different media. HVAC systems are commonly referred to as air-to-air or air-to-water systems, depending on a system's heat exchange medium. Of the two media, water is more efficient than air.

HVAC systems come in two major forms: package units, or independent, self-contained equipment providing for both the heat exchange and distribution of air; and central systems, in which the heat exchange element is in one location, with remote equipment for the actual air distribution.

Package units

Package units, being self-contained, must be relatively close to the areas they serve for both energy and economic efficiency. As the conditioned air is transmitted through a distribution system typically consisting of metal ducts, the shorter the duct length, the more efficient the transfer of air. The shape of the duct and the number of bends contribute to the efficiency of air movement. Round ducts are more efficient than square or rectangular ducts, as each bend or turn in a duct reduces airflow. The length and size of the duct system have an economic impact, as the space

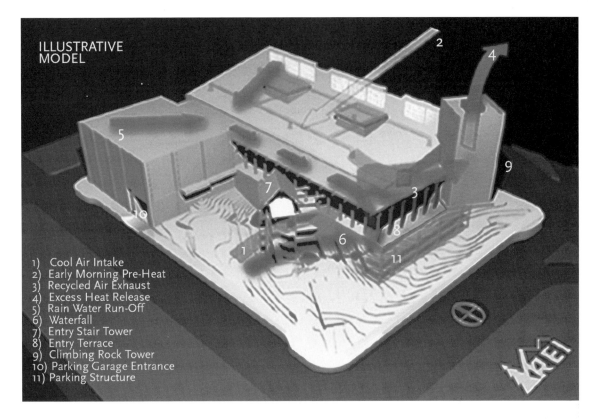

ILLUSTRATIVE
MODEL

1) Cool Air Intake
2) Early Morning Pre-Heat
3) Recycled Air Exhaust
4) Excess Heat Release
5) Rain Water Run-Off
6) Waterfall
7) Entry Stair Tower
8) Entry Terrace
9) Climbing Rock Tower
10) Parking Garage Entrance
11) Parking Structure

required for the duct system reduces the amount of usable area for a tenant. This is of particular importance in multistory projects served by a package unit.

Central systems

Central systems operate through the piping of a cooling medium to remote equipment for the distribution of conditioned air. The heat exchange for central systems is typically based on the mechanical exchange of heat through chillers, or by the exchange of heat by evaporation through cooling towers. Central systems are well suited for projects of multiple stories, where the cooling medium can be circulated in relatively small pipes to localized air-handling units, thereby minimizing space requirements for distribution.

Air distribution systems

Air distribution systems comprise five types: single-zone, multizone, variable air volume (VAV), dual duct, and induction.

Single-zone system

A single-zone system supplies air at one temperature to the distribution system, which may encompass the entire building or a portion of it. This system is typically used in simple applications such as single-family residences and small tenant shops. The initial cost is relatively low.

Multizone system

In a multizone system, a multiple duct distribution system is used to supply areas requiring more than one zone of

▲ REI Illustrative Model, REI Seattle, includes a 5° off-optimum temperature spread to reduce energy use, and 5 percent of store volume (wall and reception) is not directly cooled or heated. A stack effect is used for cooling adjacent retail waste air at the climbing wall. The design also incorporates passive solar preheating and solar control. (Image: Mithun Architects.)

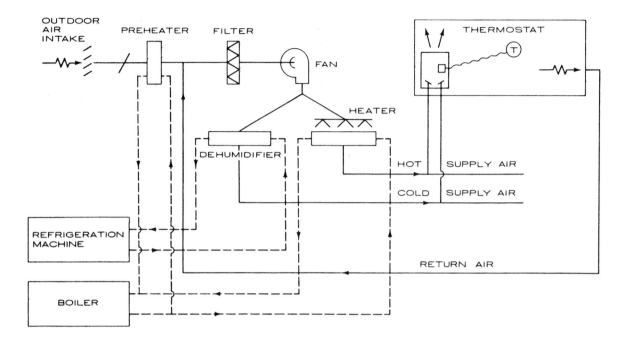

▲ Dual-duct system. The air-handling unit has a hot deck and a cold deck to produce the hot supply air and the cold supply air, which will be distributed to a mixing box located in the space via dual duct systems. The mixing box controlled by room thermostat supplies air of the proper temperature to the room to maintain the set point. (Illustration: Joseph R. Loring & Associates, Inc.).

control. The supply duct to each zone may be either a single or a dual duct. If the supply is a single duct, the duct is split just before reaching the distribution terminal. One branch has a heating coil and the other a cooling coil. Dampers control the incoming air pressure. The initial cost and energy usage are relatively high.

Variable air volume (VAV) system

A VAV system uses a single duct distribution system to supply conditioned air at a constant temperature to multiple points of distribution. Each distribution point has a VAV control box, which regulates the volume of air entering the area served, thereby allowing individual temperature control. This system is typically used in multitenant projects of one or two stories. The initial cost and energy usage are relatively low.

Dual duct system

A dual duct system uses two supply ducts, one for heated air and the other for cooled air. At each distribution point, temperature-controlled dampers mix the air to the desired temperature. The initial cost and energy usage are relatively high.

Induction system

An induction system uses forced air that is thermostatically controlled to temper its flow by heating or cooling the interior air.

Hydronic distribution systems

Hydronic systems use water as a supply medium, routed from the central heat exchange element to remote distribution terminals. These systems are more suited to larger area distribution, as compared with air systems. Hydronic systems may serve either single or multiple zones. They range from one-pipe to four-pipe systems.

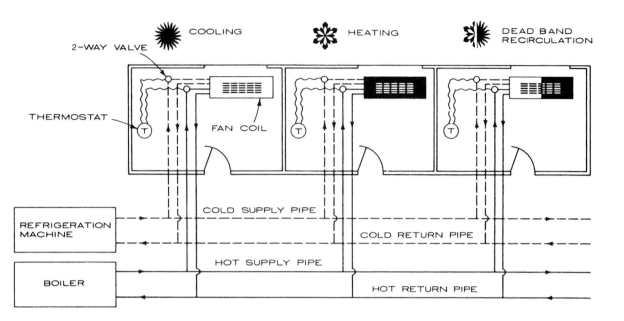

One-pipe

In one-pipe systems, distribution terminals have supply and return lines teed off the main supply line. The connection of the terminals may be in parallel or in series.

Two-pipe

In two-pipe systems, distribution terminals are supplied by a single-temperature supply line. Water circulates through the terminal and is returned by a separate return line.

Three-pipe

In thee-pipe systems, two separate pipes supply heated and cooled water, which are mixed just prior to entering the distribution terminal. The water that circulates through the terminal is returned in a common return pipe.

Four-pipe

In four-pipe systems, two separate pipes supply heated and cooler water. One supply is allowed to circulate through the terminal. Two pipes are provided for return.

Control Systems

HVAC systems are commonly designed with control systems to allow for centralized and energy-efficient operations. The control system monitors the variable being controlled, such as air temperature, and determines if the variable is at the desired level, or if a change is required. If a change is necessary, a signal is sent to the element, such as a valve or other regulator, which implements the change.

Tenant Mechanical Systems

Individual tenants in retail projects typically have a connection point—provided by the owner within their area—which

▲ Four-pipe fan coil unit system. Fan coil units are provided with chilled water or hot water from the respective loops via closing or opening the two-way control valves in the runoffs. In the dead band of the thermostat, both valves will be off and the unit will be running in the recirculation mode. (Illustration: Joseph R. Loring & Associates, Inc.)

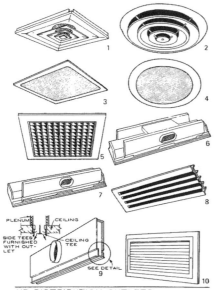

AIR DISTRIBUTION OUTLETS

KEY

1 RECTANGULAR LOUVERED FACE DIF-FUSER: Available in 1, 2, 3, or 4-way pattern, steel or aluminum. Flanged overlap frame or inserted in 2 X 2 ft or 2 X 4 ft baked enamel steel panel to fit tile modules of lay-in ceilings. Supply or return.

2 ROUND LOUVERED FACE DIFFUSER: Normal 360° air pattern with blank-off plate for other air patterns. Surface mounting for all type ceilings. Normally of steel with baked enamel finish. Supply or return.

3 RECTANGULAR PERFORATED FACE DIF-FUSER: Available in 1, 2, 3, or 4-way pattern, steel or aluminum. Flanged overlap frame or 2 X 2 ft and 2 X 4 ft for replacing tile of lay-in ceiling can be used for supply or return air.

4 ROUND PERFORATED FACE DIFFUSER: Normal 360° air pattern with blank-off plate for other air patterns. Steel or aluminum. Flanged overlap frame for all type ceilings. Can be used for supply or return air.

5 LATTICE TYPE RETURN: All aluminum square grid type return grille for ceiling installation with flanged overlap frame or of correct size to replace tile.

6 SADDLE TYPE LUMINAIRE AIR BOOT: Provides air supply from both sides of standard size luminaires. Maximum air delivery (total both sides) approximately 150 to 170 cfm for 4 ft long luminaire.

7 SINGLE SIDE TYPE LUMINAIRE AIR BOOT: Provides air supply from one side of standard size luminaires. Maximum air delivery approximately 75 cfm for 4 ft long luminaire.

8 LINEAR DIFFUSER: Extruded aluminum, anodized, duranodic, or special finishes, one way or opposite direction or vertical down air pattern. Any length with one to eight slots. Can be used for supply or return and for ceiling, sidewall, or cabinet top application.

9 INTEGRATED PLENUM TYPE OUTLET FOR "T" BAR CEILINGS: Slot type outlet, one way or two way opposite direction air pattern. Available in 24, 36, 48, and 60 in. lengths. Replaces or integrates with "T" bar. Approximately 150 to 175 cfm for 4 ft long, two-slot unit.

10 SIDEWALL OR DUCT MOUNTED REGISTER: Steel or aluminum for supply or return. Adjustable horizontal and vertical deflection. Plaster frame available. Suitable for long throw and high air volume.

▲ *Types of air-distribution outlets. (Illustration: KMA Architecture and Engineering, San Diego.)*

allows access to the project HVAC system. The distribution within the tenant area is typically the tenants' responsibility as a part of their tenant fit-out.

Distribution of heated or cooled air is typically accomplished by a network of metal ducts suspended from the structure above. The size, shape, length, and number of bends in a duct impact the efficiency of airflow. The more efficient the airflow, the less energy required to circulate the air. Round ducts are the most efficient transmitters of air, providing minimal flow resistance and allowing for well-sealed joints. Flat, oval, and rectangular ducts are not as efficient. Care should be taken to minimize bends in any ductwork. Where bends are required, a curved connection is more efficient than an angular one.

In terms of thermal comfort, the primary factors are the quantity of air being moved, the velocity at which it travels, and the perception of draft. The essential component in controlling thermal comfort is the air distribution outlet, or diffuser, which controls the final distribution of conditioned air into a space. The proper selection and placement of the air diffusers is the most critical design consideration in HVAC layout within a tenant space.

In addition to providing for the supply of conditioned air, allowances must be made for return air. Return air is air that is recirculated back to the HVAC equipment source for reuse to minimize energy consumption. Return air is handled by a plenum, using the space above the tenant ceiling, or by a ducted return. The type of construction and the building code requirements determine the type of return system required.

As a part of tenant review in multi-tenant projects, owners often require tenants to complete a form to describe the anticipated design loads for the HVAC system. This allows the owner to monitor the total requirements for any given HVAC zone and ensure adequate capacity for all tenants served within that zone.

PLUMBING SYSTEMS

Plumbing systems generally include water supply, sanitary sewer, fire sprinkler, and natural gas systems.

Water

In multilevel projects, the landlord typically provides a source of water supply to each individual tenant space. Tenants are generally responsible for constructing their own restrooms and other desired facilities. Normal retail tenants may have the water included within their base rent. Large users of water, such as restaurants and hair salons, generally have their own individual water meters and pay the utility company directly.

Sanitary Sewer

A sanitary sewer line is normally provided below each tenant space so that tenants can connect their restrooms and other facilities to the line. In many instances, such as in multilevel projects, the landlord also provides an exhaust loop for restroom ventilation that the tenant can access.

Fire Sprinklers

The need for fire sprinklers is determined by the size of the project, the types of occupancies included, the number of stories, and the type of construction.

Natural Gas

Gas is typically required only by food service tenants. Preplanning a project with the careful location of food service tenants minimizes the costs of gas distribution. Typically, each tenant has an individual gas meter and pays the utility company directly, as the amount of gas used varies significantly from tenant to tenant.

ELECTRICAL SYSTEMS

Electrical systems generally include power, telephone/cable, audiovisual, and security systems.

Power

In multitenant projects, an electrical conduit is provided from the electrical room to the tenant space. Tenants generally provide their own wire, have individual electric meters, and pay the utility company directly. In some instances, the tenant may pay the landlord if the landlord has a master meter, in which case a check meter is used to establish the tenant's actual usage. In the electrical rooms, space should be provided for additional meters to allow for subdivision of the original tenant spaces.

Telephone/Cable

The landlord typically provides a telephone panel where the main telephone service is located. A conduit is provided from the panel to each tenant space. Tenants have their own individual accounts with the telephone company and pay the utility directly.

Access to cable service is important to retailers who sell electronic goods, such as televisions, and to tenants who may use them in their premises, such as restaurants.

Audiovisual

With the increase in promotional activity, a project's audiovisual system serves as more than just a public address system. It is important to identify areas where promotions and other activities occur, so that localized sound systems can be used without undue impact on the other portions of the project. As a part of the system, theatrical lighting must also be included.

In many projects, the audio system is integrated with the life safety systems to allow for public announcements in an emergency. In such instances, the audio system must have backup power and may have to be accessible from the fire control panel or room, if such a facility exists in the project.

Security

There are many types of security systems; the degree of complexity and sophistication is generally determined by the client. Many vendors provide design services for their systems, and this is an option that may be considered. Depending on the type of system selected, the area requirements for the security room may vary significantly.

Security systems provided by the landlord generally address the safety and well-being of customers and protection of the physical premises. Security systems used by tenants tend to focus on merchandise control. The loss or theft of merchandise is commonly referred to as "shrinkage" in the retail industry.

Terrorism

Following the World Trade Center attack on September 11, 2001, terrorism became a more conscious concern worldwide. The placement of concrete barriers around buildings has become a common visible sign of this concern. As shopping centers and mixed-use projects are intended to be open, public places, the design of any security measures must be carefully considered so as not to create the appearance of an unwelcoming fortress.

Security measures are generally grouped in two broad categories: (1) physical barriers or protection and (2) operational measures. Generally all operating projects have some form of on-site security, and these systems should be reviewed in conjunction with any proposed or additional systems to promote an integrated program.

Planning for terrorism is made more difficult because the modes of terrorist attacks evolve over time; it is probably impossible to anticipate all forms of potential terrorism. Prior to September 11, probably few people were concerned about the use of commercial airline planes to attack targets. Unfortunately, it will only be through future occurrences that other potential forms of terrorism will become known.

CHAPTER 9

THE FUTURE OF RETAIL

Previous chapters show how placemaking and experience design have transformed the planning and design of retail, entertainment, and mixed-use space. The following is a look into the future.

TRENDS

Although new approaches to retail space can set trends and influence culture, retail design must also *respond* to social, political, and cultural forces. The following issues will affect the way designers create retail space over the next ten years:

- New technologies will further integrate shopping and entertainment as an aspect of daily life.

- The convergence of the information age, shifting patterns of global economics, and the dominance of American culture (and American brands) abroad will require retail designers to reconcile competing ideas—the small and the big, the American and the multicultural, the new and the old, and the local and the global.

- The challenges that face our earth—global warming, population increases, the depletion of natural resources—will call for more authentic, more communal, and more sustainable approaches to retail and mixed-use space.

These issues are explored from six viewpoints:

1. The shopper and the technological advances that will impact the shopping experience of the future

2. The store and new approaches that are changing the way retailers market and brand

3. The transition of the mall to projects with a greater mix of uses

4. The shift from suburban to urban retail space

5. The role of shopping as a global entertainment and tourist activity

6. The Internet, once a threat to "bricks and mortar" retailing, but now an inspiration

THE SHOPPER

To understand the future experience of the shopper, it is important to answer two questions: Who are the shoppers? and What do they need and want?

◀ Many retailers, such as Sur la Table, are providing enriching in-store experiences that enhance customers' purchases.

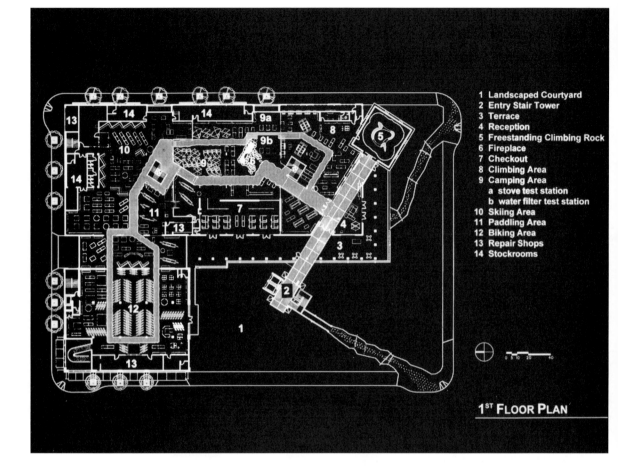

1 Landscaped Courtyard
2 Entry Stair Tower
3 Terrace
4 Reception
5 Freestanding Climbing Rock
6 Fireplace
7 Checkout
8 Climbing Area
9 Camping Area
  a stove test station
  b water filter test station
10 Skiing Area
11 Paddling Area
12 Biking Area
13 Repair Shops
14 Stockrooms

1ST FLOOR PLAN

From Need to Want

Not long ago, retailers realized that most Western consumers had one — sometimes two — of everything they needed. They recognized that a culture of *need* had been replaced by a culture of *want.*

Retailers responded by creating unique and entertaining experiences in addition to their products. It is not enough that stores serve as well-decorated warehouses filled with goods; they must invite consumers into their domains. Increasingly, retail environments must create destina-

tions with enriching experiences that accompany purchases.

The retail industry has been "responding to a customer who is looking for pleasure, escape, and relief, by offering the shopper goods and services oriented around quality experiences and choreographed environments."[1] Shoppers now go to their local electronics store to listen to CDs, watch DVDs, or order a surround-sound system. Niketown, REI, Tower Records, Apple, and other savvy retailers have added listening stations, ski

[1]"Making Mixed-Use Work," *Shopping Center Business,* August 2001, 62–67.

◀ ◀◀ REI Seattle, Seattle, Washington, includes many in-store, nonshopping amenities, such as a climbing rock, a bike test trail, and a 250-person auditorium. (Plan: Mithun. Photo: Robert Pisano.)

slopes, and other forms of retail theater to their stores.

In the future, expect to see the following:

- Changeable interiors, virtual product displays, new technology incorporating film, video, and other new media
- New distribution methods that free stores from large product displays, allowing them to become branded experiences

- Sophisticated product delivery systems requiring stores to deliver purchases, perhaps to neighborhood delivery centers, so people will not have to wait at home

User-centered Design

Retailers are developing ever more user-centered design and service-oriented approaches. Mass personalization is one of the preeminent concepts driving retailing. As retailers experiment with the concept of creating a unique experience for the shopper, they need to develop new tools to allow them to know the customer better.

Targeting Consumers

New developments in market research capabilities have allowed retailers to cater to very specific market segments. Saks Fifth Avenue, New York, has turned the entire ninth floor into Salon Z for plus-size women. J. Jill and Chico's cater to style-conscious baby boomers and beyond. To appeal to the young careerist, Ann Taylor Loft offers lower price points than Ann Taylor. Too, Inc., of The Limited, is offering Mishmash products for teens in 2,000 sq ft stores located in large shopping centers.

In the future, two demographic groups—baby boomers and ethnic

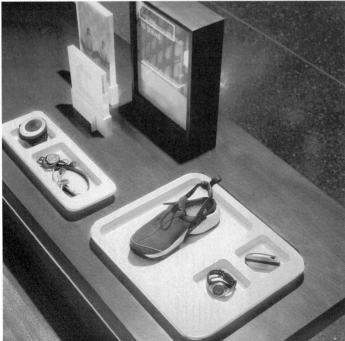

◀◀ ◀ ▲ *Lifestyle retailer Nike has created a new line of stores, Nike Goddess, specifically for women. (Photos courtesy Callison.)*

groups, especially Hispanics—will present significant opportunities for retailers.

Baby boomers

Baby boomers, aged 47–55, number 78 million and account for one-third of the U.S. population. "People over 55 are less interested in spending more time shopping than younger customers," says Candace Corlett, a principal at WSL Strategic Retail who manages the company's 50 plus marketing directions division. "It's not that they don't have the money. They have the money, but the retailing environment is not necessarily attractive to them."[2]

Over-50 consumers "have special needs," says Mark Artus, a partner at Retail Planning Associates (RPA), Columbus, Ohio. "Your vision changes, your size changes and to have retailers subtly acknowledge that—usually changes that are made to make things easier doors to open and movement of people—are just as much appreciated by younger consumers as they are by older consumers."[3]

Watch for more retailers to target the baby boomer market as Coldwater Creek has done. Coldwater Creek's store design focuses on comfort. "We use soft wood accents, slate flooring and ambient lighting. There is Native American flute music playing in the store. We have a floor-to-ceiling waterfall in each of the stores."[4]

Hispanics

Hispanics, now the fastest growing population in America, represent another powerful market segment. The number of Hispanics has increased by 58 percent to 35.5 million people since 1990; the Hispanic population is projected to increase from 12.5 percent of the U.S. population today to 21 percent by 2020.

The Hispanic market is an urban market; 80 percent of the Hispanic population resides in major urban areas like Los Angeles, New York, and Miami. As a result, successful retail environments for Hispanics are inspired by urban (not suburban) shopping patterns.

Jose Moreno, director of marketing and public affairs for San Diego's Cable Group, suggests that stores tailor their environments to appeal to Hispanic customers. For example, Plaza Fiesta in Atlanta features bold and bright colors, a large stone fountain, and rows of bodegas and stalls imitating Latin American architecture, accompanied by lively ethnic music.[5]

Tracking Behavior

Powerful data mining techniques and other technologies are transforming what retailers know about consumer preferences, thereby enabling retailers and retail designers to constantly change environments to suit unique customer needs.

Retailers are using point-of-sale data captured through bar codes and other encrypted data to inform the design and layout of stores, in effect creating custom offers and micro-targeted buying propositions.

Shopping centers that depend heavily on electronic-generated retailing, such as the new Cybercentre in Hong Kong, have

---

[2] Rachel Carlton, "Are Retailers Overlooking Baby Boomers and Their Wallets?" *Display & Design Ideas,* August 2001.

[3] Ibid.

[4] Ibid.

[5] Ibid.

spawned a form of electronic infrastructure requiring high-speed modems and extensive fiber-optic hookups.

As people become more protective of their time, shoppers grow impatient at long checkout lines. Hand-held scanners allow customers to keep track of how much they are spending, and self-scanning stations at a checkout can help them get on their way faster.

Privacy

Technologies that help track shopping behavior more effectively, however, risk encroaching on consumers' privacy.

Minority Report, a film set in the year 2054, depicted a future of marketing techniques run amok. As Nathan Bierma describes it in the *Chicago Tribune,* "Every billboard knows your name and holograms bark out personalized com-

▲ Cybercentre, the commercial and cultural town center for Hong Kong's Cyberport technology community, offers the latest in technological retailing advances, including connectivity to customers' PDAs and mobile phones to communicate new product information or sales. (Image: Jerde.)

mercials. When star Tom Cruise, for instance, enters a Gap store (still in business!), computers identify him through an eye scan, triggering a holographic saleswoman whose job it is to recite his recent purchases and suggest new ones."[6]

"This is the not-too-distant future. This is imminent," says Peter Schwartz, chairman of the Global Business Network, a futurist consulting firm. "We should be more concerned about the ability of retailers to deal in private information, as well as the ability of the government."[7]

As retailers and designers explore the powers of personalized design, branding, and marketing techniques, they will have to be increasingly aware of issues related to privacy.

THE STORE

Often, stores are where changes in demographics, technology, and culture meet, and the encounters are not always smooth. Why are stores a battleground? Because stores are where companies are at their most competitive.

Branded Environments

Many marketers believe that the most influential medium for branding is the store, where the customer makes the final decision to purchase a product. The store is also the medium that provides the most intimate and, many believe, the most emotional contact with the consumer.

Retailers are realizing that new approaches to in-store branding will help

differentiate their products. This is the battleground of extremes—where big stores compete with tiny boutiques, high art meets mass marketing, and retail space morphs into public space.

The following examples have created a "buzz" that foretells what is to come.

The lifestyle emporium

The department store of old was reborn in the 1990s as the lifestyle emporium, mixing products with experience in a unique environment. An example is the DKNY store that opened in New York in 1999. *Vogue* magazine noted, "This is what you would expect to find inside: clothes, shoes, accessories. This is what you will find, depending on the day and the trends: clothes, shoes, accessories, carrot juice, a book on Dutch design, an iMac, the latest CDs, make-your-own CDs, vintage clothes, hot-off-the-runway clothes, a sheer camisole, a see-through radio, pink candles, pink comforters, a morning yoga class, an evening reading, a Sony PlayStation, hooked up and ready to play. Donna Karan has translated 'synergy' into a shopping experience. Within four walls she's captured the wired, worldly, quirky, curious, multitasking, multimedia mindset that reflects real life right now."[8]

The flagship

In Times Square, Toys "R" Us set out to create a destination flagship store, as fabulous as the historic FAO Schwarz, that would help rebuild its brand. Billed as a

▶ The new Toys "R" Us flagship store in Times Square, New York City, which CEO John Eyler calls "the ultimate statement of our brand," includes a 60 ft tall Ferris wheel in the three-story atrium, with each car modeled on a different toy. (Photo courtesy Toys "R" Us.)

[6] Nathan Bierma, "Some Marketing Techniques Depicted in the Futuristic 'Minority Report' Seem Close at Hand, Raising New Issues of Privacy," *Chicago Tribune,* 27 June 2002.

[7] Ibid.

[8] "The Manhattan Project," *Vogue,* August 1999, 97–100.

[9] Nanette Byrnes and Christopher Palmeri, "Toys 'R' Us: A Showstopper on Broadway," *Business Week,* 24 December 2001, 54.

▲ ▶ Helmut Lang
Parfumerie, New York City,
art installation by Jenny
Holzer. (© 2002 Helmut
Lang.)

"multimillion-dollar bricks-and-mortar advertisement,"[9] the 110,000 sq ft store includes a three-story Ferris wheel and a 20 ft T. Rex. "This store will surely become a destination icon that everyone—New Yorkers and tourists alike—will surely enjoy for years to come," said CEO John Eyler.[10]

Merging experience design with media, he says, the Toys "R" Us flagship store includes feature shops to promote hot products, such as the Cabbage

Patch kids nursery, "where a 'nurse' arranges doll adoptions."[11]

Overwhelm
Some of the splashiest, brand-rich stores have been "money-draining ventures."[12] It is therefore not surprising that not everyone is enthusiastic about using the store as a brand message.

"The truth is that you can paint the sides of cows with ads if you want, but that doesn't mean you have an effective

[10] Mary Davis, "Toys 'R' Us Flagship Store Opens in New York," *Fashion Windows,* 14 November 2001.

[11] Regina Raiford, "Playhouse of the Western World," *buildings.com* (May 2002).

[12] Nanette Byrnes and Christopher Palmeri, "Toys 'R' Us: A Showstopper on Broadway," *Business Week,* 24 December 2001.

medium. It means you have a glut of worthless ad space," says Rob Frankel, branding consultant and author of *The Revenge of Brand X: How to Build a Big Time Brand—on the Web or Anywhere Else.*[13]

According to Frankel, in-store branding techniques overwhelm the consumer. "The only contribution these new media produce is ad clutter, which actually serves to reduce ad effectiveness. The average person is subjected to at least 3,000

[13] Rob Frankel, *The Revenge of Brand X: How to Build a Big Time Brand—on the Web or Anywhere Else* (Frankel & Anderson, Inc., 2000).

ad messages a day, which means the clutter is blurring ad messages into electronic wallpaper that nobody notices." [14]

Retailers are starting to agree. Puma's first retail store in Santa Monica, California, is "mostly minimalist in size and style, markedly contrasting to the uber-mall, sporting glut à la Niketown. With its squeaky-clean, spare, white walls, comparatively limited space of 3,000 square feet, and chromed-out exterior, the spot plays hip-nerd flunky to Nike's frat-boy brotherhood." [15]

The underground boutique

At Selvedge, a Levi's-owned boutique in New York City, art and cutting-edge fashion merge. With graffiti-inspired paintings on its walls and hard-to-find Levi's Vintage and Red collections on its racks, the boutique offers an antidote to the ubiquitous chain store environments. Levi's, one of America's oldest brands, is modeling its approach after innovative smaller boutique stores in Los Angeles. Shoppers looking for a respite from chain stores and the mall, which are more generic, come to stores like this to find it.

The cultural arena

As fashion, retail, and architecture merge, "architectural projects and their designers can now be seen as retail exhibits in themselves; part of the panoply of frocks, perfumes, luggage, artworks and drink that makes up the all-embracing landscape of designer consumables." [16] By incorporating quality design, and famous architects, into their identities, these retailers are using design, and designers, to differentiate their brands in the marketplace.

"Don't call it shopping or (God forbid) brand positioning," says Salon.com, "call it art." [17] "Prada," Salon.com goes on to explain, "has hired Rem Koolhaas, the renowned experimental architect, to design three new shops in San Francisco, New York, and Los Angeles. Mandarin Duck has opened a shop-cum-theme park in Paris, designed by Dutch collective Droog. Helmut Lang hired conceptual artist Jenny Holzer to jazz up its new Parfumerie. Issey Miyake's got Frank Gehry; Marni's got Future Systems. And the Apartment, a new furniture and clothing store in Soho, has turned its shop into actual performance art." [18]

Scaling down

Big box retailers, such as Wal-Mart, Home Depot, and Best Buy, are revising their traditional formats to expand into urban locations. *BusinessWeek* suggests that the strategy is driven by "real-estate constraints and demographics, but also driven by the sense that although shoppers love mega-stores' huge selection and low prices, they're tired of spending Saturday afternoons trudging through stores the size of airplane hangars." [19]

Wisconsin-based retailer Kohl's is one of "retailing's few stars, occupying a

---

[14] Rob Frankel, *The Revenge of Brand X: How to Build a Big Time Brand—on the Web or Anywhere Else* (Frankel & Anderson, Inc., 2000).

[15] "The Cat's Out of the Bag," *Detour*, February 1999, 42.

[16] Martin Pawley, "Retailers Move into the Cultural Arena," *Architectural Review* (February 2000).

[17] "Retail Redesign," *Salon.com* (25 June 2001).

[18] Ibid.

[19] "Don't Tell Kohl's There's a Slowdown," *Business Week,* 12 February 2001, 62.

niche between mall department stores such as Penney and Sears, and discounters like Wal-Mart and Target," explains *Business Week.* "Their brand was built on a simple premise: offer easy-to-navigate stores in accessible locations to time-strapped middle-class families. Kohl's focus is on crowd-pleasing items, minimizing the need to vary the product mix from region to region.[20]

Outside observers expect retailers to "face a learning curve in adapting the big-box formula to smaller spaces," but early signs are that shoppers prefer convenience to endless selection.[21]

THE MALL/MIXED-USE PROJECT

The typical shopping mall has undergone a transformation, opening the door for new mixed-use environments that integrate retail, entertainment, and "everyday" uses like grocery stores, post offices, libraries, and even schools. Caused in part by a reaction to the new consumer preferences for convenience retailing, the evolution of the mall also represents a move away from large, thematic environments toward smaller-scaled, everyday environments.

Retrofitting Existing Malls

Many developers are constructing mixed-use environments out of existing shopping malls. Regional malls, which performed well through the late 1980s, are no longer vibrant centers of suburban commerce and offer a tremendous opportunity for integration of new uses.

An example of such innovation can be found in Orange County, California, where the Planning Center in Costa Mesa discovered more than 700 obsolete malls, nearly a third of them "performing so poorly that they were destined to fall short of generating the funds needed for the most routine maintenance."[22] The Planning Center's solution: "Convert those strip centers into little villages where homes would be nestled among the stores, with parking stacked above, so those vast, unattractive paved lots could be put to much better use, maybe even as pocket parks."[23]

The Center has drafted conversions for a couple of sites. At the Target Center on Tustin Avenue in Orange, for example, it "transformed a sprawling, asphalt-dominated mixed bag with some homes scattered nearby into a sort of nontraditional town center with trees, parks and homes. In downtown Long Beach [California], a developer is building 350 residential lofts and apartments around parking garages and above shops that will replace the failed Long Beach Plaza mall."[24]

A revitalization of America's Main Street is driving the construction of many new mixed-use projects. Streets like Ventura Boulevard in Los Angeles's San Fernando Valley have grown naturally over time to become rich environments where local stores provide unique products and services to nearby residents. This successful model of retailing — a

---

[20] "Don't Tell Kohl's There's a Slowdown," *Business Week,* 12 February 2001, 62.

[21] "Honey, I Shrunk the Store," *Newsweek,* 3 June 2002, 36–37.

[22] Fran Halper, "Turning Old Strip Malls into Housing, Development," *Los Angeles Times,* 17 June 2001.

[23] Ibid.

[24] Ibid.

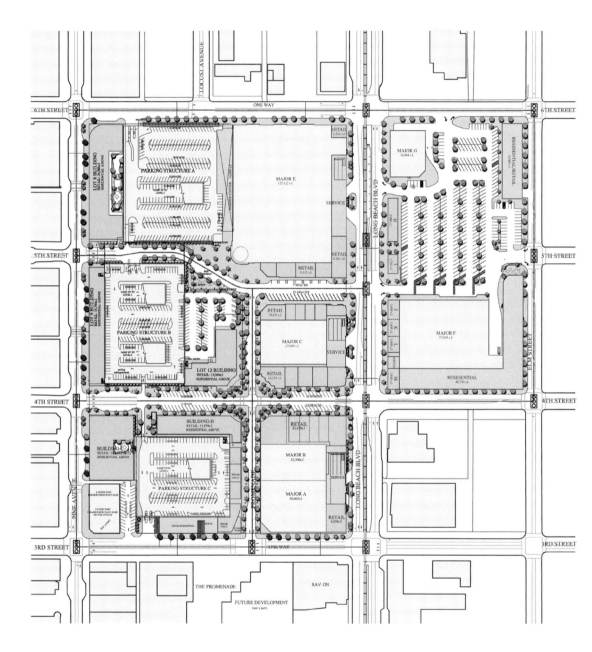

◀◀ ▲   CityPlace in Long Beach, California, was
planned by Jerde to reconnect the site of the
former Long Beach Plaza to the city's grid, opening
two streets to auto and pedestrian traffic. The
project, which was designed by Kaplan McLaughlin
Diaz, also created an urban format for Wal-Mart,
which included an art-deco facade wrapped with
smaller retailers. (Plan: KMD. Photos: Jerde).

version of the "everyday" approach—will be an inspiration for designers in the future to *design* this organic process.

Lifestyle Centers

Lifestyle centers, which create smaller, more consumer-friendly urban villages, are quickly evolving into the most viable form of the new mall. Usually built in upscale areas, they mix cachet with curb appeal. "Part main street, part fifth avenue, they combine the 'homeyness' and community of an old-time village square with the cachet of fashionable urban stores."[25]

The New Urbanist approach to town planning has been influential in the creation of this new typology. Predicting that people, tired of long commutes and impersonal surroundings, would want to return to neighborhoods, New Urbanists have created zoning guidelines for a more traditional type of living, with tree-lined streets, grocery stores, and dry cleaning services people can walk to.

THE CITY AND THE SUBURB

The transformation of the mall signals a larger cultural force, the transformation of the suburb. After nearly a half century of suburban expansion, Americans have returned to the urban. Over the last 10 years, shopping has been used as a foundation for the reinvention of urban public space in cities in America and around the world. Cities will continue to be areas for powerful retailing concepts in the future and a powerful influence on how to transform the suburbs.

Suburbs have the opportunity to develop into new economic hubs for their regions. "Older suburbs across the country are reinventing themselves as full-fledged cities and showing that they don't just rot away as new communities spring up," said Samuel Staley, project director of Older Suburbs.[26] Older suburban areas may be replacing inner cities as the melting pots of American society.

Patterns of Use

As suburbs become more urban, designers will have to offer solutions to meet the new needs of the suburban/urban consumer. The New Urbanist approach, which offers certain desirable urban characteristics like density, foot traffic, and ample public space, will likely be a good start in recreating the atmosphere of some of America's best urban neighborhoods, but may ultimately prove to be too controlled, too pristine.

The magic of the city comes from its spontaneity, its grittiness, and other characteristics that are difficult to design. In the future, retail designers will have to create successful, and *authentic,* retail and entertainment approaches for suburban town centers that are as diverse as the evolving American suburb.

THE GLOBE

Many things separate the cultures of our world, but shopping is not one of them. In fact, it can be argued that a love of shopping binds people across the globe together into one consumer culture.

Shopping as Tourism

Shopping has become a tourist activity. A recent study showed that shopping was

---

[25] "The Mall, without the Haul," *Wall Street Journal,* 25 July 2001.
[26] *Planetizen.com* (26 October 2001).

the second most popular activity for U.S. leisure travelers in foreign countries in 1997.[27] And, according to a *New York Times* article, shopping is a cause, not an effect, of the decision to travel.[28]

Consequently, retailers will increasingly create spaces for consumers *and* tourists. The Mall of America, which "attracts 43 million visitors each year, more than a third of them tourists,"[29] markets directly to the tourist consumer. The Mall of America has even developed vacation packages that include bargain airfares and hotel accommodations within walking distance.

Retail Penetration

Retail space will continue to penetrate tourist infrastructure like airports and museums. Already spreading through the world's airports is the "airport-as-mall" concept. Taking advantage of a "captive audience, caught between security checkpoint and departure, airport shops have been raking in spectacular returns," says Peter Behnke of the Airports Council International, the trade group for international airport authorities.[30]

Global Economy/Local Culture

Some Western retailing strategies adopted by overseas developers—large shopping malls, primarily—do damage by erasing local shopping patterns. As a result, for many people the existence of a shopping mall overseas indicates that American lifestyle has overpowered local culture. But the reality is that some foreign shopping malls do retain a local vernacular— an old-world flavor—lacking in most American versions.

El Salvador's Centro Comercial, for example, resembled a "second-string 1970s atrium in a midsize American suburb, with silly foundations, too many reflective surfaces and harsh fluorescent lighting," says Daisann McLane.[31] But at the entrance the similarity ends: "A white-lace-clad Baiana was ladling vatapa sauce into yummy fried balls of acaraje, Salvador's most famous snack. Inside, on a stage, a troupe of exercise instructors were kicking and jumping and gyrating to samba music, promoting a new gym. In little kiosks along the main arcade, members of different bands in Salvador's upcoming carnival were taking subscriptions."[32]

"In the United States," she goes on to say, "malls may symbolize all that is plastic and soulless about shopping, and the death of cities. But in less-developed countries, where they're almost always in cities, malls are places where tradition and modernity, local and global, mingle and morph."[33]

"Bazaar Culture" in America

In the future, some of this energy may find its way back to America, giving rise to a new global model for retail space and retail experience.

---

[27] "What to Do Abroad?" *Los Angeles Times,* 8 November 1998. (Statistics on tourism industries from the United States Commerce Department.)

[28] Ruth LaFerla, "Travel to Exotic Places and Buy, Buy, Buy," *New York Times,* 12 August 2001.

[29] Ibid.

[30] "The Airport Wants You to Shop Till You Drop," *New York Times,* 8 July 2001.

[31] Daisann McLane, "I Shop, and the World is a Better Place," *New York Times,* 30 April 2000.

[32] Ibid.

[33] Ibid.

The Los Angeles fashion district, for instance, is a place that "has more in common with 12th-century Baghdad than the California of the new millennium."[34] Described as an "80-block jumble of prewar commercial buildings, hastily constructed low-rise arcades commingled with a few modern towers," the fashion district is home to "5,000 companies employing 50,000 people and taking in $8 billion a year in wholesale and retail sales." Here you'll find immigrants realizing the American dream, building "successful businesses and new lives in an environment not dissimilar to those found in many developing countries."[35]

"What we have here is a souk," says one of the major property owners in the district. "It's open to everyone, and it's the kind of place you can go to buy something for $3 or $300." These immigrants have introduced into America the bazaar culture of their native lands. Their "love of bargaining, jostling and quick, seat-of-the-pants decision making" makes for a very unique place—the region's melting pot, and an indication of what all of Los Angeles may look like 100 years from now.[36]

THE INTERNET

As shopping connects us together, so does the Internet, which was considered the future of retailing before websites began to crash and burn. Despite the lower prices and convenience offered by the Internet, consumers are still motivated to venture outside their homes for most purchases. What is the state of virtual shopping today?

Complementary, not Competitive

The Internet's important role in shopping is illustrated by the numbers of purchases made in physical stores that were first researched and initiated on the Web. According to a recent study by Jupiter Communications, by 2005 U.S. on-line consumers will spend more than $632 billion in off-line channels as a result of research they conduct on the Internet.[37] This suggests that the Internet has a complementary, rather than a competitive role to play in bricks-and-mortar retailing.

Perhaps a more interesting version of global connectivity is the "outernet." Many of us go onto the Internet each day, but according to *Business 2.0,* "300 million transactions…occur at point-of-sale locations such as ballpark beer stands and grocery checkout counters."[38] Point-of-sale environments reach a far more diverse audience than does the Internet, and "almost everyone can be targeted by location, time of day or industry segment."[39]

Procter & Gamble has "installed two kiosks in Ohio malls as part of the company's 'Innovation Location' program, which seeks to expose young consumers to new P&G products. The kiosks were used to promote goods that were still being test marketed or weren't slated for launch for 6 to 12 months."[40]

---

[34] "A Casbah for Clothes Is Bustling in Los Angeles," *New York Times,* 20 August 2000.
[35] Ibid.
[36] Ibid.
[37] "The Web Hasn't Replaced the Storefront Quite Yet," *New York Times,* 3 October 1999.
[38] *Business 2.0* (26 June 2001).
[39] Ibid.
[40] Ibid.

Creating Community

In the end, what retail designers may learn from the Internet is something about the power of community. In *The Perfect Store: Inside eBay,* Adam Cohen describes eBay as "easily the most interesting story of the early Internet age, and one of the most important business stories of our time." [41] Just as impressive as eBay's financial success, Cohen argues, is its idealistic mission: to operate as "a perfect marketplace where all buyers are given an equal opportunity at purchasing power and where they can find a true sense of community." [42]

New approaches to retail space can set trends and influence culture. In the future, if designers focus on creating community with shopping environments, as this book proposes, then this "true sense of community" will be available off-line, in the retail spaces that populate our towns, suburbs, and cities.

---

[41] Adam Cohen, *The Perfect Store: Inside eBay* (Little, Brown & Company, 2002).
[42] Ibid.

GLOSSARY

Accent lighting Directional lighting to emphasize a particular object or draw attention to a part of the field of view.

Accessibility The ease or difficulty with which the customer reaches a given store by automobile, public transportation, or walking.

Accessories (1) Items used to complete a fashion look, such as handbags, scarves, jewelry, hats, gloves, and shoes. (2) In general, any subordinate item that adds to the usefulness or attractiveness of a principal item, such as camera lenses or automobile mud flaps.

Adaptation The process by which the retina of the eye becomes accustomed to more or less light than it was exposed to during an immediately preceding period. It results in a change in the sensitivity of the eye to light.

Add-on purchasing Extending the initial shopping intent with add-on items encouraged by visual presentation.

Aesthetic distance The entry and passage to merchandise that becomes part of the shopper's experience.

Aisle table A table in a store aisle, between departments, used to feature special promotional values. It may be used for (1) clearance items sold at a reduced price or (2) new merchandise at a popular price.

Ambience The pervading mood or environment that characterizes a store, developed to create a store image and draw customers.

Anchors The retail outlets in a shopping center that have the largest amount of square footage and are fundamental to the center's positioning strategy.

Apparel An inclusive term for clothing or garments. Includes all categories of clothing from intimate apparel to outerwear for men, women, teens, and children.

Assortment The range of choice within a particular classification of goods, such as style, color, size, and price.

Attraction The pulling force exerted by a shopping center or business district, based on merchandise availability, price advantage, physical comforts, and convenience.

Back of the house Stockrooms and other non-selling areas.

Baffle A single opaque or translucent element to shield a light source from direct view at certain angles or to absorb unwanted light.

Ballasts dimmer Special ballasts, which, used together with a dimmer control, will vary the light output of a lamp.

Basic stock The assortment of merchandise, largely staples, that is maintained at all times. This merchandise has a highly predictable sales history, with consumer demand being stable over an extended period.

Sources: Rona Ostrow and Sweetman R. Smith, *The Dictionary of Retailing* (New York: Fairchild Publications, 1985); J. Thomas Russell and W. Ronald Lane, *Kleepner's Advertising Procedure,* 14th ed. (Englewood Cliffs, N.J.: Prentice Hall, 1999).

Beam angle The angle at which 50 percent of the center beam intensity is measured and/or occurs.

Big box store Store that sells merchandise in volume, in a large square or rectangular building, usually freestanding or in or close to a shopping center.

Big ticket item Any item of merchandise that carries a high price, such as refrigerators, garden tractors, furniture, etc.

Book inventory The retail value of the inventory, presumed to be correct until physical inventory is taken.

Boutique From the French, meaning "little shop." A boutique may be a small specialty store or an area within a larger store. Emphasis is on merchandise selected for a specific customer, presented in an attractive and unified manner, and accompanied by individual attention from the sales staff.

Brand A trade name or symbol that gives a product an identity, distinguishing it in the marketplace as the product of a particular manufacturer or distributor.

Brand image The symbolic associations that a particular brand possesses and the impressions these associations have on the customer.

Breadth of selection The offering of a variety of different merchandise lines in one store or shopping center.

Brown goods Radios, television sets, and other consumer electronics.

Buyer A merchandising executive responsible for selecting and purchasing merchandise and for selling it at a profit. Among the buyer's duties are the supervision of the assistant buyers and salespeople, planning advertising and displays, stock control and pricing, and budgeting.

Capital expenditures Expenditures of money, generally on what are termed fixed assets, i.e., tangibles such as land, buildings, equipment, fixtures, furniture, etc. A characteristic of capital expenditures is that their benefits often accrue in the future.

Carriage trade The wealthy patrons of a store or other business who are accorded special services. The term derives from the private carriages in which these patrons formerly arrived.

Cashwrap A counter that houses the cash register and wrapping facilities.

Category killers Stores with a market dominance in a certain merchandise category and an in-depth selection of branded goods and house brands.

Central business district A census term referring to the area of a city or town that contains a high concentration of retail businesses, offices, theaters, etc., and high traffic flow. It consists of one or more complete census tracks. In general, it is the original retailing center of business activity.

Chain stores A group of stores, usually a dozen or more, commonly owned and centrally merchandised and managed. In the United States the largest chains are grocery stores and automobile service stations. The term has also come to be applied to large mass-merchandising organizations (J.C. Penney, Sears), franchise chains (Burger King, McDonald's), and specialty chains (Lerner Shops).

Checkout In a self-service store, an area where customers bring purchases to be tallied. Stations are either cashier-manned with a register or electronic self-scanning stations.

Circulation plan A plan showing expected customer movement throughout the sales areas. It is the basis for the location of fixtures, displays, sales counters, cashwrap desks, and other facilities.

Cladding Material applied to the outside of a building or to an interior surface.

Classification The breaking down of merchandise into categories called classes, i.e., into groups of items similar in nature or in end use, without regard to style, size, color, price, etc. The purpose of classification is to provide a basic statistical structure to facilitate merchandise control.

Closed-back window A display window backed by a wall, thus forming an enclosed, self-contained display area and eliminating any distracting background.

Closed display Merchandise exhibited under counter glass or in a case.

Closed-loop layout An arrangement of fixtures and aisles that encourages a customer to move around the outer periphery of a store. Also known as a *race-track layout.*

Closeout An offering of selected discontinued goods by the vendor to the retailer at a reduced price. This merchandise has been discontinued because of slow sales, a broken assortment, overstock, the need to make space for a new season, etc. The savings are often passed along to the consumer as a closeout sale, used to generate increased store traffic.

Color rendering Colors of objects are partly determined by the light under which they are viewed. The way in which the light "reproduces" these colors is referred to as color rendering.

Color temperature The color appearance of various light sources, defined in terms of color temperature, measured in kelvin (K). The range is from 1500 for a candle to 9000 for a northlight blue sky.

Community center A shopping center that has a wider range of facilities for the sale of soft lines (apparel) and hard lines (hardware, appliances, etc.) than a neighborhood center. Community center tenants sometimes include off-price retailers. Anchors can include a supermarket, a junior department store, a variety store, a super drugstore, or a discount department store. The center is usually configured as a strip, in a straight line, or in an "L" or "U" shape.

Consolidated metropolitan statistical area (CMSA) A group of closely related primary metropolitan statistical areas forming a cluster, such as Dade and Broward Counties in Florida.

Consumer goods Goods produced for the customer at retail level that require no further processing. They may be grouped in one of three categories: (1) convenience items (cigarettes, magazines, etc.), (2) shopping items (clothing, cars, etc.), (3) specialty items (gourmet food, etc.).

Contemporary styling An apparel classification distinguished by sophisticated, updated, and fashion-conscious style.

Contrast The relationship between the brightness of an object and its immediate background.

Convenience goods Merchandise that is consumed daily and purchased frequently, such as food and drugs. Those items generally purchased by the customer in small quantities, with the minimum of shopping and at the most accessible retail outlet; daily necessities, such as food, toiletries, and small hardware items. Although usually branded merchandise, substitutes are seen as acceptable and even interchangeable.

Convenience goods shopping center A shopping area that usually contains 30,000–75,000 sq ft of gross area and occupies 4–8 acres of land. The principal tenants are typically a supermarket and a drugstore.

Convenience goods stores Food stores, eating and drinking places, drug and proprietary stores, and service establishments.

Convenience services A category that includes frequently used personal service facilities, such as barber shops, beauty shops, shoe repair shops, and dry cleaning shops.

Convenience store A grocery store, generally small, that carries a limited line of high-demand daily necessities, is open for extended hours, and generally charges higher prices than a supermarket.

Co-op funds Manufacturer monies that are earmarked for advertising or for in-store presentation.

Coordinates Apparel separates such as skirts, sweaters, blouses, jackets, and slacks, designed to mix and match harmoniously with regard to color and fabric content.

Cost (1) Any money expended to bring merchandise into the store, including wholesale price of merchandise, freight charges, etc. (2) The price a vendor charges a retailer for goods. (3) The amount spent on producing or manufacturing a commodity.

Counter A long table or cabinet top in a store used for the display and sale of goods, and in a restaurant for the serving and preparation of food.

Counter card A sign or poster placed on a counter to promote an article for sale at that location.

Couture A term taken from the French for "dressmaking," now widely applied to apparel that is both expensive and produced in limited quantities, often by designers of wide reputation.

Cross selling A store policy that enables salespersons to sell merchandise between and among departments.

Curtain wall A wall that "hangs" on a structural frame. In the store interior, it may be installed above the wall cases to give it a "built-in" effect.

Customer Any person who buys merchandise from a store or other marketer. The customer of a retail establishment is the ultimate consumer. The store itself, however, is the customer of all the vendors with whom it does business.

Dealer An individual or firm that handles merchandise without altering it, often at the wholesale level, but sometimes at retail, e.g., automobiles, appliances, etc.

Department store A large-scale retailing institution that sells a wide variety of goods, including hard lines, and which, with some exceptions, provides its customers with extensive services. The department store takes its name from the units (departments) in which related kinds of merchandise are grouped for purposes of promotion, service, and control. Chain department stores, which include the great mass-merchandisers with their common format, have taken on many of the aspects of the traditional department store even though the profit base is the entire store rather than the individual departments. Discount department stores, characterized by low margins and self-service, sell general merchandise in such great varieties that they may also be regarded as department stores.

Depth of selection A variety of different styles, sizes, and prices in any one given merchandise line.

Destination shopper A person who sets out to buy a specific item. Retailers use in-store displays and other enticements to stimulate additional sales.

Diffuser A device on the bottom or sides of a luminaire to redirect or spread the light from a source, used to control the brightness of the source and the direction of light emitted by the luminaire.

Diffuse lighting Light that is not predominantly incident from any particular direction.

Directional lighting Illumination on a work plane or object, predominantly from a single direction.

Direct lighting Lighting by luminaries distributing 90 to 100 percent of the emitted light in the general direction of the surface to be illuminated. The term usually refers to light emitted in a downward direction.

Discount center A center in which a discount store is the major tenant in the development with additional retail space consisting of smaller retail tenants and/or a supermarket.

Display Presentation of merchandise arranged to attract customers and for ease of examination and selection. Displays can be open for self-selection or within cases.

Display signs Signs or banners on display that are at least two-sided and attached to a pole or hung from the ceiling, easily visible, facing shopper traffic.

Disposable income The proportion of a consumer's income that remains after expenditures for food, clothing, and shelter.

Dollar sales per square foot of sales area The result of dividing annual sales of an area, department, or store by the number of square feet occupied by the specific area.

Double hang Two hang rods, one over the other.

Drive aisles Flexible pathways that lead from the main aisle to departmental locations that hold prime merchandise.

Economizer A system of controls and ductwork that permits "free" cooling of a building with outside air when the outside temperature and humidity are suitable.

Energy management system An integrated group of products that regulate energy usage in a building. Options include load control, an environmental control system, or a combination of the two.

Environmental control system An integrated group of products that control a building's heating, cooling, and ventilation equipment.

Exposure (or visibility) The ability of a store to be seen and regonized by potential customers.

Exterior visibility The extent to which a storefront, marquee, or window display may be seen by a passing pedestrian or vehicular passenger.

Face-out A sloping hang rod that permits a waterfall effect for display of apparel, handbags, etc.

Facing A retail shelf designation indicating the number of times an item fits across the front of a shelf or gondola. For example, "three facings" would mean that three of the same item may be displayed side by side.

Factory outlets Manufacturers' factory outlets, once located at the factory sites, can be found in malls or shopping centers and often sell first-quality, current-season merchandise.

Fashion goods Distinctive merchandise possessing a great deal of current customer appeal. Fashion goods are characterized by a short product life span, unpredictable level of sales, the need for broad assortments to create a favorable store image, and the importance placed by consumers on style and color. Purchase of fashion goods by consumers is often done on impulse, or at least as the result of subjective buying decisions.

Fashion-oriented center A center composed of shops and boutiques carrying selected merchandise, usually of high quality and high price.

Fashion outlet A center consisting of manufacturers' retail outlet facilities where goods are sold directly to the public in stores owned and operated by the manufacturers.

Fashion/specialty center A center composed mainly of upscale apparel shops, boutiques, and craft shops carrying merchandise of high quality and price. These centers need not be anchored, although sometimes restaurants or entertainment can provide the draw for anchors. The physical design of the center is very sophisticated, emphasizing a rich décor and high-quality landscaping. Such centers are usually found in trade areas having high-income levels.

Festival/entertainment center A center consisting primarily of specialty retailers, entertainment facilities, and dining establishments.

Fixed expenses Expenses that do not fluctuate significantly despite changes in sales, service, or manufacturing activity; normally include rent, taxes, salaries, depreciation, etc.

Fixture density The ratio of the area occupied by sales fixtures to the total area of the sales space. It typically does not exceed 50 percent of the sales area.

Fixtures Tables, counters, racks, etc., used by a store to stock and display its merchandise.

Fixtures, sales The cases and displays used for merchandise presentation and storage.

Fixtures, stock Mass-produced display units.

Fixturing The selection and arrangement of store fixtures, such as racks and counters, for the purposes of display and customer convenience, especially in the case of self-service stores.

Fluorescent lamp A low-pressure mercury electric discharge lamp, tubular in shape, in which a fluorescing coating (phosphor) transforms ultraviolet energy into visible light.

Focus group Groups composed of participants who may represent either a segment or a cross section of shoppers. The trained moderator of a focus group can probe for perceptions, attitudes, and habits of shoppers, looking for the reason behind the percentages of yes and no answers.

Footcandle (fc) The basic measure used to indicate level of illumination. One footcandle is equal to 1 unit of light flux (1 lumen) distributed evenly over a 1 sq ft surface area.

Freestanding display A display unit for merchandise, often movable, with products shown on one to four sides.

Freestanding location A store site that is not physically connected to other stores in the vicinity. The store may be large, with its own parking facilities (as in highway retailing), or it may be a neighborhood retailer such as a small corner grocery store.

Full-line department or discount store A store that offers a complete selection of soft goods, housewares, domestics, drugs, shoes, hardware, paints, auto supplies, sporting goods, toys, furniture, and appliances.

Full-service store A retail store that is adequately staffed with sales and support personnel so as to provide a full range of services to the customer. These services include individual sales assistance, credit, delivery, gift wrap, installation, repair, etc.

Full-service wholesaler An independent middleman organization that carries an extensive and varied product assortment and provides services such as credit, delivery, storage, promotions, displays, etc., to the retailer.

Gazebo A display fixture, similar to a garden house, that acts as a focus point

in a department. Merchandise is often arranged in and around a gazebo in such a way as to facilitate customer access.

General merchandise stores Retail stores that sell a number of merchandise lines, such as department stores, discount department stores, and variety stores.

Gondola A counter, often two-sided, having shelves at the top and storage space at the bottom. Primary function is to display merchandise and provide room for backup stock.

Grid layout An arrangement of fixtures and aisles in a store, based on rectangles, squares, and other right-angle patterns. Often found in supermarkets and discount stores.

Grid pattern A standard way of placing fixtures on a plan.

Gross floor space Total store area, including selling and non-selling departments.

Gross leasable area (GLA) The standard unit of measure used by the shopping center industry. GLA is the total floor area designed for tenant occupancy and exclusive use, including basements, mezzanines, and upper floors. It is measured from the centerline of joint partitions and from outside wall faces. GLA is that area on which tenants pay rent.

Gross margin The difference between the total cost of merchandise and its final selling price. It may be expressed as net sales less the cost of goods sold. Inasmuch as markdowns, shortages, and discounts have been deducted in computing gross margin, the figure is not the same as maintained markup. *Gross margin* is often used synonymously with *gross profit*. The former term is more usually found in merchandising and the latter in manufacturing.

Gross profit Total receipts less the cost of goods sold, but before selling and other operating expenses have been deducted and before income taxes have been deducted. *Gross profit* is often used synonymously with *gross margin,* but *gross profit* is more common in manufacturing, *gross margin* in merchandising.

Gross sales Sales revenue before deductions have been made for returns and allowances, but after sales and excise taxes have been deducted.

Hardware Shelving and hang rod metal fixturing components.

High-intensity discharge (HID) High-intensity discharge lighting, including mercury vapor, metal halide, and high-pressure sodium light sources. Low-pressure sodium lamps are often included in the HID category.

High intensity discharge (HID) lamps A general group of lamps consisting of mercury, metal halide, and high-pressure sodium lamps.

Highly saturated colors Intense colors, generally primary or secondary. *Saturation* refers to purity, unadulterated by other colors, black, or white, which would mute the base tone.

HVAC Heating, ventilating, and air-conditioning.

Hypermarts or *hypermarchés* Large markets, usually of more than 200,000 sq ft, that carry foodstuffs and other basic commodities in depth. They are more popular in Europe than in the United States.

Impulse merchandise Items that, because of their immediate appeal to the customer, are purchased with little planning or consideration.

Incandescent filament lamp A lamp in which light is produced by a filament heated to incandescence by an electric current.

Independent store A retail outlet owned and operated by an individual, family, or partnership, or a local store that may be a publicly owned corporation that is not part of a larger chain or ownership group. The store may, however, be a member of a voluntary chain.

Indirect lighting Lighting by luminaires distributing 90 to 100 percent of the emitted light upward.

Interior display The presentation of merchandise within a store in such a way that the customer is encouraged to try the product. Interior displays are intended to stimulate unplanned purchases and to enhance the atmosphere of the store.

Intimate apparel Women's apparel in three basic categories: (1) foundations, which include bras, girdles, corsets, etc., (2) lingerie, which includes daywear (slips, panties, etc.) and sleepwear (nightgowns, pajamas, etc.), and (3) loungewear, which includes robes, housecoats, and other casual apparel for at-home entertaining.

Island A freestanding store display having space all the way around it.

Island department Generally, a space that does not have a wall backing. It can be used for subdividing a category, for bridging two categories, or as a swing area.

Junior Size range in women's apparel in odd numbers, 3 to 15, height range approximately 5'2"–5'5".

Junior department store Not as large as a conventional department store, the junior department store offers a relatively wide variety of merchandise, including soft goods (family apparel), housewares, gifts and home textiles, in a departmentalized form of organization. Prices are often moderate, and major appliances and furniture are usually not included in the merchandise offering.

Layout In retail stores, refers to the interior arrangement of departments and merchandise within departments, as well as space allocation for aisles, counters, fixtures, etc.

Lifestyle merchandising A form of retail merchandising in which the store is continually altering the merchandise mix to accommodate what the customer wants and will buy. Lifestyle merchandising recognizes that people are conscious of value, newness, and quality and that the customer's lifestyle, demographics, value system, and buying habits all play a role in his or her buying behavior.

Limited-line department or discount store A unit that concentrates on a complete selection of soft goods, housewares, drugs, and shoes.

Logo In retailing, usually the store name represented in a distinctive type design with or without other emblems or symbols. Also known as a *signature cut, sig cut,* or *logotype.*

Louver A series of baffles arranged in a geometric pattern, used to shield a lamp from view at certain angles to avoid glare.

Low-end merchandising A retailing strategy in which stores are located in low-rent areas and in which the merchandise is presented with few amenities. Goods are often displayed on dump ta-

bles or in cartons and bins, and little sales help is available.

Luminaire A complete lighting fixture including one or more lamps and a means for connection to a power source. May also include one or more ballasts and elements to position and protect the lamps and distribute their light.

Luxury goods Top-of-the-line merchandise in terms of price and quality.

Magnet The store in a shopping center or district that is the prime attractive force drawing customers to the center or district.

Major shopping district A shopping area that contains one or more major magnets or large department store units.

Mall Malls are typically enclosed, with a climate-controlled walkway between two facing strips of stores. The term represents the most common design mode for regional and superregional centers and has become an informal term for these types of centers.

Markdowns Downward revisions of selling prices.

Market A store's market is a retail trading area, i.e., a geographical entity containing potential customers.

Marketing Those activities that facilitate the exchange of goods and services as they move from producer to ultimate consumer. Activities include product development, pricing, promotion, and distribution and are carried out with the objective of making a profit.

Market penetration The amount of personal consumption expenditures that a retail operation or complex captures in a specific market area. Also called *share of the market.*

Market positioning strategy A marketing strategy that promotes an "image" of the store or shopping center.

Market segmentation The subdivision of a population (here seen as potential customers) into smaller parts having similar characteristics. These smaller segments will, in turn, exhibit homogeneous responses to various products and services.

Markup The difference between the cost paid by the store for the goods and the price at which the goods are sold to the consumer.

Mass merchandising The retailing, on a very large scale, of staple goods at prices lower than those commonly found in department and specialty stores. Mass merchandising is characterized by (1) emphasis on products whose market is not highly segmented, (2) customers who are willing to sacrifice sales assistance and store services in return for lower prices, (3) high volume and rapid stock turnover rate, and (4) a very highly competitive marketplace. Kmart, Wal-Mart, Target, and Kohl's are leading U.S. mass merchandisers.

Merchandise mix The types of merchandise offered for sale in a retail facility.

Merchandising The business of purchasing goods for inventory and resale, creating a store image, and presenting the goods to the consumer.

Merchant A person who buys and resells merchandise; a trader, dealer, retailer, storekeeper.

Metropolitan statistical area (MSA) A freestanding metropolitan area, surrounded by nonmetropolitan counties containing a city of at least 50,000. Can also refer to an urbanized area of at least 50,000 with a total metropolitan population of at least 100,000.

Mezzanine (or balcony) An area that equals less than 50 percent of the first floor of a store and is above and open to that floor. Before completing plans, the local and state building codes relating to exits, ceiling height, and other conditions should be checked.

Mixed-use development A large-scale real estate project with three or more revenue-producing uses that are mutually supporting and developed as a unit (retail, office, residential, hotel/motel, recreation); functional and physical integration of project components, including pedestrian connections; and development in conformance with a coherent plan.

Multiunit operation A retail organization in which the various branches are of relatively equal importance and in which there is no main or flagship store. All units are managed by a centrally located administrative group.

Neighborhood center A shopping area that provides for the sale of convenience goods (food, drugs, sundries) and personal services (laundry, barbering, shoe repair) for the day-to-day needs of the immediate neighborhood. It is often built around a supermarket. A neighborhood center is usually configured as a straight-line strip with no enclosed walkways or mall area, although a canopy may connect the storefronts.

Net income Income before income taxes, determined by deducting from net sales or net revenue all the expenses for the year or the accounting period.

Net selling area The area devoted to retail sales, not including storage, mechanical, or office space.

Off-price center A center consisting of retail stores that offer brand-name goods found in conventional stores, at 20–70 percent below manufacturers' suggested prices.

Open display A store's display window that is open and without a backing, thus providing an unobstructed view of the store's interior. This allows the entire store to become a display.

Open stock Merchandise kept on hand in retail stores and sold either as sets or as separate pieces. Additional and/or replacement pieces are carried in bulk over a period of several years. This policy is used most often in china, glassware, and flatware sales.

Open-to-buy (OTB) The amount (expressed in dollars or units) a buyer is permitted to order for a specified period of time. In terms of dollars, a department's open-to-buy would be the total amount budgeted less the value of goods yet to be delivered in the specified period.

Operating division A functional division of a retail store responsible for such matters as merchandise receiving, store maintenance and housekeeping, security, and certain special services such as restaurants.

Operating profit The amount remaining after expenses are subtracted from gross margin.

Optical scanning The machine reading, by a wand or fixed device, of letters and numbers (either in code or in human-readable form) and the translation of these symbols into computer language.

Outlet centers Usually located in rural areas or occasionally in tourist locations, outlet centers consist mostly of manufacturers' outlet stores selling their own brands at a discount. These centers typically are not anchored. A strip configuration is most common, although some are enclosed malls and others can be arranged in a "village" cluster.

Outpost display Merchandise displayed within the store but away from its regular selling department. Informative signs are used to direct customers to the merchandise. Sometimes the merchandise is sold directly from the outpost.

Outsize Sizes larger than the standard, for example, sizes 20–40 and 16½–26½.

Pedestrian circulation The pattern of pedestrian movements between shopping facilities.

Perimeter aisle The outside aisle in a store, off the main aisle.

Perishable Any food product that tends to spoil rapidly and therefore requires special handling such as refrigeration, freezing, etc.

Personal care item Any variety of products intended to help improve customers' grooming and appearance. Included are hair dryers, electric shavers, saunas, etc.

Planogram Instructions sent to branch stores by the parent organization detailing how much merchandise is to be stocked and how it is to be displayed. In some organizations planograms are advisory; in others, conformance to the plan is mandatory.

Point-of-purchase (POP) display An interior display of merchandise at the register, checkout counter, or other point of sale. Designed to attract customers' attention and to stimulate impulse buying. Often provided by the vendor.

Point-of-sale (POS) terminal A cash register or terminal linked to a computer. The register controls and records all sales (cash, charge, COD, layaway, etc.) at the point of sale. The terminal issues sales checks, prints transaction records, and feeds information about each transaction into the data bank of the computer.

Positioned retailing The systematic identification of a store's target market and the development of a specific merchandising strategy to meet the needs of that market.

Power center A center dominated by several large anchors, including discount department stores, off-price stores, warehouse clubs, or "category killers," i.e., stores that offer tremendous selection in a particular merchandise category at low prices. The center typically consists of several freestanding anchors and a minimum number of small specialty tenants.

Prime location An aisle position that most customers pass, where they see product displays.

Primary market population The population residing in a retail center's primary trade area, the geographic area responsible for 60–70 percent of the center's traffic.

Private brand A brand developed, owned, and controlled by the retailer or other middleman. This merchandise is generally lower in cost than other brands. The merchant becomes both the producer and the marketer, so that the manufacturer's only responsibility is to make the merchandise according to the merchant's specifications.

Product differentiation The unique features of an item of merchandise that give it a competitive edge over other products within the same classification. This may be an actual difference (such as quality) or a difference of image resulting from promotional efforts.

Productivity Annual sales per square foot of gross leasable area.

Product life cycle A theory that attempts to describe the evolution of a product from birth to decline by means of five identifiable stages: introduction of the product, growth, market maturity, saturation, and decline.

Profit center Any area of a store that contributes to the overall profit of the store, i.e., the selling areas. In department stores, the profit centers correspond to the departments. In smaller stores, profit centers may be based on product lines.

Profit per square foot of selling space The average amount of profit per week store owners get for every square foot of selling space in their store. The formula: Profit per square foot = total profit per week divided by square feet of selling space.

Promotional merchandising Short-term alterations such as reduced retail price or special events to draw traffic into the store.

Promotions Activities either within a store or outside the store calculated to stimulate sales or to generate a favorable store image.

Psychographics A description of the market based on factors such as attitudes, opinions, interests, perceptions, and lifestyles of consumers constituting that market.

Racks Permanent or semipermanent equipment, usually made of plastic or metal and designed to provide the additional needed space for merchandise.

Ready-to-wear (RTW) Ready-made clothing that is mass-produced in factories to standard size measurements so that it may be purchased from racks by consumers.

Reflector A device used to redirect the light from a lamp or luminaire by the process of reflection.

Regional center Provides shopping goods, general merchandise, apparel, furniture, and home furnishings in full depth and variety. It is often built around one full-line department store with a minimum GLA of 100,000 sq ft. A regional center typically has a GLA of 400,000 sq ft, but can contain more than 1 million sq ft. A typical center is usually enclosed, with an inward orientation of the stores, connected by a common walkway, and parking surrounds the outside perimeter.

Regional chain A chain store system whose activities are limited to a particular area or region of the country. Burdine's, which has 55 stores, operates only in Florida.

Remainders Goods that are left over and put on sale. The term is often applied to books that have been marked down, but it may be applied to other merchandise as well.

Retail (1) The sale of merchandise in small quantities to the ultimate consumer. (2) Sometimes used as a short form of *retail price*.

Retail cooperative A voluntary association of independent retailers who jointly own and operate their own wholesale facilities and/or who act together as a buying club in order to achieve the economies of large scale purchasing.

Retailing The business activity concerned primarily with selling goods and/or services to the ultimate consumer.

Includes buying goods from vendors, assembling them in a convenient location, making them available to the consumer, and other related activities. It is the final step in the marketing process.

Retail store A business that regularly offers goods for sale to the ultimate consumer. A retail store buys, stores, promotes, and sells the merchandise.

R-factor Resistance of an insulating material to heat flow. The higher the R-factor, or R-value, the more efficient the insulator.

Rounders Circular display racks used to hold large numbers of garments or other merchandise. Often capable of being turned by the customer for greater convenience and accessibility.

Sales per square foot of selling space The average amount of retail proceeds per week store owners earn from each square foot of selling space in their store. The formula: Sales per square foot = total retail sales proceeds per week divided by square feet of selling space.

Satellite stores In a shopping center, the smaller stores clustered around the large anchor stores.

Saturated area A retail trading area in which there are just enough stores to provide goods and services for the population but not so many stores that they cannot all make a fair profit.

Seasonal merchandise Goods so closely identified with a particular season or holiday that they have a very short sales life, e.g., Easter candy and novelties.

Secondary aisles Like drive aisles, these are temporary passages that can shift as the assortment balance changes and can define an area as well as lead to a focal point.

Their width varies with their distance from the main entry and the depth of stock.

Self-service Merchandise that is on open display on shelves or racks for shopper selection.

Selling area Total floor space devoted to selling activities, including aisles, fitting rooms, and adjacent stockrooms.

Service mark A word or symbol used by a firm to distinguish the services it provides from the services other organizations provide.

Shallow assortment An assortment of merchandise in which each item is stocked in small quantities.

Share of the market That portion of the available business held by a store in a particular trading area.

Shelf life The number of days that a product, particularly a food product, can be held before it begins to deteriorate. Loss of flavor, taste, and color reduce the salability of an item.

Shielding A general term including all devices used to block, diffuse, or redirect light rays, including baffles, louvers, shades, diffusers, and lenses.

Shopping center A group of architecturally unified commercial establishments planned, developed, owned, and managed as an operating unit and providing on-site parking. A center's size and orientation are generally determined by the market characteristics of the trade area it serves. The two main configurations of shopping centers are malls and open-air strip centers.

Shopping district A shopping area of varied composition. Business districts are known as "unplanned centers," and new shopping centers are normally referred to as "planned developments."

Silent salesperson A term used as a synonym for *packaging* or *graphics,* to indicate the importance of the marketing aspect of a container.

Soft goods Merchandise made from textile fabrics, e.g., apparel, piece goods, towels, sheets, etc.

Space allocation In a retail store, space is allocated first between selling and nonselling areas. Each line of merchandise is then allocated specific amounts of selling area, often on the basis of its gross profitability per square foot.

Specialty store An enterprise with a product mix narrower than that of a department store and broader than that of a single-line store. A specialty store has a clearly defined market segment as its target. Such stores offer wide assortments within their product lines, trained salespeople, credit, delivery, and other services. Neiman Marcus is an example.

Specular surface A shiny, highly polished surface that reflects light at an angle equal to that of the incident light.

Standard metropolitan statistical areas (SMSAs) Metropolitan areas defined by the federal government for purposes of data reporting and allocations of certain federal grants.

Standards and brackets Adjustable metal hardware that supports shelving and hang rods.

Staple stock Merchandise for which there is active demand at all times and which retailers always keep on hand.

Stock keeping unit (SKU) For every different style and each color within a style, a separate SKU number is given. The merchant can track the sales of inventory by each item's SKU.

Stock overage A condition in which the physical inventory of a store or department is higher than the book inventory.

Stock shortage A condition in which the physical inventory of a store or department yields a lower retail figure than the book value.

Stock turn The number of times a store needs to completely restock a consumer-goods section and permanent displays with a given product over a one-year period. The formula: Stock turns = annual case sales divided by average stock. (also see *turnover*).

Stock turnover A financial ratio commonly calculated for one year.

Store image The store as perceived by the customer. Factors that contribute to store image are store location, price ranges, and merchandise, as well as architecture, color schemes, advertising, salespeople, etc.

Strip center An attached row of stores or service outlets managed as a coherent retail entity, with on-site parking usually located in front of the stores. Open canopies may connect the storefronts, but a strip center does not have enclosed walkways linking the stores. A strip center may be configured in a straight line, or may have an "L" or "U" shape.

Superregional center A shopping area that provides an extensive variety of comparison goods, services, and recreational facilities. It contains about 750,000 sq ft of GLA. As with regional centers, the typical configuration is as an enclosed mall, frequently with multilevels.

Swing area A prime space near a store's entry that holds seasonally hot items. The life of the merchandise desirability here should be about one month.

Tabletop merchandise China, glassware, flatware, and textile products such as tablecloths and napkins.

Temporary displays Promotional free-standing displays usually kept near a store's entry from one to four weeks.

Theme/festival centers These centers typically employ a unifying theme that is carried out by the individual shops in their architectural design and, to an extent, in their merchandise. Such centers can be anchored by restaurants and entertainment facilities, and their greatest appeal is to tourists. Generally located in urban areas, these centers tend to be adapted from older, sometimes historic, buildings, and can be of mixed-use projects.

Theme setting display A retail display in which the products to be sold are presented in an environment having a particular theme or subject orientation.

Theme shopping center Characterized by distinctive architecture that carriers over into the interior design.

Toddlers Children ranging in age from 18 months to about 3 years, who wear sizes 1T–4T.

Trade area The geographic region from which the continuing patronage of a shopping area or store is obtained.

Trading up (1) A store is said to be trading up when it introduces merchandise at higher prices and, presumably, of higher quality in an effort to attract more affluent customers. (2) A salesperson is said to be trading up when he or she encourages the customer to buy more expensive merchandise.

Traffic In retail stores, *traffic* refers to the number of customers or prospective customers who either pass by or enter the store or a department within the store. In a slightly more general sense, the term *traffic* is used for the collective customer presence in a store.

Triangulate In presentation, it is the pyramiding of stock in three dimensions or using converging diagonals in two dimensions.

Turnover The number of stock turns achieved in a year. The more frequently merchandise is sold, replaced, and sold again, the more profitable the merchandising operation will be.

Unit pricing The practice of pricing merchandise (groceries, meats, etc., are common examples) relative to a common denominator, i.e., so much per pound, quart, or dozen. In addition, a label indicates the price per package or item.

Universal product code (UPC) Adopted by the food industry in 1973, the UPC is a classification system in which each product (and each size, flavor, color, etc.) is assigned a 10-digit number. The numbers are premarked on the package by the manufacturer in the form of a bar code over the 10 corresponding Arabic numerals. The bar code is readable by an optical scanner at the checkout counter, and the information it contains is transmitted to a computer. It is the computer that contains the prices, not the UPC, and it is the computer that controls the cash register.

Upscaling In upscaling, the objective is to attract the upscale customer, commonly viewed as being well educated, sophisticated in his or her tastes, and earning in excess of $60,000 a year.

Valance A horizontal band that shields lights that are directed on merchandise; or a sign band above products.

Value added The increase in the worth of the product as a result of the activities it passes through in the production/distribution chain.

Variable expenses Expenses, or costs, that vary in total in direct proportion to production or sales volume. Raw materials, cost of merchandise, piecework labor, and sales commissions are examples.

Vendor Also referred to as a *resource* or *supplier.* A vendor is a person or firm (manufacturer, importer, jobber, agent, wholesaler, etc.) from whom the retailer purchases goods.

Vertical shopping center Generally found in a downtown area, a vertical shopping center occupies the lower floors of a multiuse high-rise building, the upper floors of which may be devoted to offices and/or residential space.

Visual merchandising A retailing strategy for the in-store presentation of merchandise in such a way that it will be shown to its greatest advantage. Visual merchandising, which includes traditional display techniques, increasingly involves planning store layout and décor and activities that appeal to other senses, such as music. The object of these efforts is to increase the sale of merchandise.

Visual merchants Those responsible for the artistic presentation of a store's merchandise.

Voltage A measure of electromotive force or the pressure of electricity.

Wall display An interior display made up of posters and/or actual merchandise hung from the walls of a store. Used to attract the customer's attention and promote the sale of particular merchandise.

Watt A unit used to measure power consumption of 1 amp under pressure of 1 volt.

BIBLIOGRAPHY AND REFERENCES

Agins, Teri. 2000. *End of Fashion: How Marketing Changed the Clothing Business Forever.* New York: HarperCollins.

Barr, Vilma, and Charles E. Broudy. 1990. *Designing to Sell: A Complete Guide to Retail Store Planning and Design.* 2d ed. New York: McGraw-Hill.

———. 1995. *Time-Saver Details for Store Planning and Design.* New York: McGraw-Hill.

Barr, Vilma, and Katherine Field. 1997. *Stores: Retail Display and Design.* Glen Cove, N.Y.: PBC International.

Cohen, Nancy E. 2003. *America's Marketplace: The History of Shopping Centers.* New York: International Council of Shopping Centers and The Greenwich Publishing Group.

Diamond, Jay, and Ellen Diamond. 2003. *Contemporary Visual Merchandising and Environmental Design.* 3d ed. Upper Saddle River, N.J.: Prentice-Hall.

Doonan, Simon. 2001. *Confessions of a Window Dresser: Tales from a Life in Fashion.* New York: Penguin USA.

Forden, Sara Gay. 2001. *House of Gucci: A Sensational Story of Murder, Madness, Glamour and Greed.* New York: Perennial.

Gobé, Marc. 2001. *Emotional Branding: The New Paradigm for Connecting Brands to People.* New York: Allworth Press.

———. 2002. *Citizen Brand: 10 Commandments for Transforming Brands in a Consumer Democracy.* New York: Allworth Press.

Hannigan, John H. 1998. *Fantasy City: Pleasure and Profit in the Post-Modern Metropolis.* New York: Routledge.

Inaga, Jeffrey, Rem Koolhaas, and Sze Tsung Leong. 2002. *Great Leap Forward/Harvard Design School Project on the City 1.* Edited by Chihua Judy Chung. New York: Taschen America.

———. 2002. *Harvard Design School Guide to Shopping/Harvard Design School Project on the City 2.* Edited by Chihua Judy Chung. New York: Taschen.

Hine, Thomas. 2002. *I Want That! How We All Became Shoppers.* New York: HarperCollins.

Jerde Partnership International. 1992. *Process: Architecture, No. 101.* Tokyo: Process Architecture Co.

———. 1999. *You Are Here: The Jerde Partnership International.* London: Phaidon Press.

International Council of Shopping Centers. 1996. *ICSC Keys to Shopping Center Fundamentals.* New York: International Council of Shopping Centers. (Also available as an audiobook.)

———. 1998. *The ICSC Guide to U.S. Shopping Centers of Interest.* New York: International Council of Shopping Centers.

———. 1998. *Shopping Center Food Court Profiles.* New York: International Council of Shopping Centers.

———. 2000. *Attracting Tourists to Shopping Centers.* New York: International Council of Shopping Centers.

———. 2000. *Shopping Center Redevelopment and Renovation.* New York: International Council of Shopping Centers.

———. 2002. *Winning Shopping Center Designs.* 26th ed. New York: International Council of Shopping Centers.

Marcus, Stanley. 2001. *Minding the Store: A Memoir.* Denton: University of North Texas Press.

———. 2001. *Quest for the Best.* Denton: University of North Texas Press.

Pine, B. Joseph, II, and James H. Gilmore. 1999. *The Experience Economy: Work Is Theater and Every Business a Stage.* Boston: Harvard Business School Press.

Schmitt, Bernd H. 1999. *Experiential Marketing: How to Get Customers to Sense, Feel, Think, Act, and Relate to Your Company and Brands.* New York: The Free Press.

Underhill, Paco. 2000. *Why We Buy: The Science of Shopping.* New York: Touchstone Books.

Venturi, Robert. 1966. *Complexity and Contradiction in Architecture.* New York: The Museum of Modern Art.

Venturi, Robert, and Denise Scott Brown. 1972. *Learning from Las Vegas.* Cambridge, Mass.: MIT Press.

Weisberger, Lauren. 2003. *The Devil Wears Prada.* New York: Doubleday.

Weishar, Joseph. 1992. *Design for Effective Selling Space.* New York: McGraw-Hill.

Zaltman, Gerald. 2003. *How Customers Think: Essential Insights into the Mind of the Market.* Boston: Harvard Business School Press.

INDEX

INDEX

BUILDING TYPE BASICS FOR RETAIL AND MIXED-USE FACILITIES:

1. Program (predesign)
What are the principal programming requirements (space types and areas)?
Any special regulatory or jurisdictional concerns?
4, 31–37, 39–46, 114, 125, 127–29, 133, 141, 143–44, 150–60, 183, 204, 206, 216

2. Project process and management
What are the key components of the design and construction process?
Who is to be included on the project team?
39, 43, 73–74, 111–40, 145–48

3. Unique design concerns
What distinctive design determinants must be met? Any special circulation requirements?
1–15, 24–25, 33–35, 43, 47–62, 58–69, 97–100, 104, 106–9, 139–41, 151,
153–61, 167, 183–84, 186–87, 196, 201–12

4. Site planning/parking/landscaping
What considerations determine external access and parking? Landscaping?
18–19, 58–69, 92, 96–98, 111–12, 114, 116, 124, 130–38, 142–44,
146–51, 153–54, 159, 162–67, 173, 184, 186, 192–93

5. Codes/ADA
Which building codes and regulations apply, and what are the main applicable provisions?
(Examples: egress; electrical; plumbing; ADA; seismic; asbestos; terrorism and other hazards)
39, 46, 50, 129–30, 137, 163, 199

6. Energy/environmental challenges
What techniques in service of energy conservation and environmental sustainability
can be employed?
25, 129, 133, 194–95

7. Structure system
What classes of structural systems are appropriate?
50, 191–93

8. Mechanical systems
What are appropriate systems for heating, ventilating, and air-conditioning (HVAC) and plumbing?
Vertical transportation? Fire and smoke protection? What factors affect preliminary selection?
46, 192–99

9. Electrical/communications
What are appropriate systems for electrical service and voice and data communications?
What factors affect preliminary selection?
179, 199–200, 218